D0014527

GLENCOE LANGUAGE ARTS

Grammar AND Composition Handbook

GRADE 7

New York, New York
Columbus, Ohio
Woodland Hills, California
Peoria, Illinois

Photo Credits
Cover Index Stock; **all other photos** Amanita Pictures.

Glencoe/McGraw-Hill

A Division of The ***McGraw·Hill*** *Companies*

Printed in the United States of America.

Send all inquiries to:
Glencoe/McGraw-Hill
8787 Orion Place
Columbus, Ohio 43240

ISBN 0-07-825114-1

3 4 5 6 7 8 9 042 06 05 04 03 02

Table of Contents at a Glance

Table of Contents

Chapter 5 Adjectives 142

Chapter 6 Adverbs 156

Chapter 7 Prepositions, Conjunctions, and Interjections 171

Chapter 8 Clauses and Complex Sentences 190

Chapter 9 Verbals 205

Chapter 10 Subject-Verb Agreement 215

Chapter 11 Diagraming Sentences 227

Chapter 12 Capitalization 246

Chapter 13 Punctuation 258

Part One

Ready Reference

The **Ready Reference** consists of three parts. The **Glossary of Terms** is a list of language arts terms with definitions and examples. Page references show you where to find more information about the terms elsewhere in the book. The **Usage Glossary** lists words that are easily confused or often used incorrectly and explains how to use the words correctly. The third part is **Abbreviations**, which consists of lists of many commonly used abbreviations.

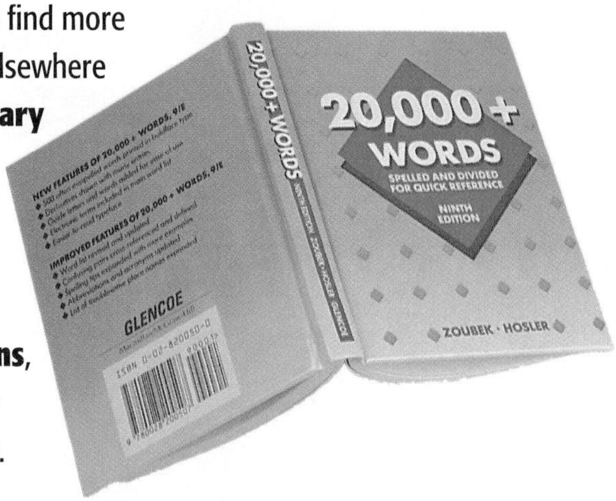

A DICTIONARY OF SYNONYMS AND ANTONYMS
by Joseph Devlin
REFERENCE
WARNER BOOKS
Merriam-Webster
Merriam-Webster's
Dictionary
Merriam-Webster
Thesau
SIGNET REFERENCE AE 6554
SLANG AND EUPHEMISM
RICHARD A. SPEARS
Merriam-Webster
Vocabulary

GLOSSARY OF TERMS

abbreviation An abbreviation is a shortened form of a word or phrase. Many abbreviations are followed by periods (pages 276–278).

EXAMPLES Mrs., Tues., Dec., NBA, ft., St., RI

abstract noun An abstract noun names an idea, a quality, or a feeling that can't be seen or touched (page 82).

EXAMPLE Her **bravery** and **courage** filled us with **admiration.**

action verb An action verb is a verb that expresses action. An action verb may consist of more than one word (pages 97–98).

EXAMPLES The director **shouts** at the members of the cast.

The lights **are flashing** above the stage.

The play **has begun.**

active voice A verb is in the active voice when the subject performs the action of the verb (pages 111–112).

EXAMPLE Thornton Wilder **composed** that play.

adjective An adjective is a word that describes, or modifies, a noun or a pronoun (pages 144–152, 164–165).

	HOW ADJECTIVES MODIFY NOUNS
WHAT KIND?	We studied **ancient** history.
HOW MANY?	I read **four** chapters.
WHICH ONE?	**That** invention changed history.

adjective clause An adjective clause is a subordinate clause that modifies, or describes, a noun or a pronoun in the main clause of a complex sentence (pages 195, 197).

EXAMPLE The Aqua-Lung, **which divers strap on,** holds oxygen.

adjective phrase An adjective phrase is a prepositional phrase or a participial phrase that modifies, or describes, a noun or a pronoun (pages 178, 206–207).

EXAMPLES The servers **at the new restaurant** are courteous. **[prepositional phrase modifying *servers*]**

The musician **seated at the piano** is Erik. **[participial phrase modifying *musician*]**

adverb An adverb is a word that modifies a verb, an adjective, or another adverb (pages 158–167, 179–180).

WHAT ADVERBS MODIFY

VERBS	People *handle* old violins **carefully.**
ADJECTIVES	**Very** *old* violins are valuable.
ADVERBS	Orchestras **almost** *always* include violins.

WAYS ADVERBS MODIFY VERBS

ADVERBS TELL	EXAMPLES
HOW	grandly, easily, completely, neatly, gratefully, sadly
WHEN	soon, now, immediately, often, never, usually, early
WHERE	here, there, everywhere, inside, downstairs, above

adverb clause An adverb clause is a subordinate clause that often modifies the verb in the main clause of a complex sentence. It tells *how, when, where, why,* or *under what conditions* the action occurs (pages 198–199).

EXAMPLE **After we won the meet,** we shook hands with our opponents.

An adverb clause can also modify an adjective or an adverb.

EXAMPLES Carson is younger **than I am. [The adverb clause *than I am* modifies the adjective *younger*.]**

Sherry walks faster **than her brother runs. [The adverb clause *than her brother runs* modifies the adverb *faster*.]**

adverb phrase An adverb phrase is a prepositional phrase that modifies a verb, an adjective, or another adverb (page 178).

	ADVERB PHRASES
MODIFIES A VERB	The servers *dress* **like movie characters.**
MODIFIES AN ADJECTIVE	The restaurant is *popular* **with young people.**
MODIFIES AN ADVERB	The restaurant opens *early* **in the morning.**

agreement Agreement is the match between grammatical forms. A verb must agree with its subject. A pronoun must agree with its antecedent (pages 73, 132–133, 181, 216–224).

EXAMPLES Both **ducks** and **swans swim** in this lake. **[subject-verb agreement]**

Jerry and his **brother** visited **their** grandparents. **[pronoun-antecedent agreement]**

antecedent An antecedent is the word a pronoun refers to. The word *antecedent* means "going before" (pages 128–130).

EXAMPLE **Max** likes to read books. **He** particularly likes novels. **[*He* refers to *Max*. *Max* is the antecedent of *He*.]**

apostrophe An apostrophe (') is a punctuation mark used in possessive nouns, possessive indefinite pronouns, and contractions. In contractions an apostrophe shows that one or more letters have been left out (pages 273–274).

EXAMPLES Shefali's friends don't always understand her.

Cameron's asking for everyone's help.

appositive An appositive is a noun that is placed next to another noun to identify it or add information about it (pages 89–90).

EXAMPLE James Madison's wife, **Dolley,** was a famous first lady.

appositive phrase An appositive phrase is a group of words that includes an appositive and other words that modify the appositive (pages 89–90).

EXAMPLE Madison, **our fourth president,** held many other offices.

article The words *a, an,* and *the* make up a special group of adjectives called articles. *A* and *an* are called **indefinite articles** because they refer to one of a general group of people, places, things, or ideas. *A* is used before words beginning with a consonant sound. *An* is used before words beginning with a vowel sound (page 147).

EXAMPLES **a** union **a** picture **an** hour **an** easel

The is called the **definite article** because it identifies specific people, places, things, or ideas (page 147).

auxiliary verb *See helping verb.*

base form A base form is the simplest form of a word. *Small* is a base form; other forms of *small* are *smaller* and *smallest. Be* is a base form; other forms of *be* are *am, is, are, was, were, being,* and *been* (pages 104, 113–116, 149–151, 163).

clause A clause is a group of words that has a subject and a verb (pages 192–201). *See also adjective clause, adverb clause, main clause, noun clause, and subordinate clause.*

closing A closing is a way to end a letter. It begins with a capital letter and is followed by a comma (page 249).

EXAMPLES

Yours truly, Sincerely, With love, Your friend,

READY REFERENCE

collective noun A collective noun names a group of people, animals, or things. It may be singular or plural, depending on the meaning of the sentence (pages 85, 220–221).

EXAMPLES The **team** shares the field with its opponent.

The **team** share their jokes with one another.

colon A colon (:) is a punctuation mark. It's used to introduce a list and to separate the hour and the minutes when you write the time of day. It's also used after the salutation of a business letter (page 269).

EXAMPLES Please buy these fruits**:** apples, bananas, grapes, peaches.

It's now exactly 2**:**43 P.M.

Dear Editor**:**

comma A comma (,) is a punctuation mark that's used to separate items or to set them off from the rest of a sentence (pages 262–267).

EXAMPLES Shoes**,** socks**,** hats**,** and gloves lay in the bottom of the closet.

Tessa's great-grandmother**,** who is ninety**,** loves to travel.

common noun A common noun names any person, place, thing, or idea. Common nouns can be either concrete or abstract (pages 81–82).

EXAMPLE **Children** learn **handwriting** in **school.**

comparative form The comparative form of an adjective compares one person or thing with another. The comparative form of an adverb compares one action with another (pages 149–152, 162–163).

EXAMPLES Is Venezuela **larger** than Peru? **[adjective]**

The pianist arrived **earlier** than the violinist. **[adverb]**

complete predicate *See predicate.*

complete subject *See subject.*

complex sentence A complex sentence has one main clause and one or more subordinate clauses (pages 193–194).

EXAMPLE Since Mariah moved to Springfield, she has made many new friends. **[*She has made many new friends* is a main clause. *Since Mariah moved to Springfield* is a subordinate clause.]**

compound-complex sentence A compound-complex sentence has two or more main clauses and one or more subordinate clauses (page 194).

EXAMPLE Ahmal has never scored a goal, but he plays soccer because he loves the game. **[The two main clauses are *Ahmal has never scored a goal* and *he plays soccer. Because he loves the game* is a subordinate clause.]**

compound noun A compound noun is a noun made of two or more words (pages 82, 85).

EXAMPLES storybook, showcase, bookmark
ice cream, dining room, high school
sister-in-law, seventh-grader, push-ups

compound predicate A compound predicate consists of two or more simple predicates, or verbs, that have the same subject. The verbs may be connected by *and, or, but, both . . . and, either . . . or,* or *neither . . . nor* (page 73).

EXAMPLE Many students **read** the novel *Jane Eyre* and **enjoy** it.

compound sentence A compound sentence is a sentence that contains two or more main clauses joined by a comma and a coordinating conjunction or by a semicolon (pages 75, 181, 183–184, 192).

READY REFERENCE

EXAMPLES **Eudora Welty is a novelist,** but **she also writes essays.** **[A comma and the coordinating conjunction *but* join the two main clauses, *Eudora Welty is a novelist* and *she also writes essays.*]**

Eudora Welty is a novelist; she also writes essays.

compound subject A compound subject consists of two or more simple subjects that have the same predicate. The subjects may be joined by *and, or, both . . . and, either . . . or,* or *neither . . . nor* (pages 73, 181, 223–224).

EXAMPLE **Charlotte Brontë** and **Emily Brontë** were sisters.

compound verb *See compound predicate.*

concrete noun A concrete noun names something you can see or touch (page 82).

EXAMPLE **Julio** wore a **cap** on his **head** and a **scarf** around his **neck.**

conjunction A conjunction is a connecting word. *See coordinating conjunction, correlative conjunction, and subordinating conjunction.*

conjunctive adverb A conjunctive adverb may be used to join the simple sentences in a compound sentence (pages 183–184).

EXAMPLE The school cafeteria sometimes serves Chinese food; **however,** these meals are not very tasty.

contraction A contraction is a word formed from one or more words by omitting one or more letters and substituting an apostrophe (pages 87–88, 166, 274).

EXAMPLES We **can't** find the map. **[*Can't* is a contraction of *cannot.*]**

Carmella's visited every state. **[*Carmella's* is a contraction of *Carmella has.*]**

coordinating conjunction A coordinating conjunction is a word used to connect compound parts of a sentence. *And, but, or, nor,* and *for* are coordinating conjunctions. *So* and *yet* are also sometimes used as coordinating conjunctions (pages 181, 223–224).

EXAMPLE Juan **or** Lisa collects the money **and** distributes the tickets.

correlative conjunction Correlative conjunctions are pairs of words used to connect compound parts of a sentence. Correlative conjunctions include *both . . . and, either . . . or, neither . . . nor,* and *not only . . . but also* (pages 181, 223–224).

EXAMPLE Examples of great architecture exist in **both** New York **and** Paris.

dash A dash (—) is a punctuation mark. It's usually used in pairs to set off a sudden break or change in thought or speech (page 275).

EXAMPLE Billy Adams—he lives next door—is our team manager.

declarative sentence A declarative sentence makes a statement. It ends with a period (pages 66, 261).

EXAMPLE Edgar Allan Poe wrote suspenseful short stories.

demonstrative adjective A demonstrative adjective points out something and modifies a noun by answering the question *which one?* or *which ones? This, that, these,* and *those* are demonstrative adjectives when they modify nouns (page 147).

EXAMPLES Take **this** umbrella with you. **That** answer is wrong.
Take **these** boots too. **Those** clouds are lovely.

READY REFERENCE

demonstrative pronoun A demonstrative pronoun is a pronoun that points out something. *This, that, these,* and *those* are demonstrative pronouns when they take the place of nouns (pages 136, 148).

EXAMPLES Take **this** with you. **That** is the wrong answer.
Take **these** too. **Those** are lovely clouds.

dependent clause *See subordinate clause.*

direct address Direct address is a name used in speaking directly to a person. Direct address may also be a word or a phrase used in place of a name. Words used in direct address are set off by commas (page 263).

EXAMPLES **Suzy,** please hand me a dish towel.
Here, **my dear mother,** is your birthday present.
Don't do that again, **Samson.**

direct object A direct object receives the action of a verb. It answers the question *whom?* or *what?* after an action verb (pages 98–100).

EXAMPLE The actor rehearsed his **lines** from the play.

direct quotation A direct quotation gives a speaker's exact words (pages 248, 270).

EXAMPLE **"Spiders,"** explained Raul, **"have eight legs."**

double negative A double negative is the use of two negative words to express the same idea. Only one negative word is necessary (pages 166–167).

EXAMPLES

INCORRECT I **don't** have **no** homework.
CORRECT I **don't** have **any** homework.
CORRECT I have **no** homework.

end mark An end mark is a punctuation mark used at the end of a sentence. Periods, question marks, and exclamation points are end marks (pages 66–67, 261).

EXAMPLES Tell me a story.

Where have you been?

What a hot day this has been!

essential clause An essential clause is a clause that is necessary to make the meaning of a sentence clear. Don't use commas to set off essential clauses (page 197).

EXAMPLE The girl **who is standing beside the coach** is our best swimmer.

essential phrase An essential phrase is a phrase that is necessary to make the meaning of a sentence clear. Don't use commas to set off essential phrases (page 207).

EXAMPLE The boy **seated at the piano** is Erik.

exclamation point An exclamation point (!) is a punctuation mark used to end a sentence that shows strong feeling (exclamatory). It's also used after strong interjections (pages 67, 261).

EXAMPLES My! What a hot day it is!

exclamatory sentence An exclamatory sentence expresses strong feeling. It ends with an exclamation point (pages 67, 261).

EXAMPLES What a great writer Poe was!

How I enjoy his stories!

future perfect tense The future perfect tense of a verb expresses action that will be completed before another future event begins (page 110).

EXAMPLE The production **will have closed** by next week.

future tense The future tense of a verb expresses action that will take place in the future (page 110).

EXAMPLE Mr. and Mrs. Pao **will attend** the performance.

gender The gender of a noun may be masculine (male), feminine (female), or neuter (referring to things) (page 130).

EXAMPLES boy (male), woman (female), desk (neuter)

gerund A gerund is a verb form that ends in *-ing* and is used as a noun (pages 208–209).

EXAMPLE **Exercising** builds strength, endurance, and flexibility.

gerund phrase A gerund phrase is a group of words that includes a gerund and other words that complete its meaning (pages 208–209).

EXAMPLE **Exercising on a bike** is fun for all ages.

helping verb A helping verb is a verb that helps the main verb express action or make a statement (pages 104–106, 217).

EXAMPLES Telma **is acting** in another play today. **[*Is* is the helping verb; *acting* is the main verb.]**

Emilio **has written** a story. **[*Has* is the helping verb; *written* is the main verb.]**

hyphen A hyphen (-) is a punctuation mark that's used in some compound words (page 275).

EXAMPLE Mrs. Gilmore's **mother-in-law** is **sixty-two** years old.

imperative sentence An imperative sentence gives a command or makes a request. It ends with a period (pages 66, 72, 261).

EXAMPLE Read "The Pit and the Pendulum."

indefinite pronoun An indefinite pronoun is a pronoun that does not refer to a particular person, place, or thing (pages 132–133, 222, 274).

SOME INDEFINITE PRONOUNS

SINGULAR			PLURAL
another	everybody	no one	both
anybody	everyone	nothing	few
anyone	everything	one	many
anything	much	somebody	others
each	neither	someone	several
either	nobody	something	
SINGULAR OR PLURAL	all, any, most, none, some		

indirect object An indirect object answers the question *to whom?* or *for whom?* or *to what?* or *for what?* an action is done (page 100).

EXAMPLE Friends sent the **actors** flowers.

indirect quotation An indirect quotation does not give a speaker's exact words (page 248).

EXAMPLE Raul said **that spiders have eight legs.**

READY REFERENCE

READY REFERENCE

infinitive An infinitive is formed with the word *to* and the base form of a verb. Infinitives are often used as nouns in sentences (pages 210–211).

EXAMPLE **To write** is Alice's ambition.

infinitive phrase An infinitive phrase is a group of words that includes an infinitive and other words that complete its meaning (pages 210–211).

EXAMPLE **To write a great novel** was Alice's ambition.

intensive pronoun An intensive pronoun ends with *-self* or *-selves* and is used to draw special attention to a noun or a pronoun already named (page 134).

EXAMPLE Yolanda **herself** repaired the engine.

interjection An interjection is a word or group of words that expresses emotion. It has no grammatical connection to other words in a sentence (pages 185–186, 261).

EXAMPLE **Good grief!** My favorite restaurant has closed.

interrogative pronoun An interrogative pronoun is a pronoun used to introduce an interrogative sentence. *Who, whom, which, what,* and *whose* are interrogative pronouns (pages 135–136).

EXAMPLE **Who** borrowed the book?

interrogative sentence An interrogative sentence asks a question. It ends with a question mark (pages 66, 71–72, 219, 261).

EXAMPLE Did Poe also write poetry?

intransitive verb An intransitive verb is a verb that does not have a direct object (pages 98–99).

EXAMPLE The audience **applauds** loudly.

inverted sentence An inverted sentence is a sentence in which the subject follows the verb (pages 72, 218–219).

EXAMPLES There **are** many **immigrants** among my ancestors.

Across the ocean **sailed** the three **ships.**

irregular verb An irregular verb is a verb whose past tense and past participle are formed in a way other than by adding *-d* or *-ed* to the base form (pages 113–116).

SOME IRREGULAR VERBS

BASE	PAST	PAST PARTICIPLE
go	went	gone
write	wrote	written
begin	began	begun

italics Italics are printed letters that slant to the right. *This sentence is printed in italic type.* Italics are used for the titles of certain kinds of published works and works of art. In handwriting, underlining is a substitute for italics (page 272).

EXAMPLE On the desk were a copy of *Robinson Crusoe* and several issues of *Time* magazine.

linking verb A linking verb connects the subject of a sentence with a noun or an adjective in the predicate (pages 101–102).

EXAMPLE Juana Ortiz **was** the director.

main clause A main clause has a subject and a predicate and can stand alone as a sentence (pages 192–194).

EXAMPLE After the storm passed, **the governor surveyed the damage.**

READY REFERENCE

main verb A main verb is the last word in a verb phrase. If a verb stands alone, it's a main verb (pages 104–106, 217).

EXAMPLES The professor is **studying** ancient history.

The professor **studies** ancient history.

negative word A negative word expresses the idea of "no" or "not" (pages 166–167).

SOME COMMON NEGATIVE WORDS

barely	no	no one	nowhere
hardly	nobody	not	scarcely
never	none	nothing	

nonessential clause A nonessential clause is a clause that is not necessary to make the meaning of a sentence clear. Use commas to set off nonessential clauses (pages 197, 265).

EXAMPLE Janice**, who is standing beside the coach,** is our best swimmer.

nonessential phrase A nonessential phrase is a phrase that is not necessary to make the meaning of a sentence clear. Use commas to set off nonessential phrases (pages 207, 263, 264).

EXAMPLE Erik**, dreaming of fame,** sits at the piano.

nonrestrictive clause *See nonessential clause.*

nonrestrictive phrase *See nonessential phrase.*

noun A noun is a word that names a person, a place, a thing, or an idea (pages 81–90).

NOUNS

PERSONS	sister, mayor, player, coach, pianist, children
PLACES	park, zoo, lake, school, playground, desert, city
THINGS	magazine, boots, rose, pencil, peach, baseball, car
IDEAS	honesty, truth, democracy, pride, maturity, progress

noun clause A noun clause is a subordinate clause used as a noun (pages 200–201).

EXAMPLE **Whoever plays hockey** wears protective equipment.

number Number is the form of a word that shows whether it's singular or plural (page 130).

EXAMPLES **This book is a mystery.** [singular words]

These books are mysteries. [plural words]

object An object is a noun or a pronoun that follows a verb or a preposition. *See direct object, indirect object, and object of a preposition.*

EXAMPLE Mario gave the **horse** a **carrot** for a **treat.** [*Horse* is an indirect object; *carrot* is a direct object; *treat* is the object of a preposition.]

object of a preposition The object of a preposition is the noun or pronoun that ends a prepositional phrase (pages 175, 176–177).

EXAMPLE Hang the painting outside the **auditorium.**

object pronoun *Me, us, you, him, her, it, them,* and *whom* are object pronouns. Object pronouns are used as direct objects, indirect objects, and objects of prepositions (pages 125–127, 176–177).

EXAMPLE Sally gave **her** and **me** a picture of **them.**

parentheses Parentheses ( ) are punctuation marks used to set off words that define or explain another word (page 276).

EXAMPLE This container holds one gallon **(**3.785 liters**)**.

participial phrase A participial phrase is a group of words that includes a participle and other words that complete its meaning (pages 206–207, 263).

EXAMPLE **Sitting at the piano,** Erik loses himself in the music.

participle A participle is a verb form that can act as the main verb in a verb phrase or as an adjective to modify a noun or a pronoun (pages 206–207, 263). *See also past participle and present participle.*

EXAMPLES Erik has **played** several pieces on the piano. **[main verb]**

His **playing** skill improves daily. **[adjective]**

passive voice A verb is in the passive voice when the subject receives the action of the verb (pages 111–112).

EXAMPLE That play **was composed** by Thornton Wilder.

past participle A past participle is usually formed by adding *-d* or *-ed* to the base form of a verb. Some past participles are formed irregularly. When the past participle acts as a verb, one or more helping verbs are always used before the past participle. A past participle may also be used as an adjective (pages 104–105, 113–116, 145, 206–207).

EXAMPLES Kimi has **baked** cookies for us. **[*Baked* is the past participle of *bake*.]**

Mrs. Gonzales had **planted** tomatoes in the spring. **[*Planted* is the past participle of *plant*.]**

Two students have **written** a play. **[*Written* is the past participle of *write*.]**

Erik practices on a **rented** piano. **[*Rented* is an adjective modifying *piano*.]**

past perfect tense The past perfect tense of a verb expresses action that happened before another action or event in the past (page 109).

EXAMPLES The actors **had rehearsed** for many weeks.

We **had** just **arrived** when the play started.

past progressive The past progressive form of a verb expresses action or a condition that was continuing at some time in the past (page 107).

EXAMPLE We **were watching** a scary show.

past tense The past tense of a verb expresses action that already happened (pages 103, 113–116).

EXAMPLE The actors **rehearsed.**

perfect tenses The perfect tenses are the present perfect tense, the past perfect tense, and the future perfect tense. The perfect tenses consist of a form of the verb *have* and a past participle (pages 108–110).

EXAMPLES Lynn **has played** the trumpet for three years. **[present perfect]**

His father **had played** the trumpet as a boy. **[past perfect]**

By the end of high school, Lynn **will have played** the trumpet for seven years. **[future perfect]**

period A period (.) is a punctuation mark used to end a sentence that makes a statement (declarative) or gives a command (imperative). It's also used at the end of many abbreviations (pages 66, 261, 276–278).

EXAMPLES The day was hot and humid**.** **[declarative]**

Bring me some lemonade**.** **[imperative]**

personal pronoun A personal pronoun is a pronoun that refers to people or things. *I, me, you, he, she, him, her, it, we, us, they,* and *them* are personal pronouns (pages 125–126).

EXAMPLE **I** saw **you** with **her** and **him.**

phrase A phrase is a group of words that is used as a single part of speech and does not contain a verb and its subject. *See adjective phrase, adverb phrase, appositive phrase, gerund phrase, infinitive phrase, participial phrase, prepositional phrase, and verb phrase.*

EXAMPLE Three students **wearing backpacks were hiking through the woods.** **[*Wearing backpacks* is a participial phrase acting as an adjective to modify the noun *students. Were hiking* is a verb phrase. *Through the woods* is a prepositional phrase acting as an adverb to modify the verb *were hiking.*]**

plural noun A plural noun is a noun that means more than one of something (pages 83–88).

EXAMPLE The **students** and their **parents** heard the **candidates** give their **speeches.**

possessive noun A possessive noun is a noun that shows ownership (pages 86–88, 273).

EXAMPLE **Tiffany's** friend distributed the **children's** toys.

possessive pronoun A possessive pronoun is a pronoun that shows ownership. *My, mine, our, ours, your, yours, his, her, hers, its, their, theirs,* and *whose* are possessive pronouns (pages 131, 274).

predicate The predicate part of a sentence tells what the subject does or has. It can also tell what the subject is or is like. The **complete predicate** includes all the words in the predicate of a sentence. The **simple predicate** is the main word or word group in the complete predicate. The simple predicate is always a verb (pages 68–73).

EXAMPLE Emily Dickinson **wrote hundreds of poems.** **[The complete predicate is *wrote hundreds of poems.* The simple predicate is *wrote.*]**

predicate adjective A predicate adjective is an adjective that follows a linking verb and modifies the subject of the sentence (pages 101–102, 145).

EXAMPLE Ms. Ortiz is **stern** but **fair.**

predicate noun A predicate noun is a noun that follows a linking verb and renames or identifies the subject of the sentence (pages 101–102).

EXAMPLE Ms. Ortiz is the **director.**

preposition A preposition is a word that relates a noun or a pronoun to another word in a sentence (pages 174–180).

EXAMPLE A boy **with** red hair stood **near** the window.

prepositional phrase A prepositional phrase is a group of words that begins with a preposition and ends with a noun or a pronoun, which is called the **object of the preposition** (pages 174–180, 218–219, 263).

EXAMPLE Hang the painting **outside the new auditorium.**

present participle A present participle is formed by adding *-ing* to the base form of a verb. A helping verb is always used with the present participle when it acts as a verb. A present participle may also be used as an adjective (pages 104–105, 145, 206–207).

EXAMPLES Mr. Omara is **teaching** algebra this year. **[*Teaching* is the present participle of *teach*.]**

The students were **making** decorations. **[*Making* is the present participle of *make*.]**

Erik's **playing** skill improves daily. **[*Playing* is an adjective modifying *skill*.]**

present perfect tense The present perfect tense of a verb expresses action that happened at an indefinite time in the past (page 108).

EXAMPLE The actors **have rehearsed** for many hours.

READY REFERENCE

present progressive The present progressive form of a verb expresses action or a condition that is continuing in the present (pages 106–107, 110).

EXAMPLE Althea **is finishing** her song.

present tense The present tense of a verb expresses action that happens regularly. It can also express a general truth (pages 103, 110).

EXAMPLE A great actor **wins** awards.

principal parts of a verb The principal parts of a verb are the base form, the present participle, the past, and the past participle. The principal parts are used to form verb tenses (pages 104, 113–116).

BASE	PRESENT PARTICIPLE	PAST	PAST PARTICIPLE
play	playing	played	played
go	going	went	gone

progressive forms Progressive forms of verbs express continuing action. They consist of a form of the verb *be* and a present participle (pages 106–107). *See also past progressive and present progressive.*

EXAMPLES Carla **is leaving,** but Mr. and Mrs. Tsai **are staying.**

Ahmed **was studying,** but his brothers **were playing** basketball.

pronoun A pronoun is a word that takes the place of one or more nouns (pages 125–136).

EXAMPLE Max likes books. **He** particularly enjoys novels. **[The pronoun *He* takes the place of the noun *Max*.]**

proper adjective A proper adjective is an adjective formed from a proper noun. It begins with a capital letter (pages 145–146, 254).

EXAMPLE The **Florida** sun beat down on the **Japanese** tourists.

proper noun A proper noun names a particular person, place, thing, or idea. The first word and all other important words in a proper noun are capitalized (pages 81–82, 250–254).

EXAMPLE Did **Edgar Allan Poe** ever see the **Statue of Liberty**?

question mark A question mark (?) is a punctuation mark used to end a sentence that asks a question (interrogative) (pages 66, 261).

EXAMPLE Do you like green eggs and ham**?**

quotation marks Quotation marks (" ") are punctuation marks used to enclose the exact words of a speaker. They're also used for certain titles (pages 270–271).

EXAMPLES **"**A spider,**"** said Sean, **"**has eight legs.**"**
Have you read the story **"**To Build a Fire**"**?

reflexive pronoun A reflexive pronoun ends with *-self* or *-selves* and refers to the subject of a sentence. In a sentence with a reflexive pronoun, the action of the verb returns to the subject (page 134).

EXAMPLE Yolanda bought **herself** a book on engine repair.

regular verb A regular verb is a verb whose past tense and past participle are formed by adding *-d* or *-ed* (page 103).

EXAMPLES I **believed** her.
The twins **have learned** a lesson.

relative pronoun A relative pronoun is a pronoun that may be used to introduce an adjective clause (page 195).

EXAMPLE Divers prefer equipment **that** is lightweight.

restrictive clause *See essential clause.*

restrictive phrase *See essential phrase.*

READY REFERENCE

run-on sentence A run-on sentence is two or more sentences incorrectly written as one sentence (page 75).

EXAMPLES Welty wrote novels, she wrote essays. **[run-on]**
Welty wrote novels she wrote essays. **[run-on]**
Welty wrote novels. She wrote essays. **[correct]**
Welty wrote novels, and she wrote essays. **[correct]**
Welty wrote novels; she wrote essays. **[correct]**

salutation A salutation is the greeting in a letter. The first word and any proper nouns in a salutation should be capitalized (pages 249, 267).

EXAMPLES My dear aunt Julia, Dear Professor Higgins:

semicolon A semicolon (;) is a punctuation mark used to join the main clauses of a compound sentence (pages 268–269).

EXAMPLE Kendra weeded the garden; Geronimo mowed the lawn.

sentence A sentence is a group of words that expresses a complete thought (pages 66–68).

EXAMPLE Edgar Allan Poe wrote many short stories.

sentence fragment A sentence fragment does not express a complete thought. It may also be missing a subject, a predicate, or both (page 68).

EXAMPLES The poems. **[fragment]**
Lay in Dickinson's bureau for years. **[fragment]**
The poems lay in Dickinson's bureau for years. **[sentence]**

simple predicate *See predicate.*

simple sentence A simple sentence has one subject and one predicate (pages 74, 192).

EXAMPLE Eudora Welty lived in Jackson, Mississippi.

simple subject *See subject.*

singular noun A singular noun is a noun that means only one of something (pages 83–86).

EXAMPLE The **child** and his **father** saw a **rabbit** in the **garden.**

subject The subject part of a sentence names whom or what the sentence is about. The **complete subject** includes all the words in the subject of a sentence. The **simple subject** is the main word or word group in the complete subject (pages 68–73, 216–224).

EXAMPLE **A large ship with many sails** appeared on the horizon. **[The complete subject is *A large ship with many sails.* The simple subject is *ship*.]**

subject pronoun *I, we, you, he, she, it, they,* and *who* are subject pronouns. Subject pronouns are used as subjects and predicate pronouns (pages 125–127).

EXAMPLE **He** and **I** know **who you** are.

subordinate clause A subordinate clause is a group of words that has a subject and a predicate but does not express a complete thought and cannot stand alone as a sentence. A subordinate clause is always combined with a main clause in a sentence (pages 193–201).

EXAMPLE Mariah, **who moved here from Montana,** is very popular.

subordinating conjunction A subordinating conjunction is a word that is used to introduce a subordinate clause (page 199).

SUBORDINATING CONJUNCTIONS

after	because	though	whenever
although	before	till	where
as	if	unless	whereas
as if	since	until	wherever
as though	than	when	while

superlative form The superlative form of an adjective compares one person or thing with several others. The superlative form of an adverb compares one action with several others (pages 149–152, 162–163).

READY REFERENCE

READY REFERENCE

EXAMPLES Is Brazil the **richest** country in South America? **[adjective]**

The drummer arrived **earliest** of all the players. **[adverb]**

tense Tense shows the time of the action of a verb (pages 103–110).

EXAMPLES The team often **wins** games. **[present tense]**

The team **won** the game. **[past tense]**

The team **will win** this game. **[future tense]**

transitive verb A transitive verb is an action verb that transfers action to a direct object (pages 98–99).

EXAMPLE The audience **applauds** the actors.

verb A verb is a word that expresses action or a state of being (pages 97–116, 216–224).

EXAMPLES Juanita **plays** soccer.

Kwami **is** a good student.

verbal A verbal is a verb form used as a noun, an adjective, or an adverb. Participles, gerunds, and infinitives are verbals (pages 206–211).

EXAMPLES The **swimming** instructor showed us **diving** techniques. **[participles used as adjectives]**

Mr. McCoy teaches **swimming** and **diving. [gerunds used as nouns]**

Mr. McCoy taught us **to swim** and **to dive. [infinitives used as nouns]**

verb phrase A verb phrase consists of one or more helping verbs followed by a main verb (page 105).

EXAMPLE Telma **is acting** in another play today. **[*Is* is the helping verb; *acting* is the main verb.]**

voice *See active voice and passive voice.*

USAGE GLOSSARY

READY REFERENCE

This glossary will guide you in choosing between words that are often confused. It will also tell you about certain words and expressions you should avoid when you speak or write for school or business.

a, an Use *a* before words that begin with a consonant sound. Use *an* before words that begin with a vowel sound.

EXAMPLES **a** poem, **a** house, **a** yacht, **a** union, **a** one-track mind

an apple, **an** icicle, **an** honor, **an** umbrella, **an** only child

accept, except *Accept* is a verb that means "to receive" or "to agree to." *Except* is a preposition that means "but." *Except* may also be a verb that means "to leave out or exclude."

EXAMPLES Please **accept** this gift.

Will you **accept** our decision?

Everyone will be there **except** you. **[preposition]**

Some students may be **excepted** from taking physical education. **[verb]**

advice, advise *Advice,* a noun, means "an opinion offered as a guide." *Advise,* a verb, means "to give advice."

EXAMPLE Why should I **advise** you when you never accept my **advice**?

affect, effect *Affect* is a verb that means "to cause a change in" or "to influence the emotions of." *Effect* may be a noun or a verb. As a noun, it means "result." As a verb, it means "to bring about or accomplish."

EXAMPLES The mayor's policies have **affected** every city agency.

The mayor's policies have had a positive **effect** on every city agency. **[noun]**

READY REFERENCE

The mayor has **effected** positive changes in every city agency. **[verb]**

ain't *Ain't* is unacceptable in speaking and writing unless you're quoting someone's exact words or writing dialogue. Use *I'm not; you, we,* or *they aren't; he, she,* or *it isn't.*

all ready, already *All ready* means "completely ready." *Already* means "before" or "by this time."

EXAMPLE The band was **all ready** to play its last number, but the fans were **already** leaving the stadium.

all right, alright The spelling *alright* is not acceptable in formal writing. Use *all right.*

EXAMPLE Don't worry; everything will be **all right.**

all together, altogether Use *all together* to mean "in a group." Use *altogether* to mean "completely" or "in all."

EXAMPLES Let's cheer **all together.**

You are being **altogether** silly.

I have three dollars in quarters and two dollars in dimes; that's five dollars **altogether.**

almost, most Don't use *most* in place of *almost.*

EXAMPLE Marty **almost [*not* most]** always makes the honor roll.

a lot, alot *A lot* should always be written as two words. It means "a large number or amount." Avoid using *a lot* in formal writing; be specific.

EXAMPLES **A lot** of snow fell last night.

Ten inches of snow fell last night.

altar, alter An *altar* is a raised structure at which religious ceremonies are performed. *Alter* means "to change."

EXAMPLES The bride and groom approached the **altar.**

Mom **altered** my old coat to fit my little sister.

among, between Use *among* to show a relationship in which more than two persons or things are considered as a group.

EXAMPLES The committee will distribute the used clothing **among** the poor families in the community.

There was confusion **among** the players on the field.

In general, use *between* to show a relationship involving two persons or things, to compare one person or thing with an entire group, or to compare more than two items within a single group.

EXAMPLES Mr. and Mrs. Ohara live halfway **between** Seattle and Portland. **[relationship involving two places]**

What was the difference **between** Elvis Presley and other singers of the twentieth century? **[one person compared with a group]**

Emilio could not decide **between** the collie, the cocker spaniel, and the beagle. **[items within a group]**

anxious, eager *Anxious* means "fearful." It is not a synonym for *eager*, which means "filled with enthusiasm."

EXAMPLES Jean was **anxious** about her test results.

Kirk was **eager [*not* anxious]** to visit his cousin.

anyways, anywheres, everywheres, nowheres, somewheres Write these words without the final *s: anyway, anywhere, everywhere, nowhere, somewhere.*

a while, awhile Use *a while* after a preposition. Use *awhile* as an adverb.

EXAMPLES She read for **a while.**

She read **awhile.**

READY REFERENCE

B

bad, badly *Bad* is an adjective; use it before nouns and after linking verbs to modify the subject. *Badly* is an adverb; use it to modify action verbs.

EXAMPLES Clara felt **bad** about the broken vase.

The team performed **badly** in the first half.

bare, bear *Bare* means "naked." A *bear* is an animal.

EXAMPLES Don't expose your **bare** skin to the sun.

There are many **bears** in Yellowstone National Park.

base, bass One meaning of *base* is "a part on which something rests or stands." *Bass* pronounced to rhyme with *face* is a type of voice. When *bass* is pronounced to rhyme with *glass,* it's a kind of fish.

EXAMPLES Who is playing first **base**?

We need a **bass** singer for the part.

We caught several **bass** on our fishing trip.

beside, besides *Beside* means "at the side of" or "next to." *Besides* means "in addition to."

EXAMPLES Katrina sat **beside** her brother at the table.

Besides apples and bananas, the lunchroom serves dry cereal and doughnuts.

blew, blue *Blue* is the color of a clear sky. *Blew* is the past tense of *blow.*

EXAMPLES She wore a **blue** shirt.

The dead leaves **blew** along the driveway.

boar, bore A *boar* is a male pig. *Bore* means "to tire out with dullness"; it can also mean "a dull person."

EXAMPLES Wild **boars** are common in parts of Africa.

Please don't **bore** me with your silly jokes.

bow When *bow* is pronounced to rhyme with *low*, it means "a knot with two loops" or "an instrument for shooting arrows." When *bow* rhymes with *how*, it means "to bend at the waist."

EXAMPLES Can you tie a good **bow**?

Have you ever shot an arrow with a **bow**?

Actors **bow** at the end of a play.

brake, break As a noun, a *brake* is a device for stopping something or slowing it down. As a verb, *brake* means "to stop or slow down"; its principal parts are *brake, braking, braked*, and *braked.* The noun *break* has several meanings: "the result of breaking," "a fortunate chance," "a short rest." The verb *break* also has many meanings. A few are "to smash or shatter," "to destroy or disrupt," "to force a way through or into," "to surpass or excel." Its principal parts are *break, breaking, broke,* and *broken.*

EXAMPLES Rachel, please put a **brake** on your enthusiasm. **[noun]**

He couldn't **brake** the car in time to avoid the accident. **[verb]**

To fix the **break** in the drainpipe will cost a great deal of money. **[noun]**

Don't **break** my concentration while I'm studying. **[verb]**

bring, take *Bring* means "to carry from a distant place to a closer one." *Take* means "to carry from a nearby place to a more distant one."

EXAMPLES Will you **bring** me some perfume when you return from Paris?

Remember to **take** your passport when you go to Europe.

bust, busted Don't use these words in place of *break*, *broke*, *broken*, or *burst*.

EXAMPLES Don't **break** **[*not* bust]** that vase!

Who **broke** **[*not* busted]** this vase?

Someone has **broken** **[*not* busted]** this vase.

The balloon **burst** **[*not* busted]** with a loud pop.

The child **burst** **[*not* busted]** into tears.

buy, by *Buy* is a verb. *By* is a preposition.

EXAMPLES I'll **buy** the gift tomorrow.

Stand **by** me.

can, may *Can* indicates ability. *May* expresses permission or possibility.

EXAMPLES I **can** tie six kinds of knots.

"You **may** be excused," said Dad. **[permission]**

Luanna **may** play in the band next year. **[possibility]**

"We don't say 'CAN I,' Jeffy. It's 'MAY I' 'cause this is May."

capital, capitol A *capital* is a city that is the seat of a government. *Capitol,* on the other hand, refers only to a building in which a legislature meets.

EXAMPLES What is the **capital** of Vermont?

The **capitol** has a gold dome.

cent, scent, sent A *cent* is a penny. A *scent* is an odor. *Sent* is the past tense and past participle of *send*.

EXAMPLES I haven't got one **cent** in my pocket.

The **scent** of a skunk is unpleasant.

I **sent** my grandma a birthday card.

choose, chose *Choose* is the base form; *chose* is the past tense. The principal parts are *choose, choosing, chose,* and *chosen.*

EXAMPLES Please **choose** a poem to recite in class.

Brian **chose** to recite a poem by Emily Dickinson.

cite, sight, site *Cite* means "to quote an authority." *Sight* is the act of seeing or the ability to see; it can also mean "to see" and "something seen." A *site* is a location; it also means "to place or locate."

EXAMPLES Consuela **cited** three sources of information in her report.

My **sight** is perfect.

The board of education has chosen a **site** for the new high school.

clothes, cloths *Clothes* are what you wear. *Cloths* are pieces of fabric.

EXAMPLES Please hang all your **clothes** in your closet.

Use these **cloths** to wash the car.

coarse, course *Coarse* means "rough." *Course* can mean "a school subject," "a path or way," "order or development," or "part of a meal." *Course* is also used in the phrase *of course.*

EXAMPLES To begin, I'll need some **coarse** sandpaper.

I'd like to take a photography **course.**

The hikers chose a difficult **course** through the mountains.

complement, complementary; compliment, complimentary As a noun, *complement* means "something that completes"; as a verb, it means "to complete." As a noun, *compliment* means "a flattering remark"; as a verb, it means "to praise." *Complementary* and *complimentary* are the adjective forms of the words.

EXAMPLES This flowered scarf will be the perfect **complement** for your outfit. **[noun]**

This flowered scarf **complements** your outfit perfectly. **[verb]**

Phyllis received many **compliments** on her speech. **[noun]**

Many people **complimented** Phyllis on her speech. **[verb]**

consul; council, councilor; counsel, counselor A *consul* is a government official living in a foreign city to protect his or her country's interests and citizens. A *council* is a group of people gathered for the purpose of giving advice. A *councilor* is one who serves on a council. As a noun, *counsel* means "advice." As a verb, *counsel* means "to give advice." A *counselor* is one who gives counsel.

EXAMPLES The **consul** protested to the foreign government about the treatment of her fellow citizens.

The city **council** met to discuss the lack of parking facilities at the sports field.

The defendant received **counsel** from his attorney. **[noun]**

The attorney **counseled** his client to plead innocent. **[verb]**

could of, might of, must of, should of, would of After the words *could, might, must, should,* and *would,* use the helping verb *have* or its contraction, *'ve,* not the word *of.*

EXAMPLES **Could** you **have** prevented the accident?

You **might have** swerved to avoid the other car.

You **must have** seen it coming.

I **should've** warned you.

READY REFERENCE

dear, deer *Dear* is a word of affection and is used to begin a letter. It can also mean "expensive." A *deer* is an animal.

EXAMPLES Talia is my **dear** friend.

We saw a **deer** at the edge of the woods.

desert, dessert *Desert* has two meanings. As a noun, it means "dry, arid land" and is stressed on the first syllable. As a verb, it means "to leave" or "to abandon" and is stressed on the second syllable. A *dessert* is something sweet eaten after a meal.

EXAMPLES This photograph shows a sandstorm in the **desert.** [noun]

I won't **desert** you in your time of need. [verb]

Strawberry shortcake was served for **dessert.**

diner, dinner A *diner* is someone who dines or a place to eat. A *dinner* is a meal.

EXAMPLES The **diners** at the corner **diner** enjoy the friendly atmosphere.

Dinner will be served at eight.

doe, dough A *doe* is a female deer. *Dough* is a mixture of flour and a liquid.

EXAMPLES A **doe** and a stag were visible among the trees.

Knead the **dough** for three minutes.

doesn't, don't *Doesn't* is a contraction of *does not.* It is used with *he, she, it,* and all singular nouns. *Don't* is a contraction of *do not.* It is used with *I, you, we, they,* and all plural nouns.

EXAMPLES She **doesn't** know the answer to your question.

The twins **don't** like broccoli.

eye, I An *eye* is what you see with; it's also a small opening in a needle. *I* is a personal pronoun.

EXAMPLE **I** have something in my **eye.**

fewer, less Use *fewer* with nouns that can be counted. Use *less* with nouns that can't be counted.

EXAMPLES There are **fewer** students in my English class than in my math class.

I used **less** sugar than the recipe recommended.

flour, flower *Flour* is used to bake bread. A *flower* grows in a garden.

EXAMPLES Sift two cups of **flour** into a bowl.

A daisy is a **flower.**

for, four *For* is a preposition. *Four* is a number.

EXAMPLES Wait **for** me.

I have **four** grandparents.

formally, formerly *Formally* is the adverb form of *formal,* which has several meanings: "according to custom, rule, or etiquette," "requiring special ceremony or fancy clothing," "official." *Formerly* means "previously."

EXAMPLES The class officers will be **formally** installed on Thursday.

Mrs. Johnson was **formerly** Miss Malone.

go, say Don't use forms of *go* in place of forms of *say*.

EXAMPLES I tell her the answer, and she **says [*not* goes]**, "I don't believe you."

I told her the news, and she **said [*not* went]**, "Are you serious?"

good, well *Good* is an adjective; use it before nouns and after linking verbs to modify the subject. *Well* is an adverb; use it to modify action verbs. *Well* may also be an adjective meaning "in good health."

EXAMPLES You look **good** in that costume.

Joby plays the piano **well.**

You're looking **well** in spite of your cold.

grate, great A *grate* is a framework of bars set over an opening. *Grate* also means "to shred by rubbing against a rough surface." *Great* means "wonderful" or "large."

EXAMPLES The little girl dropped her lollipop through the **grate.**

Will you **grate** this cheese for me?

You did a **great** job!

had of Don't use *of* between *had* and a past participle.

EXAMPLE I wish I **had known [*not* had of known]** about this sooner.

had ought, hadn't ought, shouldn't ought *Ought* never needs a helping verb. Use *ought* by itself.

EXAMPLES You **ought** to win the match easily.

You **ought** not to blame yourself. *or* You **shouldn't** blame yourself.

hardly, scarcely *Hardly* and *scarcely* have negative meanings. They shouldn't be used with other negative words, like *not* or the contraction *n't*, to express the same idea.

EXAMPLES I **can [*not* can't] hardly** lift this box.

The driver **could [*not* couldn't] scarcely** see through the thick fog.

he, she, it, they Don't use a pronoun subject immediately after a noun subject, as in *The **girls they** baked the cookies.* Omit the unnecessary pronoun: *The **girls** baked the cookies.*

hear, here *Hear* is a verb meaning "to be aware of sound by means of the ear." *Here* is an adverb meaning "in or at this place."

EXAMPLES I can **hear** you perfectly well.

Please put your books **here.**

how come In formal speech and writing, use *why* instead of *how come.*

EXAMPLE **Why** weren't you at the meeting? **[*not* How come you weren't at the meeting?]**

in, into, in to Use *in* to mean "inside" or "within." Use *into* to show movement from the outside to a point within. Don't write *into* when you mean *in to.*

EXAMPLES Jeanine was sitting outdoors **in** a lawn chair.

When it got too hot, she went **into** the house.

She went **in to** get out of the heat.

its, it's *Its* is the possessive form of *it. It's* is a contraction of *it is* or *it has.*

EXAMPLES The dishwasher has finished **its** cycle.

It's [It is] raining again.

It's [It has] been a pleasure to meet you, Ms. Donatello.

kind of, sort of Don't use these expressions as adverbs. Use *somewhat* or *rather* instead.

EXAMPLE We were **rather** sorry to see him go. **[*not* We were kind of sorry to see him go.]**

knead, need *Knead* means "to mix or work into a uniform mass." As a noun, a *need* is a requirement. As a verb, *need* means "to require."

EXAMPLES **Knead** the clay to make it soft.

I **need** a new jacket.

knew, new *Knew* is the past tense of *know. New* means "unused" or "unfamiliar."

EXAMPLES I **knew** the answer.

I need a **new** pencil.

There's a **new** student in our class.

knight, night A *knight* was a warrior of the Middle Ages. *Night* is the time of day during which it is dark.

EXAMPLES A handsome **knight** rescued the fair maiden.

Night fell, and the moon rose.

lay, lie *Lay* means "to put" or "to place." Its principal parts are *lay, laying, laid,* and *laid.* Forms of *lay* are usually followed by a direct object. *Lie* means "to recline" or "to be positioned." Its principal parts are *lie, lying, lay,* and *lain.* Forms of *lie* are never followed by a direct object.

EXAMPLES **Lay** your coat on the bed.

The children are **laying** their beach towels in the sun to dry.

Dad **laid** the baby in her crib.

Myrna had **laid** the book beside her purse.

Lie down for a few minutes.

The lake **lies** to the north.

The dog is **lying** on the back porch.

This morning I **lay** in bed listening to the birds.

You have **lain** on the couch for an hour.

lead, led As a noun, *lead* has two pronunciations and several meanings. When it's pronounced to rhyme with *head,* it means "a metallic element." When it's pronounced to rhyme with *bead,* it can mean "position of being in first place in a race or contest," "example," "clue," "leash," or "the main role in a play."

EXAMPLES **Lead** is no longer allowed as an ingredient in paint.

Jason took the **lead** as the runners entered the stadium.

Follow my **lead.**

The detective had no **leads** in the case.

Only dogs on **leads** are permitted in the park.

Who will win the **lead** in the play?

As a verb, *lead* means "to show the way," "to guide or conduct," "to be first." Its principal parts are *lead, leading, led,* and *led.*

EXAMPLES Ms. Bachman **leads** the orchestra.

The trainer was **leading** the horse around the track.

An usher **led** us to our seats.

Gray has **led** the league in hitting for two years.

READY REFERENCE

learn, teach *Learn* means "to receive knowledge." *Teach* means "to give knowledge."

EXAMPLES Manny **learned** to play the piano at the age of six.

Ms. Guerrero **teaches** American history.

leave, let *Leave* means "to go away." *Let* means "to allow to."

EXAMPLES I'll miss you when you **leave.**

Let me help you with those heavy bags.

like, as, as if, as though *Like* can be a verb or a preposition. It should not be used as a subordinating conjunction. Use *as, as if,* or *as though* to introduce a subordinate clause.

EXAMPLES I **like** piano music. **[verb]**

Teresa plays the piano **like** a professional. **[preposition]**

Moira plays **as** **[*not* like]** her teacher taught her to play.

He looked at me **as if** **[*not* like]** he'd never seen me before.

loose, lose The adjective *loose* means "free," "not firmly attached," or "not fitting tightly." The verb *lose* means "to misplace" or "to fail to win."

EXAMPLES Don't **lose** that **loose** button on your shirt.

If we **lose** this game, we'll be out of the tournament.

mail, male *Mail* is what turns up in your mailbox. *Mail* also means "send." A *male* is a boy or a man.

EXAMPLES We received four pieces of **mail** today.

Sunny **mailed** a gift to her aunt Netta.

The **males** in the chorus wore red ties.

main, mane *Main* means "most important." A *mane* is the long hair on the neck of certain animals.

READY REFERENCE

EXAMPLES What is your **main** job around the house?

The horse's **mane** was braided with colorful ribbons.

many, much Use *many* with nouns that can be counted. Use *much* with nouns that can't be counted.

EXAMPLES **Many** of the events are entertaining.

Much of the money goes to charity.

meat, meet *Meat* is food from an animal. Some meanings of *meet* are "to come face to face with," "to make the acquaintance of," and "to keep an appointment."

EXAMPLES Some people don't eat **meat.**

Meet me at the library at three o'clock.

minute The word *minute* (min´it) means "sixty seconds" or "a short period of time." The word *minute* (mī nōōt´) means "very small."

EXAMPLES I'll be with you in a **minute.**

Don't bother me with **minute** details.

object *Object* is stressed on the first syllable when it means "a thing." *Object* is stressed on the second syllable when it means "oppose."

EXAMPLES Have you ever seen an unidentified flying **object**?

Mom **objected** to the proposal.

of Don't use *of* after the prepositions *off, inside,* and *outside.*

EXAMPLES He jumped **off [*not* off of]** the diving board.

The cat found a mouse **inside [*not* inside of]** the garage.

Outside [*not* outside of] the school, there is an old-fashioned drinking fountain.

off Don't use *off* in place of *from.*

EXAMPLE I'll borrow some money **from [*not* off]** my brother.

ought to of Don't use *of* in place of *have* after *ought to.*

EXAMPLE You **ought to have [*not* ought to of]** known better.

pair, pare, pear A *pair* is two. *Pare* means "to peel." A *pear* is a fruit.

EXAMPLES I bought a new **pair** of socks.

Pare the potatoes and cut them in quarters.

Would you like a **pear** or a banana?

passed, past *Passed* is the past tense and the past participle of the verb *pass. Past* can be an adjective, a preposition, an adverb, or a noun.

EXAMPLES We **passed** your house on the way to school. **[verb]**

The **past** week has been a busy one for me. **[adjective]**

We drove **past** your house. **[preposition]**

At what time did you drive **past**? **[adverb]**

I love Great-grandma's stories about the **past. [noun]**

pause, paws A *pause* is a short space of time. *Pause* also means "to wait for a short time." *Paws* are animal feet.

EXAMPLES We **pause** now for station identification.

I wiped the dog's muddy **paws.**

peace, piece *Peace* means "calmness" or "the absence of conflict." A *piece* is a part of something.

EXAMPLES We enjoy the **peace** of the countryside.

The two nations have finally made **peace.**

May I have another **piece** of pie?

READY REFERENCE

plain, plane *Plain* means "not fancy," "clear," or "a large area of flat land." A *plane* is an airplane or a device for smoothing wood; it can also mean "a two-dimensional figure."

EXAMPLES He wore a **plain** blue tie.

The solution is perfectly **plain** to me.

Buffalo once roamed the **plains.**

We took a **plane** to Chicago.

Jeff used a **plane** to smooth the rough wood.

How do you find the area of a **plane** with four equal sides?

precede, proceed *Precede* means "to go before" or "to come before." *Proceed* means "to continue" or "to move along."

EXAMPLE Our band **preceded** the decorated floats as the parade **proceeded** through town.

principal, principle As a noun, *principal* means "head of a school." As an adjective, *principal* means "main" or "chief." *Principle* is a noun meaning "basic truth or belief" or "rule of conduct."

EXAMPLES Mr. Washington, our **principal,** will speak at the morning assembly. **[noun]**

What was your **principal** reason for joining the club? **[adjective]**

The **principle** of fair play is important in sports.

quiet, quit, quite The adjective *quiet* means "silent" or "motionless." The verb *quit* means "to stop" or "to give up or resign." The adverb *quite* means "very" or "completely."

EXAMPLES Please be **quiet** so I can think.

Shirelle has **quit** the swim team.

We were **quite** sorry to lose her.

raise, rise *Raise* means "to cause to move upward." It can also mean "to breed or grow" and "to bring up or rear." Its principal parts are *raise, raising, raised,* and *raised.* Forms of *raise* are usually followed by a direct object. *Rise* means "to move upward." Its principal parts are *rise, rising, rose,* and *risen.* Forms of *rise* are never followed by a direct object.

EXAMPLES **Raise** your hand if you know the answer.

My uncle is **raising** chickens.

Grandma and Grandpa Schwartz **raised** nine children.

Steam **rises** from boiling water.

The sun is **rising.**

The children **rose** from their seats when the principal entered the room.

In a short time, Loretta had **risen** to the rank of captain.

rap, wrap *Rap* means "to knock." *Wrap* means "to cover."

EXAMPLES **Rap** on the door.

Wrap the presents.

read, reed *Read* means "to understand the meaning of something written" or "to speak aloud something that is written or printed." A *reed* is a stalk of tall grass.

EXAMPLES Will you **read** Jimmy a story?

We found a frog in the **reeds** beside the lake.

real, really *Real* is an adjective; use it before nouns and after linking verbs to modify the subject. *Really* is an adverb; use it to modify action verbs, adjectives, and other adverbs.

EXAMPLES Winona has **real** musical talent.

She is **really** talented.

real, reel *Real* means "actual." A *reel* is a spool to wind something on, such as a fishing line.

EXAMPLES I have a **real** four-leaf clover.

My dad bought me a new fishing **reel.**

reason is because Don't use *because* after *reason is.* Use *that* after *reason is,* or use *because* alone.

EXAMPLES The **reason** I'm tired is **that** I didn't sleep well last night.

I'm tired **because** I didn't sleep well last night.

row When *row* is pronounced to rhyme with *low,* it means "a series of things arranged in a line" or "to move a boat by using oars." When *row* is pronounced to rhyme with *how,* it means "a noisy quarrel."

EXAMPLES We sat in the last **row** of the theater.

Let's **row** across the lake.

My sister and I had a serious **row** yesterday, but today we've forgotten about it.

sail, sale A *sail* is part of a boat. It also means "to travel in a boat." A *sale* is a transfer of ownership in exchange for money.

EXAMPLES As the boat **sails** away, the crew raise the **sails.**

The **sale** of the house was completed on Friday.

sea, see A *sea* is a body of water. *See* means "to be aware of with the eyes."

EXAMPLES The **sea** is rough today.

I can **see** you.

set, sit *Set* means "to place" or "to put." Its principal parts are *set, setting, set,* and *set.* Forms of *set* are usually followed by a direct object. *Sit* means "to place oneself in a seated position." Its principal parts are *sit, sitting, sat,* and *sat.* Forms of *sit* are not followed by a direct object.

EXAMPLES Lani **set** the pots on the stove.

The children **sit** quietly at the table.

sew, sow *Sew* means "to work with needle and thread." When *sow* is pronounced to rhyme with *how,* it means "a female pig." When *sow* is pronounced to rhyme with *low,* it means "to plant."

EXAMPLES Can you **sew** a button on a shirt?

The **sow** has five piglets.

Some farmers **sow** corn in their fields.

shined, shone, shown Both *shined* and *shone* are past tense forms and past participles of *shine.* Use *shined* when you mean "polished"; use *shone* in all other instances.

EXAMPLES Clete **shined** his shoes.

The sun **shone** brightly.

Her face **shone** with happiness.

Shown is the past participle of *show;* its principal parts are *show, showing, showed,* and *shown.*

EXAMPLES You **showed** me these photographs yesterday.

You have **shown** me these photographs before.

some, somewhat Don't use *some* as an adverb in place of *somewhat.*

EXAMPLE The team has improved **somewhat** [*not* some] since last season.

son, sun A *son* is a male child. A *sun* is a star.

EXAMPLES Kino is Mr. and Mrs. Akawa's **son.**

Our **sun** is 93 million miles away.

READY REFERENCE

stationary, stationery *Stationary* means "fixed" or "unmoving." *Stationery* is writing paper.

EXAMPLES This classroom has **stationary** desks.

Rhonda likes to write letters on pretty **stationery.**

sure, surely *Sure* is an adjective; use it before nouns and after linking verbs to modify the subject. *Surely* is an adverb; use it to modify action verbs, adjectives, and other adverbs.

EXAMPLES Are you **sure** about that answer?

You are **surely** smart.

tail, tale A *tail* is what a dog wags. A *tale* is a story.

EXAMPLES The dog's **tail** curled over its back.

Everyone knows the **tale** of Goldilocks and the three bears.

tear When *tear* is pronounced to rhyme with *ear,* it's a drop of fluid from the eye. When *tear* is pronounced to rhyme with *bear,* it means "a rip" or "to rip."

EXAMPLES A **tear** fell from the child's eye.

Tear this rag in half.

than, then *Than* is a conjunction used to introduce the second part of a comparison. *Then* is an adverb meaning "at that time."

EXAMPLES LaTrisha is taller **than** LaToya.

My grandmother was a young girl **then.**

that, which, who *That* may refer to people or things. *Which* refers only to things. *Who* refers only to people.

EXAMPLES The poet **that** wrote *Leaves of Grass* is Walt Whitman.

I have already seen the movie **that** is playing at the Palace.

The new play, **which** closed after a week, received poor reviews.

Students **who** do well on the test will receive scholarships.

that there, this here Don't use *there* or *here* after *that, this, those,* or *these.*

EXAMPLES I can't decide whether to read **this [*not* this here]** magazine or **that [*not* that there]** book.

Fold **these [*not* these here]** towels and hang **those [*not* those there]** shirts in the closet.

their, there, they're *Their* is a possessive form of *they;* it's used to modify nouns. *There* means "in or at that place." *They're* is a contraction of *they are.*

EXAMPLES A hurricane damaged **their** house.

Put your books **there.**

They're our next-door neighbors.

theirs, there's *Theirs* is a possessive form of *they* used as a pronoun. *There's* is a contraction of *there is* or *there has.*

EXAMPLES **Theirs** is the white house with the green shutters.

There's [There is] your friend Chad.

There's [There has] been an accident.

them Don't use *them* as an adjective in place of *those.*

EXAMPLE I'll take one of **those [*not* them]** hamburgers.

this kind, these kinds Use the singular forms *this* and *that* with the singular nouns *kind, sort,* and *type.* Use the plural forms *these* and *those* with the plural nouns *kinds, sorts,* and *types.*

EXAMPLES Use **this kind** of lightbulb in your lamp.

Do you like **these kinds** of lamps?

Many Pakistani restaurants serve **that sort** of food.

Those sorts of foods are nutritious.

This type of dog makes a good pet.

These types of dogs are good with children.

thorough, through *Thorough* means "complete." *Through* is a preposition meaning "into at one side and out at another."

EXAMPLES We gave the bedrooms a **thorough** cleaning.

A breeze blew **through** the house.

threw, through *Threw* is the past tense of *throw. Through* is a preposition meaning "into at one side and out at another." *Through* can also mean "finished."

EXAMPLES Lacey **threw** the ball.

Ira walked **through** the room.

At last I'm **through** with my homework.

to, too, two *To* means "in the direction of"; it is also part of the infinitive form of a verb. *Too* means "very" or "also." *Two* is the number after *one.*

EXAMPLES Jaleela walks **to** school.

She likes **to** study.

The soup is **too** salty.

May I go **too**?

We have **two** kittens.

try and Use *try to.*

EXAMPLE Please **try to [*not* try and]** be on time.

unless, without Don't use *without* in place of *unless.*

EXAMPLE **Unless [*not* Without]** I clean my room, I can't go to the mall.

used to, use to The correct form is *used to.*

EXAMPLE We **used to [*not* use to]** live in Cleveland, Ohio.

waist, waste Your *waist* is where you wear your belt. As a noun, *waste* means "careless or unnecessary spending" or "trash." As a verb, it means "to spend or use carelessly or unnecessarily."

EXAMPLES She tied a colorful scarf around her **waist.**

Buying that computer game was a **waste** of money.

Put your **waste** in the dumpster.

Don't **waste** time worrying.

wait, weight *Wait* means "to stay or remain." *Weight* is a measurement.

EXAMPLES **Wait** right here.

Her **weight** is 110 pounds.

wait for, wait on *Wait for* means "to remain in a place looking forward to something expected." *Wait on* means "to act as a server."

EXAMPLES **Wait for** me at the bus stop.

Nat and Tammy **wait on** diners at The Golden Griddle.

way, ways Use *way,* not *ways,* in referring to distance.

EXAMPLE It's a long **way [*not* ways]** to Tipperary.

weak, week *Weak* means "feeble" or "not strong." A *week* is seven days.

EXAMPLE She felt **weak** for a **week** after the operation.

weather, whether *Weather* is the condition of the atmosphere. *Whether* means "if"; it is also used to introduce the first of two choices.

EXAMPLES The **weather** in Portland is mild and rainy.

Tell me **whether** you can go.

I can't decide **whether** to go or stay.

when, where Don't use *when* or *where* incorrectly in writing a definition.

EXAMPLES A compliment is a flattering remark. **[*not* A compliment is when you make a flattering remark.]**

Spelunking is the hobby of exploring caves. **[*not* Spelunking is where you explore caves.]**

where Don't use *where* in place of *that.*

EXAMPLE I see **that [*not* where]** the Yankees are in first place in their division.

where . . . at Don't use *at* after *where.*

EXAMPLE **Where** is your mother? **[*not* Where is your mother at?]**

who's, whose *Who's* is a contraction of *who is* or *who has.* *Whose* is the possessive form of *who.*

EXAMPLES **Who's [Who is]** conducting the orchestra?

Who's [Who has] read this book?

Whose umbrella is this?

wind When *wind* has a short-*i* sound, it means "moving air." When *wind* has a long-*i* sound, it means "to wrap around."

EXAMPLES The **wind** is strong today.

Wind the bandage around your ankle.

wood, would *Wood* comes from trees. *Would* is a helping verb.

EXAMPLE **Would** you prefer a **wood** bookcase or a metal one?

wound When *wound* is pronounced to rhyme with *sound,* it is the past tense of *wind.* The word *wound* (wo͞ond) means "an injury in which the skin is broken."

EXAMPLE I **wound** the bandage around my ankle to cover the **wound.**

your, you're *Your* is a possessive form of *you. You're* is a contraction of *you are.*

EXAMPLES **Your** arguments are convincing.

You're doing a fine job.

ABBREVIATIONS

An abbreviation is a short way to write a word or a group of words. Abbreviations should be used sparingly in formal writing except for a few that are actually more appropriate than their longer forms. These are *Mr., Mrs.,* and *Dr. (doctor)* before names, *A.M.* and *P.M.,* and *B.C.* and *A.D.*

Some abbreviations are written with capital letters and periods, and some with capital letters and no periods; some are written with lowercase letters and periods, and some with lowercase letters and no periods. A few may be written in any one of these four ways and still be acceptable. For example, to abbreviate *miles per hour,* you may write *MPH, M.P.H., mph,* or *m.p.h.*

Some abbreviations may be spelled in more than one way. For example, *Tuesday* may be abbreviated *Tues.* or *Tue. Thursday* may be written *Thurs.* or *Thu.* In the following lists, only the most common way of writing each abbreviation is given.

When you need information about an abbreviation, consult a dictionary. Some dictionaries list abbreviations in a special section in the back. Others list them in the main part of the book.

MONTHS

Jan.	January	none	July
Feb.	February	Aug.	August
Mar.	March	Sept.	September
Apr.	April	Oct.	October
none	May	Nov.	November
none	June	Dec.	December

DAYS

Sun.	Sunday	Thurs.	Thursday
Mon.	Monday	Fri.	Friday
Tues.	Tuesday	Sat.	Saturday
Wed.	Wednesday		

TIME AND DIRECTION

CDT	central daylight time
CST	central standard time
DST	daylight saving time
EDT	eastern daylight time
EST	eastern standard time
MDT	mountain daylight time
MST	mountain standard time
PDT	Pacific daylight time
PST	Pacific standard time
ST	standard time
NE	northeast
NW	northwest
SE	southeast
SW	southwest
A.D.	in the year of the Lord (Latin *anno Domini*)
B.C.	before Christ
B.C.E.	before the common era
C.E.	common era
A.M.	before noon (Latin *ante meridiem*)
P.M.	after noon (Latin *post meridiem*)

MEASUREMENT

The same abbreviation is used for both the singular and the plural meaning of measurements. Therefore, *ft.* stands for both *foot* and *feet,* and *in.* stands for both *inch* and *inches.* Note that abbreviations of metric measurements are commonly written without periods. U.S. measurements, on the other hand, are usually written with periods.

Metric System

Mass and Weight

t	metric ton
kg	kilogram
g	gram
cg	centigram
mg	milligram

Capacity

kl	kiloliter
l	liter
cl	centiliter
ml	milliliter

Length

km	kilometer
m	meter
cm	centimeter
mm	millimeter

U.S. Weights and Measures

Weight

wt.	weight
lb.	pound
oz.	ounce

Capacity

gal.	gallon
qt.	quart
pt.	pint
c.	cup
tbsp.	tablespoon
tsp.	teaspoon
fl. oz.	fluid ounce

Length

mi.	mile
rd.	rod
yd.	yard
ft.	foot
in.	inch

MISCELLANEOUS MEASUREMENTS

p.s.i.	pounds per square inch
MPH	miles per hour
MPG	miles per gallon
rpm	revolutions per minute
C	Celsius, centigrade
F	Fahrenheit
K	Kelvin
kn	knot

COMPUTER AND INTERNET

CPU	central processing unit
CRT	cathode ray tube
DOS	disk operating system
e-mail	electronic mail
K	kilobyte
URL	uniform resource locator
DVD	digital video disc
d.p.i.	dots per inch
WWW	World Wide Web
ISP	Internet service provider
DNS	domain name system

ADDITIONAL ABBREVIATIONS

ac	alternating current
dc	direct current
AM	amplitude modulation
FM	frequency modulation
ASAP	as soon as possible
e.g.	for example (Latin *exempli gratia*)
etc.	and others, and so forth (Latin *et cetera*)
i.e.	that is (Latin *id est*)
Inc.	incorporated
ISBN	International Standard Book Number

lc	lowercase
misc.	miscellaneous
p.	page
pp.	pages
R.S.V.P.	please reply (French *répondez s'il vous plaît*)
SOS	international distress signal
TM	trademark
uc	uppercase
vs.	versus
w/o	without

UNITED STATES (U.S.)

In most cases, state names and street addresses should be spelled out. The postal abbreviations in the following list should be used with ZIP codes in addressing envelopes. They may also be used with ZIP codes for return addresses and inside addresses in business letters. The traditional state abbreviations are seldom used nowadays, but occasionally it's helpful to know them.

State	Traditional	Postal
Alabama	Ala.	AL
Alaska	none	AK
Arizona	Ariz.	AZ
Arkansas	Ark.	AR
California	Calif.	CA
Colorado	Colo.	CO
Connecticut	Conn.	CT
Delaware	Del.	DE
District of Columbia	D.C.	DC
Florida	Fla.	FL
Georgia	Ga.	GA
Hawaii	none	HI
Idaho	none	ID
Illinois	Ill.	IL
Indiana	Ind.	IN

Iowa	none	IA
Kansas	Kans.	KS
Kentucky	Ky.	KY
Louisiana	La.	LA
Maine	none	ME
Maryland	Md.	MD
Massachusetts	Mass.	MA
Michigan	Mich.	MI
Minnesota	Minn.	MN
Mississippi	Miss.	MS
Missouri	Mo.	MO
Montana	Mont.	MT
Nebraska	Nebr.	NE
Nevada	Nev.	NV
New Hampshire	N.H.	NH
New Jersey	N.J.	NJ
New Mexico	N. Mex.	NM
New York	N.Y.	NY
North Carolina	N.C.	NC
North Dakota	N. Dak.	ND
Ohio	none	OH
Oklahoma	Okla.	OK
Oregon	Oreg.	OR
Pennsylvania	Pa.	PA
Rhode Island	R.I.	RI
South Carolina	S.C.	SC
South Dakota	S. Dak.	SD
Tennessee	Tenn.	TN
Texas	Tex.	TX
Utah	none	UT
Vermont	Vt.	VT
Virginia	Va.	VA
Washington	Wash.	WA
West Virginia	W. Va.	WV
Wisconsin	Wis.	WI
Wyoming	Wyo.	WY

Part Two

Grammar, Usage, and Mechanics

Chapter 1

Subjects, Predicates, and Sentences

PRETEST Kinds of Sentences

Write declarative, interrogative, imperative, *or* exclamatory *to identify each sentence.*

1. When did Michael Jordan join the Chicago Bulls?
2. Watch Jordan shoot free throws.
3. What a great jumper Jordan is!
4. My favorite team is the Boston Celtics.
5. Dad prefers baseball to basketball.

PRETEST Sentences and Sentence Fragments

Write sentence *or* fragment *for each item. Rewrite each fragment to make it a sentence.*

6. Edgar Allan Poe wrote poems and stories.
7. The American Revolution or the Civil War.

8. My dog is very smart.
9. Dan and Debi play softball in the summer.
10. Knows the answer to many questions.
11. Sally and her seven brothers.
12. Of the tall buildings.
13. Earthquakes occur in California.
14. Ancient Egyptians built boats from reeds.
15. Saw several movies about the Old West.

PRETEST Subjects and Predicates

Write each sentence. Underline the simple subjects once and the simple predicates twice.

16. There is a fly in your soup.
17. This dictionary has a red cover.
18. Yesterday Somally and Johanna tutored Monica for an hour.
19. Did the girls take the test and pass it?
20. Wait for them here.
21. Venus and Serena Williams play professional tennis.
22. Over the net flies the ball.
23. Here are a trophy and two ribbons from last year.
24. Are the five Great Lakes Huron, Ontario, Michigan, Erie, and Superior?
25. Find and name the capital of your state.

GRAMMAR/USAGE/MECHANICS

PRETEST Simple, Compound, and Run-on Sentences

Write simple, compound, *or* run-on *to identify each numbered item. If an item is a run-on, rewrite it correctly.*

26. The family vacations every summer in Myrtle Beach, South Carolina.
27. Heavy rains fell all day the river overflowed its banks.
28. All mammals are animals, but not all animals are mammals.

29. My sister and I pitched the tent and gathered wood for a fire.
30. Suyuan is a champion gymnast her brother doesn't enjoy sports.
31. Did you finish your homework, or did you talk on the phone for an hour?
32. The fire crackled and sputtered in the fireplace, and the clock struck twelve.
33. Some plants grow in poor soil and eat insects for food.
34. The Venus's-flytrap attracts insects, the leaves of the plant then snap shut around their prey.
35. The settlers planted corn and wheat, but bad weather and insect pests destroyed their crops.

1.1 KINDS OF SENTENCES

A **sentence** is a group of words that expresses a complete thought.

Different kinds of sentences have different purposes. A sentence can make a statement, ask a question, or give a command. A sentence can also express strong feeling. All sentences begin with a capital letter and end with a punctuation mark. The punctuation mark depends on the purpose of the sentence.

A **declarative sentence** makes a statement. It ends with a period.

EXAMPLE Edgar Allan Poe wrote suspenseful short stories.

An **interrogative sentence** asks a question. It ends with a question mark.

EXAMPLE Did Poe also write poetry?

An **imperative sentence** gives a command or makes a request. It ends with a period.

EXAMPLE Read "The Pit and the Pendulum."

An **exclamatory sentence** expresses strong feeling. It ends with an exclamation point.

EXAMPLE What a great writer Poe was!

EXAMPLE How I enjoy his stories!

"MY INVENTION IS EVEN MORE REMARKABLE THAN YOURS. IT IS THE SIMPLE DECLARATIVE SENTENCE."

PRACTICE Identifying Kinds of Sentences

Write declarative, interrogative, imperative, *or* exclamatory *to identify each sentence.*

1. Are elephants the largest land animals?
2. You can reach California by traveling west.
3. Don't forget your mother's birthday.
4. Bring me those papers on the desk.
5. How hot it is today!

6. Have you ever seen a live kangaroo?
7. What a great fireworks display that was!
8. Construction of the new school will begin in the spring.
9. My little brother's favorite movie is *The Lion King*.
10. Let me help you with those heavy suitcases.

1.2 SENTENCES AND SENTENCE FRAGMENTS

Every sentence has two parts: a subject and a predicate.

EXAMPLE Emily Dickinson (Subject) wrote poetry. (Predicate) — Sentence

The **subject part** of a sentence names whom or what the sentence is about.

The **predicate part** of a sentence tells what the subject does or has. It can also tell what the subject is or is like.

A **sentence fragment** does not express a complete thought. It may also be missing a subject, a predicate, or both.

CORRECTING SENTENCE FRAGMENTS

FRAGMENT	PROBLEM	SENTENCE
The poems.	The fragment lacks a predicate. *What did the poems do?*	The poems lay in Dickinson's bureau for years.
Wrote about her emotions.	The fragment lacks a subject. *Who wrote about her emotions?*	This famous poet wrote about her emotions.
Of meaning.	The fragment lacks a subject and a predicate.	Her poems contain many layers of meaning.

GRAMMAR/USAGE/MECHANICS

PRACTICE Identifying Sentences and Fragments

Write sentence *or* fragment *for each item. Write each sentence and underline the subject part once and the predicate part twice. For each fragment, add a subject or a predicate or both to make it a sentence.*

1. Mr. Wilson teaches life science at the middle school.
2. Over the river and through the woods.
3. Showed me a book about pioneers in Montana.
4. Am having a good time at summer camp.
5. Jacob writes a letter to his parents once a week.
6. Frogs begin life as tadpoles.
7. This unusual photograph shows a sandstorm in the desert.
8. Everywhere on this planet and throughout the solar system.
9. Won the game by just two points.
10. A huge green and white beach umbrella.

GRAMMAR/USAGE/MECHANICS

1.3 SUBJECTS AND PREDICATES

A sentence consists of a subject and a predicate that together express a complete thought. Both a subject and a predicate may consist of more than one word.

	Complete Subject	Complete Predicate
EXAMPLE	Charles Dickens's **novels**	**are** still popular today.
EXAMPLE	My English **teacher**	**wrote** an article about Dickens.

The **complete subject** includes all the words in the subject of a sentence.

The **complete predicate** includes all the words in the predicate of a sentence.

Not all words in the subject or the predicate are equally important.

Complete Subject / Complete Predicate

EXAMPLE The young **Charles Dickens** **wrote** many articles.

Simple Subject / Simple Predicate

The **simple subject** is the main word or word group in the complete subject.

The simple subject is usually a noun or a pronoun. A **noun** is a word that names a person, a place, a thing, or an idea. A **pronoun** is a word that takes the place of one or more nouns.

The **simple predicate** is the main word or word group in the complete predicate.

The simple predicate is always a verb. A **verb** is a word that expresses action or a state of being.

Sometimes the simple subject is the same as the complete subject. Sometimes the simple predicate is the same as the complete predicate.

GRAMMAR/USAGE/MECHANICS

PRACTICE Identifying Complete Subjects and Complete Predicates

Write each sentence. Underline the complete subject once and the complete predicate twice.

1. The purple mountains appeared misty in the distance.
2. Emilio cheered for his sister's teammates.
3. A big raccoon crawled out of the hole.
4. Ms. Hayashida is our math teacher.
5. I like strawberry shortcake with cream.
6. The Snake River flows through southern Idaho.
7. You seem sad today.

8. This dictionary has 1,559 pages.
9. The young detective searched the room for clues.
10. The fresh yellow butter melted.

PRACTICE **Identifying Simple Subjects and Simple Predicates**

Write each sentence. Underline the simple subject once and the simple predicate twice.

1. Thirteen pink candles decorated Lisa's birthday cake.
2. This collie's name is Misty Moonlight.
3. Some teachers assign homework every day.
4. The boys' soccer team lost only one game this season.
5. His bushy beard stretched to his waistline.
6. Daffodils swayed in the brisk breeze.
7. Jefferson Middle School has a new principal.
8. That tall blond boy plays a trombone in the band.
9. My library book disappeared.
10. Computer games give me many hours of fun and entertainment.

1.4 IDENTIFYING THE SUBJECT

In most sentences, the subject comes before the predicate.

EXAMPLE Washington Irving [Subject] described New York in his stories. [Predicate]

Other kinds of sentences, such as questions, begin with part or all of the predicate. The subject comes next, followed by the rest of the predicate.

EXAMPLE Are [Predicate] people [Subject] still reading his stories? [Predicate]

To locate the subject of a question, rearrange the words to form a statement.

PREDICATE	SUBJECT	PREDICATE
Did	Irving	write many funny stories?
	Irving	did write many funny stories.

The predicate also comes before the subject in sentences with inverted word order and in declarative sentences that begin with *Here is, Here are, There is,* and *There are.*

EXAMPLE Over the paper raced [Predicate] Irving's pen. [Subject]

EXAMPLE There is [Predicate] Irving's original manuscript. [Subject]

In imperative sentences (requests and commands), the subject is usually not stated. The predicate is the entire sentence. The word *you* is understood to be the subject.

EXAMPLE (You) [Understood Subject] Look for the author's name on the cover. [Predicate]

GRAMMAR/USAGE/MECHANICS

PRACTICE Identifying the Subject

Write each sentence. Underline the complete subject. Write (You) *before any sentence with an understood subject.*

1. Does your brother deliver the morning paper?
2. Into the tall grass crawled the little garter snake.
3. Call me this afternoon at three o'clock.
4. Has the mail arrived yet?
5. The Beatles introduced many popular songs.
6. Here is a famous painting by Grant Wood.
7. From the bottom of the sea rose a hideous monster.
8. Define the words *numerator* and *denominator.*
9. A personal computer is a useful tool for a writer.
10. There are rules for this game.

1.5 COMPOUND SUBJECTS AND COMPOUND PREDICATES

A sentence may have more than one simple subject or simple predicate.

A **compound subject** consists of two or more simple subjects that have the same predicate. The subjects may be joined by *and, or, both . . . and, either . . . or,* or *neither . . . nor.*

Compound Subject

EXAMPLE **Charlotte Brontë** and **Emily Brontë** were sisters.

When the two simple subjects are joined by *and* or by *both . . . and,* the compound subject is plural. Use the plural form of the verb to agree with the plural compound subject.

When simple subjects are joined by *or, either . . . or,* or *neither . . . nor,* the verb must agree with the nearer simple subject.

EXAMPLE Neither **Charlotte** nor **Emily is** my favorite author.

EXAMPLE Neither her **sisters** nor **Charlotte was** outgoing.

EXAMPLE Neither **Charlotte** nor her **sisters were** outgoing.

In the first sentence, *Emily* is the nearer subject, so the singular form of the verb is used. In the second sentence, *Charlotte* is the nearer subject, so the singular form of the verb is used here too. In the third sentence, *sisters* is the nearer subject, so the plural form of the verb is used.

A **compound predicate** consists of two or more simple predicates, or verbs, that have the same subject. The verbs may be connected by *and, or, but, both . . . and, either . . . or,* or *neither . . . nor.*

Compound Predicate

EXAMPLE Many students **read** and **enjoy** novels.

The compound predicate in this sentence consists of *read* and *enjoy.* Both verbs agree with the plural subject, *students.*

GRAMMAR/USAGE/MECHANICS

PRACTICE Identifying Compound Subjects and Compound Predicates

Write each sentence, using the correct form of the verb in parentheses. Then underline the compound subjects once and the compound predicates twice.

1. Rita Dove and Robert Frost (is, are) two famous American poets.
2. The hotel guests either (reads, read) or (naps, nap) in the afternoon.
3. Both owls and raccoons (hunts, hunt) at night.
4. The chef or his assistants (bakes, bake) and (decorates, decorate) the wedding cakes.
5. Althea (works, work) hard during the week but (relaxes, relax) on Saturday and Sunday.
6. The players or the coach (thanks, thank) the cheerleaders.
7. Some students neither (revises, revise) nor (proofreads, proofread) their compositions.
8. The brothers and sisters both (plays, play) and (sings, sing) together.
9. Either Ruth or Betty (feeds, feed) the children and (puts, put) them to bed.
10. Neither the three sisters nor their brother (weeds, weed) the garden or (mows, mow) the lawn.

1.6 SIMPLE, COMPOUND, AND RUN-ON SENTENCES

A **simple sentence** has one subject and one predicate.

Simple Sentence

EXAMPLE Eudora Welty lived in Jackson, Mississippi.

A simple sentence may have a compound subject, a compound predicate, or both, as in the following example.

Simple Sentence

EXAMPLE **Jeff** and **I** **read** and **enjoy** Welty's stories.

Compound Subject Compound Predicate

A **compound sentence** is a sentence that contains two or more simple sentences joined by a comma and a coordinating conjunction (*and, but, or*) or by a semicolon.

Compound Sentence

EXAMPLE Welty is a novelist, but she also writes essays.

EXAMPLE Welty is a novelist; she also writes essays.

Simple Sentence — Simple Sentence

A run-on sentence is two or more sentences incorrectly written as one sentence. To correct a run-on, write separate sentences or combine the sentences.

CORRECTING RUN-ON SENTENCES	
RUN-ON	**CORRECT**
Welty wrote novels she wrote essays. Welty wrote novels, she wrote essays.	Welty wrote novels**. S**he wrote essays. Welty wrote novels**, and** she wrote essays. Welty wrote novels**;** she wrote essays.

GRAMMAR/USAGE/MECHANICS

PRACTICE Identifying Simple, Compound, and Run-on Sentences

Write simple, compound, *or* run-on *to identify each numbered item. If an item is a run-on, rewrite it correctly.*

1. The school bus stops at the corner of my street.
2. LaToya missed the basket, but Laura caught the rebound.
3. We went to a movie then we stopped for a snack.
4. Ms. Martin's class made the posters, and Mr. Rossi's class sold tickets.
5. Lawyers prepare their cases and defend their clients in court.

6. Cars and trucks stream across the bridge and disappear into the tunnel.
7. Did George Washington really chop down his father's cherry tree, or is that story just a legend?
8. Dad washes dishes by hand Mom puts them in the dishwasher.
9. The wind howls, and the hikers huddle in their tents and drink hot soup.
10. The engine sputters and coughs, the car jerks forward and then stops.

GRAMMAR/USAGE/MECHANICS

PRACTICE Proofreading

Rewrite the following passage, correcting errors in spelling, capitalization, grammar, and usage. Add any missing punctuation. Write legibly to be sure one letter is not mistaken for another. There are ten errors.

Arnold Adoff

[1]Arnold Adoff grew up in New York City. [2]As a boy, he liked books and Jewish poetry. [3]What did Adoff study in college [4]He received a degree in history and government, then he went to Columbia University for further study. [5]for many years, he was a teacher in the public schools of New York. [6]Now he travel, lectures, and writes poetry. [7]His poetry has received an award from the National Council of Teachers of English. [8]According to Adoff, a poem should be read three times and you should listen for its music and rhythm. [9]Two of his books are *Sports Pages* and *All the Colors of the Race.*

[10]Adoff married the writer Virginia Hamilton, author of *M. C. Higgins, the Great,* in 1960. [11]Mr. and Mrs. Adoff lives in Yellow Springs, Ohio. [12]A small college town. [13]They have two grown-up children, Leigh and Jaime

[14]Adoff's wife writes her books on a computer but Adoff prefers his old familiar typewriter. [15]Many of his poems have a definate physical shape. [16]Perhaps he can compose such poems more easily with a typewriter.

POSTTEST Kinds of Sentences

Write declarative, interrogative, imperative, *or* exclamatory *to identify each sentence.*

1. Some dinosaurs may have weighed a hundred tons!
2. A large car weighs about a ton and a half.
3. How much does a rhinoceros weigh?
4. Take me to the zoo.
5. You can see many unusual animals in a zoo.

POSTTEST Sentences and Sentence Fragments

Write sentence *or* fragment *for each item. Rewrite each fragment to make it a sentence.*

6. Beneath the surface of the lake.
7. The story of a dog.
8. A volcanic eruption destroyed the city.
9. Lived there all his life.
10. The tall, thin boy is my cousin.
11. The three tiny kittens have a new home.
12. The icy track down the mountain.
13. Geraldo washed the car.
14. In the beautiful blue sky.
15. Practices every morning.

POSTTEST Subjects and Predicates

Write each sentence. Underline the simple subjects once and the simple predicates twice.

16. Have Kawa and Tyrone studied American history this year?
17. In 1842 pioneers and their animals traveled on the Oregon Trail.
18. Then came the railroads.
19. Through the mountains sped the trains.

20. In 1925 Nellie Tayloe Ross became the governor of Wyoming.
21. She was the first female governor in the United States.
22. Name another female governor.
23. Annie Oakley performed in Buffalo Bill's Wild West Show in 1885 and amazed the crowds with her rifle.
24. Here is a model of her rifle.
25. When did this performer die?

POSTTEST Simple, Compound, and Run-on Sentences

Write simple, compound, *or* run-on *to identify each numbered item. If an item is a run-on, rewrite it correctly.*

26. Seventy-six trombones led the big parade.
27. My mother works as a dental assistant, and my father drives a truck.
28. I made an outline for my report then I wrote the introduction.
29. Several aunts and uncles and all my grandparents live in other states.
30. Jake and Sally grilled hot dogs and made a salad.
31. Perry makes his bed every morning Sandra always leaves her room in a mess.
32. The dog barked and growled, the thief turned and ran.
33. Did Serena prepare this meal by herself, or did her brother help her?
34. Silvia lost her watch, but Jeremiah found it and returned it.
35. Mr. and Mrs. Montoya raise Irish setters, and their son and daughter feed and exercise the animals.

Chapter 2

Nouns

PRETEST Kinds of Nouns

Write each noun. Label the common nouns C *and the proper nouns* P.

1. In the tiny house in Cleveland, Grandma Palavinskas baked strudel with her daughter.
2. The success of the project will depend on hard work by all members of the team.
3. The friendship between the two girls from Orlando began in kindergarten.
4. Men and women throughout the world wear makeup for different reasons.
5. A vacation at Disney World will be fun for the whole family.

PRETEST Possessive Nouns

Write the possessive form of the noun in parentheses.

6. This store sells only (women) shoes.
7. My (mom) responsibilities allow her little free time.

8. (Chris) father works in a bakery.
9. The doctor set (Jessica) broken leg.
10. What is the (store) policy on returns?
11. The (Williamses) house is on the north side of Buffalo Road.
12. Did you hear the (judge) instructions to the jury?
13. The counselors scheduled the (campers) activities in advance.
14. Mrs. (Cassirer) daughter designed her own Web page.
15. The airline delivered the (passengers) baggage to the wrong city.

GRAMMAR/USAGE/MECHANICS

PRETEST Recognizing Plurals, Possessives, and Contractions

Identify the italicized word in each sentence by writing plural noun, singular possessive noun, plural possessive noun, *or* contraction.

16. The *Women's* National Basketball Association allowed women into professional basketball.
17. How shall we celebrate *Mei-Ling's* birthday?
18. *Edwin's* won three races today.
19. There will be a dinner for the *volunteers* on Thursday.
20. Will you attend the *writers'* conference?
21. Please clean the *cat's* litter box.
22. John *Dixon's* the president of the company.
23. The *mall's* location is convenient.
24. Workers clean the *horses'* stables twice a day.
25. The *Smiths* have three children in high school.

PRETEST Appositives

Write the appositive or appositive phrase in each sentence.

26. Soccer's world championship, the World Cup occurs every four years.
27. The scientific community admired Albert Einstein, a United States immigrant.

28. The rock group Fudd will perform tonight in the high school auditorium.
29. A mighty volcano, Kilauea destroys homes and plant life with its lava flows.
30. Harold talks constantly about computer games, his favorite subject.
31. Have you ever read the short story "Rikki-tikki-tavi"?
32. A champion golfer, Babe Didrikson Zaharias is probably the greatest female athlete of all time.
33. Tamika visited her cousin Bernard.
34. Harry Houdini, a famous magician, specialized in escape tricks.
35. The poet Shel Silverstein wrote *Where the Sidewalk Ends.*

2.1 KINDS OF NOUNS

A **noun** is a word that names a person, a place, a thing, or an idea.

NOUNS	
PERSONS	sister, mayor, player, coach, pianist, children
PLACES	park, zoo, lake, school, playground, desert, city
THINGS	magazine, boots, rose, pencil, peach, baseball, car
IDEAS	honesty, truth, democracy, pride, maturity, progress

A **common noun** names *any* person, place, thing, or idea.
A **proper noun** names a *particular* person, place, thing, or idea.

The first word and all other important words in a proper noun are capitalized: *Edgar Allan Poe, Statue of Liberty.*

Common nouns can be either concrete or abstract.

Concrete nouns name things you can see or touch.

Abstract nouns name ideas, qualities, and feelings that can't be seen or touched.

KINDS OF NOUNS

COMMON NOUNS		PROPER NOUNS
Abstract	**Concrete**	
truth	document	Supreme Court
courage	crown	Queen Elizabeth I
time	snow	December
history	museum	Museum of Modern Art
entertainment	actor	Meryl Streep
education	school	Howard University
comedy	comedian	Jerry Seinfeld
friendship	friend	Jessica
tragedy	ship	*Titanic*

GRAMMAR/USAGE/MECHANICS

Compound nouns are nouns made of two or more words.

A compound noun can be one word, like *storybook,* or more than one word, like *ice cream.* A compound noun can also be joined by one or more hyphens, like *runner-up.*

COMPOUND NOUNS

ONE WORD	housekeeper, showcase, bookmark, outdoors, teammate
MORE THAN ONE WORD	post office, dining room, maid of honor, high school
HYPHENATED	sister-in-law, great-aunt, kilowatt-hour, walkie-talkie

PRACTICE Identifying Common and Proper Nouns

Write each noun. Label the common nouns C *and the proper nouns* P.

1. Paul rolled his wheelchair up the ramp and into the Weston Municipal Building.
2. The Empire State Building in New York City was once the tallest structure in the world.
3. Friendship and loyalty are two qualities most people admire.
4. Buy your fruits and flowers at Friendly Farm Market in Clarkville.
5. Abraham Lincoln served as president during the Civil War.
6. Harry bought several souvenirs during his visit to Disney World.
7. The United Nations encourages peace and cooperation among nations.
8. My mom sometimes calls Pizza Pantry for a quick delivery.
9. Grandma Faith often describes memories of her youth on a farm in Kansas.
10. The librarian recommended *Treasure Island,* a book by Robert Louis Stevenson.

2.2 SINGULAR AND PLURAL NOUNS

A **singular noun** names one person, place, thing, or idea. A **plural noun** names more than one.

To form the plural of most nouns, you simply add *-s.* Other plural nouns are formed in different ways.

FORMING PLURAL NOUNS

NOUNS ENDING WITH	TO FORM PLURAL	EXAMPLES		
s, z, ch, sh, x	Add ***-es.***	bus bus**es**	buzz buzz**es**	box box**es**
o preceded by a vowel	Add ***-s.***	rodeo rodeo**s**	studio studio**s**	radio radio**s**
o preceded by a consonant	Usually add ***-es.***	hero hero**es**	potato potato**es**	echo echo**es**
	Sometimes add ***-s.***	zero zero**s**	photo photo**s**	piano piano**s**
y preceded by a vowel	Add ***-s.***	day day**s**	turkey turkey**s**	toy toy**s**
y preceded by a consonant	Usually change ***y*** to ***i*** and add ***-es.***	city cit**ies**	diary diar**ies**	penny penn**ies**
f or ***fe***	Usually change ***f*** to ***v*** and add ***-s*** or ***-es.***	wife wi**ves**	leaf lea**ves**	half hal**ves**
	Sometimes add ***-s.***	roof roof**s**	chief chief**s**	belief belief**s**

To form the plural of compound nouns written as one word, usually add *-s* or *-es.* To form the plural of compound nouns that are written as more than one word or are hyphenated, make the main noun in the compound word plural, or check a dictionary.

COMPOUND NOUNS	
ONE WORD	doorbell**s**, necklace**s**, rosebush**es**; *Exception:* passer**s**by
MORE THAN ONE WORD	post office**s**, dining room**s**, maid**s** of honor, high school**s**
HYPHENATED	brother**s**-in-law, great-aunt**s**, eighth-grader**s**, push-up**s**

Words such as *family* and *team* are called collective nouns.

A **collective noun** names a group of people, animals, or things.

A collective noun subject may be followed by a singular verb or a plural verb, depending on the meaning. The subject is singular when the members of the group act as a single unit. The subject is plural when each member of the group acts separately. Other words in a sentence can sometimes help you decide whether a collective noun is singular or plural.

EXAMPLE The **team shares** the field with **its** opponent. **[shares, its, singular]**

EXAMPLE The **team share their** jokes with one another. **[share, their, plural]**

PRACTICE Forming Plural Nouns

Write the plural form of each noun.

1. mailbox
2. belief
3. country
4. banana
5. leaf
6. valley
7. bush
8. mother-in-law
9. potato
10. radio

GRAMMAR/USAGE/MECHANICS

PRACTICE Identifying Collective Nouns

Write each collective noun. Label it S *if it's singular and* P *if it's plural.*

1. The science club meets after school.
2. The jury vote by secret ballot.
3. The Sanchez family goes to all the football games.
4. The teaching staff plans the graduation ceremonies.
5. The team take their positions on the field.
6. The committee interview community leaders.
7. The crowd cheers.
8. The class give their reports.
9. The herd enters the barn.
10. The orchestra tune their instruments.

2.3 POSSESSIVE NOUNS

A noun can show ownership or possession of things or qualities. This kind of noun is called a possessive noun.

A **possessive noun** tells who or what owns or has something.

Possessive nouns may be common nouns or proper nouns. They may also be singular or plural. Notice the possessive nouns in the following sentences:

SINGULAR NOUN	**Rita** has a book about baseball.
SINGULAR POSSESSIVE NOUN	**Rita's** book is about baseball.
PLURAL NOUN	Several **cities** have baseball teams.
PLURAL POSSESSIVE NOUN	These **cities'** teams attract fans.

Possessive nouns are formed in one of two ways. To form the possessive of singular nouns and plural nouns not ending in *s*, add an apostrophe and *s ('s)*. To form the possessive of plural nouns ending in *s*, add just an apostrophe at the end of the word.

FORMING POSSESSIVE NOUNS

NOUNS	TO FORM POSSESSIVE	EXAMPLES
All singular nouns; plural nouns not ending in ***s***	Add an apostrophe and ***s*** *(**'s**)*.	a girl–a girl**'s** name Germany–Germany**'s** exports the bus–the bus**'s** capacity Ms. Ames–Ms. Ames**'s** class children–children**'s** toys women–women**'s** coats
Plural nouns ending in ***s***	Add just an apostrophe (**'**) at the end of the plural noun.	babies–babies**'** birth weight the Joneses–the Joneses**'** car

PRACTICE Writing Possessive Nouns

Write the possessive form of the noun in parentheses.

1. The teacher read (Doris) composition.
2. I took my little brother to the (children) story hour at the library.
3. The (Barkleys) house stands on the corner.
4. Is (Dallas) climate hot enough for you?
5. My (parents) cars are parked in the driveway.
6. The (judge) decision is final.
7. You will find (men) suits on the third floor.
8. Return this key to the (boys) locker room.
9. I have seen many of (Florida) tourist attractions.
10. I got (Tiger Woods) autograph!

2.4 RECOGNIZING PLURALS, POSSESSIVES, AND CONTRACTIONS

Most plural nouns, all possessive nouns, and certain contractions end with the sound of *s.* These words may sound alike, but their spellings and meanings are different.

NOUN FORMS AND CONTRACTIONS

	EXAMPLE	MEANING
Plural Noun	The **students** wrote a play.	more than one student
Plural Possessive Noun	The **students'** play is good.	the play by several students
Singular Possessive Noun	I saw the **student's** performance.	the performance of one student
Contraction	This **student's** the author. This **student's** written other plays.	This student is the author. This student has written other plays.

A **contraction** is a word made by combining two words and leaving out one or more letters. An apostrophe shows where the letters have been omitted.

Plural nouns don't have an apostrophe. Contractions and singular possessive nouns look exactly alike. Some plural possessive nouns end with *'s*, and some end with just an apostrophe. You can tell these words apart by the way they're used in a sentence.

NOUN FORMS AND CONTRACTIONS

PLURAL NOUNS	CONTRACTIONS	SINGULAR POSSESSIVE NOUNS	PLURAL POSSESSIVE NOUNS
speakers	speaker's	speaker's	speakers'
women	woman's	woman's	women's
echoes	echo's	echo's	echoes'
countries	country's	country's	countries'

PRACTICE Identifying Plurals, Possessives, and Contractions

Identify the italicized word in each sentence by writing plural noun, singular possessive noun, plural possessive noun, *or* contraction.

1. The *nurses'* committee will meet on Monday.
2. *Keely's* parents attend all her softball games.
3. My *aunt's* left for a trip to China.
4. Many *students* volunteer throughout the community.
5. No opponent has defeated the *girls'* basketball team.
6. Have you found the *dog's* leash?
7. *Harrison's* washing the family car.
8. The principal called the *boy's* parents.
9. The *astronauts'* voyage to the moon was a success.
10. The *Pattons* moved to Santa Fe last month.

GRAMMAR/USAGE/MECHANICS

2.5 APPOSITIVES

An **appositive** is a noun that is placed next to another noun to identify it or add information about it.

EXAMPLE James Madison's wife, **Dolley,** was a famous first lady.

The noun *Dolley* identifies the noun next to it, *wife.* In this sentence, *Dolley* is an appositive.

An **appositive phrase** is a group of words that includes an appositive and other words that modify the appositive.

EXAMPLE Madison, **our fourth president,** held many other offices.

The words *our* and *fourth* modify the appositive *president.* The phrase *our fourth president* is an appositive phrase. It identifies the noun *Madison.*

An appositive or an appositive phrase can appear anywhere in a sentence as long as it appears next to the noun it identifies.

EXAMPLE **Our fourth president,** Madison held many other offices.

EXAMPLE Many historians have studied the life of Madison**, our fourth president.**

Appositives and appositive phrases are usually set off with commas. If the appositive is essential to the meaning of the sentence, however, commas are not used.

EXAMPLE Madison's friend **Thomas Jefferson** was president before Madison.

EXAMPLE Madison's father**, James Madison,** was a plantation owner.

Obviously, Madison had more than one friend, so the appositive, *Thomas Jefferson,* is needed to identify this particular friend. No commas are needed. However, Madison had only one father. The father's name is not needed to identify him. Therefore, commas are needed.

GRAMMAR/USAGE/MECHANICS

PRACTICE Identifying Appositives

Write each sentence. Underline the appositive or appositive phrase and add appropriate commas. Circle the noun the appositive identifies.

1. Manuel Ortiz an artist will display his works at the library.
2. Jane Nakamura the president's assistant spoke at the banquet.
3. The entertainer Will Rogers was famous for his political jokes.
4. In euchre a lively card game jacks are the high cards.
5. Mr. Wells explained his latest invention a time machine.
6. A mystery writer Agatha Christie composed clever plots.
7. Aunt Carmella my mother's sister is a veterinarian in San Antonio.
8. My favorite athlete is the baseball player Ken Griffey Jr.
9. Harry's dog a cocker spaniel won a blue ribbon.
10. An industrious young man Jimmy already runs his own business.

PRACTICE Proofreading

Rewrite the following passage, correcting errors in spelling, capitalization, grammar, and usage. Add any missing punctuation. Write legibly to be sure one letter is not mistaken for another. There are ten errors.

Gary Soto

[1]Gary Soto grew up in Fresno, California. [2]Sotos grandparents were born in Mexico and worked in the United States. [3]His parent's were born in the United States. [4]Soto often heard his family and friends speak Spanish, but Soto never learned Spanish in school.

[5]Soto read a poem, "Unwanted," by the poet edward field. [6]Then he wrote poetry. [7]Soto also wrote storys. [8]At the age of twenty, he enrolled at California State University. [9]At the university, Philip Levine another poet taught Soto more about poetry.

[10]Soto has achieved sucess as a poet. [11]This poets won many awards for his writing. [12]The Academy of American Poets award prizes every year. [13]Soto won a prize in 1975. [14]Another organization the Guggenheim Foundation gave him money for a year in Mexico. [15]Gabriel García Márquez a Colombian writer influenced Gary Soto.

POSTTEST Kinds of Nouns

Write each noun. Label the common nouns C *and the proper nouns* P.

1. The monarch butterfly travels four thousand miles during its migration.
2. Many sporting events are held at the Meadowlands in New Jersey.
3. Anika values the love of her family, her friendship with Ricardi, and the relaxation of an afternoon without homework.
4. Susan B. Anthony fought for the rights of women.
5. A psychiatrist is a medical doctor with four additional years of preparation in a hospital.

POSTTEST Possessive Nouns

Write the possessive form of the noun in parentheses.

6. Do you like this (artist) style?
7. We went directly to the (boys) shoe department.
8. The (Harrises) van is parked in the driveway.
9. (Mwanakweli) flower business showed a profit in the first year.
10. The heavy rain seeped through the (tents) fabric.
11. One of (Arkansas) tourist attractions is Mammoth Springs.
12. The (children) toys were scattered everywhere.
13. Did you enjoy (Ross) report on turtles?
14. The (photographer) subject, a three-year-old girl, smiled at her puppy.
15. Ms. Montaldo belongs to the (nurses) association.

GRAMMAR/USAGE/MECHANICS

POSTTEST Recognizing Plurals, Possessives, and Contractions

Identify the italicized word in each sentence by writing plural noun, singular possessive noun, plural possessive noun, *or* contraction.

16. We're collecting *children's* toys for the hospital.
17. *Tecumseh's* diplomatic skills unified tribes from Florida to the Great Lakes.
18. *Dad's* worked at the same job for fifteen years.
19. Which of these *singers* is your favorite?
20. The *workers'* helmets were bright yellow.
21. I put some food in the *hamster's* cage.
22. Ms. *Esteban's* our new principal.
23. The *car's* brakes are in need of repair.
24. I found three *robins'* nests in the garden.
25. The *Wilsons* have two dalmation puppies.

POSTTEST Appositives

Write the appositive or appositive phrase in each sentence.

26. Everyone likes Mr. Swallow, our band director.

27. The third store from the corner, a bakery, is our destination.

28. Our best player, Jason Tran, broke his ankle.

29. A round tent, the yurt is a Mongolian house.

30. The architect Frank Lloyd Wright designed a house over a waterfall.

31. An "unsinkable" ship, the *Titanic* hit an iceberg on its first voyage and sank.

32. The popular singer Linda Ronstadt performs in a variety of musical styles.

33. The city of Shanghai lies at the mouth of China's longest river, the Yangtze.

34. The American colonist David Bushnell built a submarine in 1776.

35. A starchy vegetable, the potato is also a source of vitamins.

Chapter 3

Verbs

PRETEST Action Verbs and Linking Verbs

Write each verb. Label the action verbs A *and the linking verbs* L.

1. The temperature rose to a hundred.
2. Dorothy remembered the dream.
3. The actor's face looks familiar.
4. Enrico looked into the next room.
5. The children were quiet.
6. Every culture has its own myths, legends, and fairy tales.
7. The weather grew cold.
8. The twins are visiting their grandparents.
9. Maria Tallchief became a famous ballerina.
10. Our cat has disappeared again.

PRETEST Direct Objects, Indirect Objects, Predicate Nouns, and Predicate Adjectives

Identify the italicized word in each sentence by writing direct object, indirect object, predicate noun, *or* predicate adjective.

11. Ants at a picnic are *pests.*
12. The workers built a *house*.
13. A tornado's winds are *dangerous*.
14. The new mother fed her seven *infants* formula from a bottle.
15. Tiger Woods has shown the *world* his talent.
16. The science field trip was *sensational.*
17. Follow your favorite *sports* on this channel.
18. Mother Teresa was a religious *woman*.
19. We rode a *train* from Boston to Providence.
20. The ancient Roman gladiator was a powerful *fighter.*

PRETEST Present and Past Tenses and Progressive Forms

Write the verb. Then write present tense, past tense, present progressive, *or* past progressive *to identify it.*

21. Tom Whittaker, a man with an artificial right foot, was climbing Mount Everest.
22. Athletes in ancient Greece participated in the first Olympic Games.
23. The human hyoid bone, a bone above the larynx, touches no other bone.
24. Sumiko and her brother were building a tree house.
25. Kou was making a pumpkin pie with his father.
26. These birds fly south for the winter.
27. Someone measured the depth of the Pacific Ocean.
28. We are recording our thoughts in our journals.
29. Ogun, a seventh-grader, is acting in plays.
30. I am enjoying my vacation.

PRETEST Perfect and Future Tenses

Write the verb. Then write present perfect, past perfect, future, *or* future perfect *to identify it.*

31. By two o'clock, we had finished our chores.
32. We shall visit the dinosaur display at the museum.
33. Emily's neighbor has raised cattle all her life.
34. The student council has decorated the gymnasium.
35. Who will win the next election?
36. The Egyptian mummy had vanished from the tomb.
37. By this time tomorrow, I shall have finished my report.
38. The train will have departed by ten o'clock tonight.
39. We have attended every football game this season.
40. The two actors had rehearsed the play for five weeks.

PRETEST Irregular Verbs

Write the correct verb form from the choices in parentheses.

41. We (flew, flown) our kites on the windiest day in March.
42. All the campers (swam, swum) a mile on Friday afternoon.
43. The sprinter had (sprang, sprung) out of the blocks in record time.
44. The boxer has (hit, hitted) the punching bag one hundred times this morning.
45. A dreadful storm (began, begun) just after midnight.
46. The small fangs of the centipede have (stinged, stung) me.
47. Antony had (cut, cutted) the lawn with the lawnmower.
48. The Morgan twins have (sang, sung) in the choir for three years.
49. Oniwaki has (spoke, spoken) three languages in one conversation!
50. The balloon (burst, bursted).

3.1 ACTION VERBS

You may have heard the movie director's call for "lights, camera, *action!*" The actions in movies and plays can be expressed by verbs. If a word expresses action and tells what a subject does, it's an action verb.

An **action verb** is a word that expresses action. An action verb may be made up of more than one word.

Notice the action verbs in the following sentences.

EXAMPLE The director **shouts** at the members of the cast.

EXAMPLE The lights **are flashing** above the stage.

EXAMPLE The audience **arrived** in time for the performance.

EXAMPLE Several singers **have memorized** the lyrics of a song.

Action verbs can express physical actions, such as *shout* and *arrive.* They can also express mental activities, such as *memorize* and *forget.*

GRAMMAR/USAGE/MECHANICS

ACTION VERBS	
PHYSICAL	shout, flash, arrive, talk, applaud, act, sing, dance
MENTAL	remember, forget, think, memorize, read, dream, appreciate

FRANK & ERNEST® by Bob Thaves

FRANK AND ERNEST reprinted by permission of Newspaper Enterprise Association, Inc.

Have, has, and *had* are often used before other verbs. They can also be used as action verbs when they tell that the subject owns or holds something.

EXAMPLE The actors already **have** their costumes.

EXAMPLE The director **has** a script in her back pocket.

EXAMPLE Rosa **had** a theater program from 1920.

PRACTICE Identifying Action Verbs

Write the action verbs.

1. Mom and Dad play golf on Saturday.
2. Six juicy hamburgers sizzled on the grill.
3. The workers cleaned the pool last week.
4. David had scored twelve points.
5. Our neighbors have a new car.
6. The ceremony began at two o'clock.
7. The cafeteria staff prepares lunch for the entire school.
8. Serena has read thirty books this year.
9. The icy rain blew through the open window.
10. Josh and his sister are arranging the flowers.

3.2 TRANSITIVE AND INTRANSITIVE VERBS

In some sentences, the predicate consists of only an action verb.

EXAMPLE The actor **rehearsed.**

Most sentences provide more information. The predicate often names who or what receives the action of the verb.

EXAMPLE The actor rehearsed his **lines** from the play.

The word *lines* tells what the actor rehearsed. *Lines* is a direct object.

A **direct object** receives the action of a verb. It answers the question *whom?* or *what?* after an action verb.

A sentence may have a compound direct object. That is, a sentence may have more than one direct object.

EXAMPLE We saw **Maurice** and **Inez** in the audience.

When an action verb transfers action to a direct object, the verb is transitive. When an action verb has no direct object, the verb is intransitive.

A **transitive verb** has a direct object.
An **intransitive verb** does not have a direct object.

Most action verbs can be transitive or intransitive. A verb can be labeled transitive or intransitive only by examining its use in a particular sentence.

EXAMPLE The audience **applauds** the actors. **[transitive]**

EXAMPLE The audience **applauds** loudly. **[intransitive]**

GRAMMAR/USAGE/MECHANICS

PRACTICE Recognizing Transitive and Intransitive Verbs

For each sentence, write the action verb. Then write T *if the verb is transitive or* I *if the verb is intransitive. If the verb is transitive, write the direct object or objects.*

1. A transitive verb has a direct object.
2. Jason forgot his homework.
3. Three plastic deer stood in the garden.
4. Horatio achieved his success with hard work and luck.
5. The stone goose wore a bright yellow raincoat.
6. The porpoises jump through hoops.
7. The high school drama club performed the play for the middle school students.
8. The baby cried loudly from her crib in the next room.
9. Jackie ordered a vanilla shake and a hot dog with mustard.
10. Little Miss Muffet sat on a tuffet.

3.3 INDIRECT OBJECTS

A direct object answers the question *whom?* or *what?* after an action verb.

EXAMPLE Friends sent **flowers.**

In some sentences, an indirect object also follows an action verb.

An **indirect object** answers the question *to whom?* or *for whom?* or *to what?* or *for what?* an action is done.

EXAMPLE Friends sent the **actors** flowers.

The direct object in the sentence is *flowers.* The indirect object is *actors. Actors* answers the question *to whom?* after the action verb *sent.*

A sentence may have a compound indirect object. In the sentence below, *cast* and *orchestra* are indirect objects. The direct object is *thanks.*

EXAMPLE Ms. Ortiz gave the **cast** and the **orchestra** her thanks.

An indirect object appears only in a sentence that has a direct object. Two clues can help you recognize an indirect object. First, an indirect object always comes between the verb and the direct object. Second, you can put the word *to* or *for* before an indirect object and change its position. The sentence will still have the same meaning, but it will no longer have an indirect object.

EXAMPLE Friends **sent** the **director flowers.** **[*Director* is an indirect object.]**

EXAMPLE Friends sent flowers **to the director.** **[*Director* is not an indirect object.]**

You know that in the first sentence *director* is the indirect object because it comes between the verb and the direct object and because it can be placed after the word *to,* as in the second sentence.

PRACTICE Identifying Direct and Indirect Objects

Write the indirect objects and underline them. Then write the direct objects.

1. Kareem gave the crowd a big smile.
2. The eager salesperson sold the couple a new car.
3. The company promises its employees annual pay increases.
4. Ms. Nishimura served her guests a traditional meal.
5. Sharlene made her brother and his friend costumes for the play.
6. Mrs. Kowalski fed her favorite horse a carrot.
7. The Harrisons have left the university their art collection.
8. The parents' club bought the school three new computers.
9. Muhammad writes his cousin a letter once a month.
10. Satch threw the last batter a slow curveball.

3.4 LINKING VERBS AND PREDICATE WORDS

A **linking verb** connects the subject of a sentence with a noun or an adjective in the predicate.

EXAMPLE Juana Ortiz **was** the **director.**

EXAMPLE Ms. Ortiz **is imaginative.**

In the first sentence, the verb *was* links the noun *director* to the subject. *Director* identifies the subject. In the second sentence, the verb *is* links the adjective *imaginative* to the subject. *Imaginative* describes the subject.

A **predicate noun** is a noun that follows a linking verb. It renames or identifies the subject.

A **predicate adjective** is an adjective that follows a linking verb. It describes, or modifies, the subject.

A sentence may contain a compound predicate noun or a compound predicate adjective.

EXAMPLE Ms. Ortiz is a **teacher** and a **musician.** **[compound predicate noun]**

EXAMPLE Ms. Ortiz is **stern** but **fair.** **[compound predicate adjective]**

COMMON LINKING VERBS			
be (am, is, are,	seem	taste	sound
was, were)	appear	feel	grow
become	look	smell	turn

Most of these verbs can also be used as action verbs.

EXAMPLE The director **sounded** angry. **[linking verb]**

EXAMPLE The director **sounded** the alarm. **[action verb]**

NOTE Two other linking verbs are *remain* and *stay.*

GRAMMAR/USAGE/MECHANICS

PRACTICE Identifying Verbs, Predicate Nouns, and Predicate Adjectives

For each sentence, write the verb. Label the verb A *if it's an action verb or* L *if it's a linking verb. If it's a linking verb, write the predicate noun or the predicate adjective. Label a predicate noun* PN. *Label a predicate adjective* PA.

1. Douglas looks handsome in his pirate costume.
2. Carly is a singer and a dancer.
3. A shadowy figure appeared in the gloom.
4. The band sounds wonderful today.
5. Suddenly Zelda smelled smoke.
6. Ouida Sebestyen became a writer late in life.

7. Mr. Menendez grows huge pumpkins in his garden.
8. Sereta felt nervous before her performance.
9. Harry's horse seems a sure winner in the next race.
10. The leaves turn red and yellow in the fall.

3.5 PRESENT AND PAST TENSES

The verb in a sentence expresses action. It also tells when the action takes place. The form of a verb that shows the time of the action is called the **tense** of the verb.

The **present tense** of a verb expresses action that happens regularly. It can also express a general truth.

EXAMPLE A great actor **wins** awards.

In the present tense, the base form of a verb is used with all plural subjects and the pronouns *I* and *you.* For singular subjects other than *I* and *you,* *-s* or *-es* is usually added to the base form of the verb. Remember that a verb must agree in number with its subject.

PRESENT TENSE FORMS

SINGULAR	PLURAL
I **walk.**	We **walk.**
You **walk.**	You **walk.**
He, she, *or* it **walks.**	They **walk.**

The **past tense** of a verb expresses action that already happened.

The past tense of many verbs is formed by adding *-d* or *-ed* to the base form of the verb.

EXAMPLE The actors **rehearsed.** Ms. Ortiz **directed.**

GRAMMAR/USAGE/MECHANICS

PRACTICE Identifying Present and Past Tenses

For each sentence, write the verb. Then write present *or* past *to identify its tense.*

1. I like pizza with everything.
2. James and Betsy waited twenty minutes for the bus.
3. Millions of people around the world are poor.
4. You borrowed too many books from the library.
5. Tulips and daffodils bloom in the spring.
6. I enjoyed my visit to Aunt Ethel's horse farm.
7. The cruise passengers dine between six and eight.
8. Captain James Cook explored the South Pacific in the eighteenth century.
9. Amos or Tara mows the lawn once a week.
10. The Pattersons moved here in April.

3.6 MAIN VERBS AND HELPING VERBS

Verbs have four principal parts that are used to form all tenses. Notice how the principal parts of a verb are formed.

PRINCIPAL PARTS OF VERBS

BASE FORM	PRESENT PARTICIPLE	PAST	PAST PARTICIPLE
act	acting	acted	acted

You can use the base form and the past alone to form the present and past tenses. The present participle and the past participle can be combined with helping verbs to form other tenses.

A **helping verb** helps the main verb express action or make a statement.

A **verb phrase** consists of one or more helping verbs followed by a main verb.

EXAMPLE Telma **is acting** in another play today.

The word *is* is the helping verb, and the present participle *acting* is the main verb. Together they form a verb phrase.

The most common helping verbs are *be, have,* and *do.* Forms of the helping verb *be* are *am, is,* and *are* in the present and *was* and *were* in the past. These helping verbs often combine with the present participle of the main verb.

GRAMMAR/USAGE/MECHANICS

BE AND THE PRESENT PARTICIPLE

SINGULAR	PLURAL	SINGULAR	PLURAL
I **am** learning.	We **are** learning.	I **was** learning.	We **were** learning.
You **are** learning.	You **are** learning.	You **were** learning.	You **were** learning.
She **is** learning.	They **are** learning.	He **was** learning.	They **were** learning.

The helping verb *have* combines with the past participle of the main verb. Forms of the helping verb *have* are *have* and *has* in the present and *had* in the past.

HAVE AND THE PAST PARTICIPLE

SINGULAR	PLURAL	SINGULAR	PLURAL
I **have** learned.	We **have** learned.	I **had** learned.	We **had** learned.
You **have** learned.	You **have** learned.	You **had** learned.	You **had** learned.
She **has** learned.	They **have** learned.	He **had** learned.	They **had** learned.

Forms of the helping verb *do* are *do* and *does* in the present and *did* in the past. The helping verb *do* combines with the base form of a verb: *I do believe you. She does believe you. They did believe you.*

NOTE Other helping verbs are *can, could, may, might, must, should,* and *would.*

PRACTICE Identifying Main Verbs and Helping Verbs

Write each verb phrase. Underline the helping verb. Write base form, present participle, *or* past participle *to identify the main verb.*

1. DeeDee is planning her science project.
2. Silvia Chin has solved several mysteries for the police.
3. The students were measuring the area of their classroom.
4. The pioneers had journeyed over two thousand miles.
5. Did you feed the dog?
6. I am reading a good baseball story.
7. We do need your help, Jason.
8. A boy with red hair was walking across the football field.
9. The mayor and the city council are cooperating on the project.
10. Have you discovered the secret of success?

3.7 PROGRESSIVE FORMS

You know that the present tense of a verb can express action that occurs repeatedly. To express action that is taking place at the present time, use the present progressive form of the verb.

The **present progressive form** of a verb expresses action or a condition that is continuing in the present.

EXAMPLE Althea **is finishing** her song.

The present progressive form of a verb consists of the helping verb *am*, *are*, or *is* and the present participle of the main verb.

PRESENT PROGRESSIVE FORMS

SINGULAR	PLURAL
I **am watching.**	We **are watching.**
You **are watching.**	You **are watching.**
He, she, *or* it **is watching.**	They **are watching.**

The **past progressive form** of a verb expresses action or a condition that was continuing at some time in the past.

EXAMPLE We **were watching** a scary show.

The past progressive form of a verb consists of the helping verb *was* or *were* and the present participle of the main verb.

PAST PROGRESSIVE FORMS

SINGULAR	PLURAL
I **was working.**	We **were working.**
You **were working.**	You **were working.**
He, she, *or* it **was working.**	They **were working.**

GRAMMAR/USAGE/MECHANICS

PRACTICE Using Progressive Forms

Rewrite the sentence using the progressive form of the verb. If the verb is in the present tense, change it to the present progressive form. If the verb is in the past tense, change it to the past progressive form.

1. Sean plays computer games.
2. The horses trotted around the track.
3. This machine worked yesterday.
4. Serena hurried to her dance class.
5. Harry and Sally take piano lessons.
6. The Ryans vacation at the beach.
7. Sharon and Joel cleaned the garage.
8. Courtney visits her grandmother.
9. I watch television with my best friend.
10. Billy typed a letter to his cousin.

3.8 PRESENT PERFECT AND PAST PERFECT TENSES

The **present perfect tense** of a verb expresses action that happened at an indefinite time in the past.

EXAMPLE The actor **has rehearsed** for many hours.

EXAMPLE Lori and Pam **have watched** *Grease* five times.

The present perfect tense consists of the helping verb *have* or *has* and the past participle of the main verb.

PRESENT PERFECT TENSE	
SINGULAR	**PLURAL**
I **have watched.**	We **have watched.**
You **have watched.**	You **have watched.**
He, she, *or* it **has watched.**	They **have watched.**

The **past perfect tense** of a verb expresses action that happened before another action or event in the past.

The past perfect tense is often used in sentences that contain a past-tense verb in another part of the sentence.

EXAMPLE The actors **had rehearsed** for many weeks.

EXAMPLE We **had** just **arrived** when the play **started.**

The past perfect tense of a verb consists of the helping verb *had* and the past participle of the main verb.

PAST PERFECT TENSE	
SINGULAR	**PLURAL**
I **had started.**	We **had started.**
You **had started.**	You **had started.**
He, she, *or* it **had started.**	They **had started.**

GRAMMAR/USAGE/MECHANICS

PRACTICE Identifying Perfect Tenses

Write the verb. Then write present perfect *or* past perfect *to identify the tense.*

1. Harry has saved a hundred dollars for a new bike.
2. The chef had decorated the wedding cake earlier in the day.
3. I have wanted a camera of my own for a long time.
4. Jerry has checked his spelling twice.
5. You have mentioned your fabulous aunt Harriet many times.
6. I had packed my lunch during the evening news.
7. Kay and Ben have collected several hundred aluminum cans.
8. Davis had bunted on his last trip to the plate.

9. Mitsuko has combed her hair three times.
10. Around midnight the butler had locked all the doors and windows.

3.9 EXPRESSING FUTURE TIME

The **future tense** of a verb expresses action that will take place in the future.

EXAMPLE We **shall attend** the performance.

EXAMPLE The actors **will show** their talents.

The future tense of a verb is formed by using the helping verb *will* before the base form of a verb. The helping verb *shall* is sometimes used when the subject is *I* or *we.*

There are other ways to show that an action will happen in the future. *Tomorrow, next year,* and *later* are all words that indicate a future time. These words are called **time words,** and they may be used with the present tense to express future time.

EXAMPLE Our show **opens next week.**

EXAMPLE **Tomorrow** we **start** rehearsals.

The present progressive form can also be used with time words to express future actions.

EXAMPLE Our show **is opening next week.**

EXAMPLE **Tomorrow** we **are starting** rehearsals.

Another way to talk about the future is with the future perfect tense.

The **future perfect tense** of a verb expresses action that will be completed before another future event begins.

EXAMPLE By Thursday I **shall have performed** six times.

EXAMPLE The production **will have closed** by next week.

The future perfect tense is formed by using *will have* or *shall have* before the past participle of a verb.

PRACTICE Identifying Verb Tenses

Write the verb. Then write present, future, present progressive, *or* future perfect *to identify the verb tense.*

1. We shall arrive in Denver around noon.
2. The new comedy show *Oscar and Larry* begins next Monday night on Channel 3.
3. Bonita's flute lessons are ending in April.
4. By October the construction workers will have finished the new school.
5. Workers in the downtown area will watch the parade from their office windows.
6. Dad is interviewing for a new job tomorrow.
7. I go to the dentist's office at three o'clock today.
8. I shall have applied three coats of paint to these walls by tomorrow afternoon.
9. Marge and Homer will be the team leaders.
10. By the end of this course, you will have learned the fox-trot and the waltz.

3.10 ACTIVE AND PASSIVE VOICE

A verb is in the **active voice** when the subject performs the action of the verb.

EXAMPLE Thornton Wilder **composed** that play.

A verb is in the **passive voice** when the subject receives the action of the verb.

EXAMPLE That play **was composed** by Thornton Wilder.

In the first example, the author, Thornton Wilder, seems more important because *Thornton Wilder* is the subject of the sentence. In the second example, the play seems more important because *play* is the subject of the sentence.

Notice that verbs in the passive voice consist of a form of *be* and the past participle. Often a phrase beginning with *by* follows the verb in the passive voice.

EXAMPLE I am puzzled **by your question.** **[passive voice]**

EXAMPLE Your question puzzles me. **[active voice]**

EXAMPLE The puppy is frightened **by loud noises.** **[passive voice]**

EXAMPLE Loud noises frighten the puppy. **[active voice]**

EXAMPLE Plays are performed **by actors.** **[passive voice]**

EXAMPLE Actors perform plays. **[active voice]**

EXAMPLE This painting was purchased **by Ms. Jones.** **[passive voice]**

EXAMPLE Ms. Jones purchased this painting. **[active voice]**

The active voice is usually a stronger, more direct way to express ideas. Use the passive voice if you want to stress the receiver of the action or if you don't know who performed the action.

EXAMPLE *Our Town* **was performed.** **[You may want to stress the play.]**

EXAMPLE The actors **were fired.** **[You may not know who fired the actors.]**

PRACTICE Using Active and Passive Voice

Rewrite each sentence, changing the verb from active to passive or from passive to active.

1. Most of the town was destroyed by a tornado.
2. Elias Howe invented the sewing machine.
3. Radium and polonium were discovered by Marie Curie.
4. The speech was delivered by Dr. Galbraith.
5. Mario Mendoza played a minuet by Mozart.
6. Irving Berlin composed the song "God Bless America."
7. The song was performed many times by Kate Smith.
8. Voters often reject tax proposals.
9. The judge settles all disputes.
10. These flowers were planted by our 4-H club.

3.11 IRREGULAR VERBS

The irregular verbs listed here are grouped according to the way their past tense and past participle are formed.

IRREGULAR VERBS			
PATTERN	**BASE FORM**	**PAST**	**PAST PARTICIPLE**
One vowel changes to form the past and the past participle.	begin	began	begun
	drink	drank	drunk
	ring	rang	rung
	shrink	shrank *or* shrunk	shrunk
	sing	sang	sung
	sink	sank	sunk
	spring	sprang *or* sprung	sprung
	swim	swam	swum
The past and the past participle are the same.	bring	brought	brought
	build	built	built
	buy	bought	bought
	catch	caught	caught
	creep	crept	crept
	feel	felt	felt
	fight	fought	fought
	find	found	found
	get	got	got *or* gotten
	have	had	had
	hold	held	held
	keep	kept	kept
	lay	laid	laid
	lead	led	led
	leave	left	left
	lend	lent	lent
	lose	lost	lost
	make	made	made
	meet	met	met
	pay	paid	paid
	say	said	said

PATTERN	BASE FORM	PAST	PAST PARTICIPLE
The past and the past participle are the same.	seek	sought	sought
	sell	sold	sold
	send	sent	sent
	sit	sat	sat
	sleep	slept	slept
	spend	spent	spent
	spin	spun	spun
	stand	stood	stood
	sting	stung	stung
	swing	swung	swung
	teach	taught	taught
	tell	told	told
	think	thought	thought
	win	won	won

PRACTICE Using Irregular Verbs I

Write the correct verb form from the choices in parentheses.

1. The center fielder (catched, caught) several fly balls.
2. The chorus (sang, sung) three selections from *My Fair Lady.*
3. The last bell (rang, rung) at three o'clock.
4. How many people have (swam, swum) the English Channel?
5. The jockey (lead, led) his horse to the winner's circle.
6. Ms. Delgado has (teached, taught) us many useful things about photography.
7. Mary Lou had (brung, brought) treats for everyone.
8. This wool sweater has (shrank, shrunk) two sizes.
9. Lars (drank, drunk) a quart of milk after the game.
10. The Tigers had (winned, won) the championship for the last three years.

3.12 MORE IRREGULAR VERBS

Here are some more irregular verbs.

IRREGULAR VERBS

PATTERN	BASE FORM	PAST	PAST PARTICIPLE
The base form and the past participle are the same.	become	became	become
	come	came	come
	run	ran	run
The past ends in *ew*, and the past participle ends in *wn*.	blow	blew	blown
	draw	drew	drawn
	fly	flew	flown
	grow	grew	grown
	know	knew	known
	throw	threw	thrown
The past participle ends in *en*.	bite	bit	bitten *or* bit
	break	broke	broken
	choose	chose	chosen
	drive	drove	driven
	eat	ate	eaten
	fall	fell	fallen
	freeze	froze	frozen
	give	gave	given
	ride	rode	ridden
	rise	rose	risen
	see	saw	seen
	shake	shook	shaken
	speak	spoke	spoken
	steal	stole	stolen
	take	took	taken
	write	wrote	written

PATTERN	BASE FORM	PAST	PAST PARTICIPLE
The past and the past participle don't follow any pattern.	be	was, were	been
	do	did	done
	go	went	gone
	lie	lay	lain
	tear	tore	torn
	wear	wore	worn
The base form, the past, and the past participle are the same.	burst	burst	burst
	cost	cost	cost
	cut	cut	cut
	hit	hit	hit
	hurt	hurt	hurt
	let	let	let
	put	put	put
	read	read	read
	set	set	set
	spread	spread	spread

FRANK AND ERNEST reprinted by permission of Newspaper Enterprise Association, Inc.

PRACTICE Using Irregular Verbs II

Write the correct verb form from the choices in parentheses.

1. The answer (came, come) to me in a flash.
2. The twins have (broke, broken) Mom's favorite teacup.

3. Nathan (ran, run) the three blocks to the library.
4. I (saw, seen) that movie last week.
5. The math team has (went, gone) to a competition in River City.
6. Cinderella had finally (became, become) a princess.
7. Dad has (wore, worn) the same suit for five years.
8. The children (bursted, burst) all the balloons.
9. I never (did, done) a back dive before.
10. Little Freddy had (fell, fallen) into a mud puddle.

GRAMMAR/USAGE/MECHANICS

PRACTICE Proofreading

Rewrite the following passage, correcting errors in spelling, capitalization, grammar, and usage. Add any missing punctuation. Write legibly to be sure one letter is not mistaken for another. There are ten errors.

Carl Sandburg

[1]Carl Sandburg liked simple poems [2]His parents came from Sweden. [3]They had chose the United States as their home. [4]Sandburg grew up in Illinois. [5]By the age of eighteen, he had leaved home. [6]He traveled across the country, and he often catched rides on trains.

[7]At the age of twenty, Sandburg joined the army. [8]He served breifly in Puerto Rico. [9]Then he returned home and attended Lombard College.

[10]As a boy, Sandburg had thunk about the name Carl. [11]It sounded too foreign, so he taked the name Charles. [12]At the age of thirty, he married a teacher. [13]She liked the name Carl. [14]He used this name again, and he become proud of his Swedish ancestors.

[15]Sandburg won the Pulitzer Prize for poetry in 1951. [16]He did not just write poems. [17]He also gone across the country. [18]He collected and sung American folk songs.

POSTTEST Action Verbs and Linking Verbs

Write each verb. Label the action verbs A *and the linking verbs* L.

1. Chuon Chuon jogs for her health.
2. My uncle is a plumber.
3. Tomorrow Chuon Chuon and Verta have a softball practice.
4. Shelby feels unhappy.
5. Nick felt the dog's tongue on his hand.
6. Grass needs rain.
7. Without rain, grass turns yellow.
8. Mom is watering her plants.
9. Jaime has written his cousin a letter.
10. Antonia seems a friendly person.

POSTTEST Direct Objects, Indirect Objects, Predicate Nouns, and Predicate Adjectives

Identify the italicized word in each sentence by writing direct object, indirect object, predicate noun, *or* predicate adjective.

11. A screwdriver seems a useful *tool.*
12. The kindergarten student made his *mother* a present.
13. The heat grew *unbearable.*
14. The children catch *fireflies* on summer nights.
15. A crocodile is a large *reptile* with many teeth.
16. The students suddenly became *serious.*
17. This banana feels *mushy.*
18. The guide showed the *class* the new dinosaur exhibit.
19. Many movies and television series have dramatized western *heroes.*
20. The western hero often has a favorite *horse.*

POSTTEST Present and Past Tenses and Progressive Forms

Write the verb. Then write present tense, past tense, present progressive, *or* past progressive *to identify it.*

21. Developers planned the route of the first transcontinental road, the Lincoln Highway, in 1913.
22. The band members are practicing in the gym.
23. I am writing a report on hot-air balloons.
24. The fire destroyed the neighborhood flower shop.
25. In a single contraction, the heart pumps about two ounces of blood.
26. The stoplight was causing traffic problems.
27. The professional athletes were boasting about their talent.
28. Workers make bulletproof glass with two sheets of plate glass and a layer of resin.
29. Jake was studying for an important test.
30. The dinosaur exhibit is traveling from city to city.

POSTTEST Perfect and Future Tenses

Write the verb. Then write present perfect, past perfect, future, *or* future perfect *to identify it.*

31. Wildlife has disappeared from this area.
32. I shall greet the guests at the door.
33. I had finished my homework by six o'clock.
34. In the excitement, Mr. Parmesi had misplaced his key.
35. By next week, I will have memorized all my lines for the play.
36. The offer for a free can of dog food will expire next Monday.
37. The chef has selected the perfect ingredients for the taco salad.

38. By Thursday evening, the workers will have signed a new contract.
39. The passengers had boarded the ship early in the morning.
40. I have tested the trombone, the saxophone, the flute, and the trumpet.

POSTTEST Irregular Verbs

Write the correct verb form from the choices in parentheses.

41. The awards program (began, begun) at eight o'clock.
42. The Milwaukee Brewers (won, winned) the baseball game in the eighteenth inning!
43. Christopher Pike has (wrote, written) a number of scary stories.
44. The enormous Hoover Dam has (holded, held) back the waters of the Colorado River for more than fifty years.
45. I (drank, drunk) too many soft drinks.
46. The detective (catched, caught) the computer thief with a clever trap.
47. She had (wore, worn) her best dress to the awards ceremony.
48. A soft pad (broke, breaked) the fall of the pole-vaulter.
49. I (leaved, left) my umbrella on the bus.
50. Mom has (keeped, kept) every one of my letters.

Chapter 4

Pronouns

PRETEST Personal Pronouns

Write each personal pronoun. Then write one of the following phrases to identify the pronoun: subject pronoun as subject, subject pronoun as predicate pronoun, object pronoun as direct object, object pronoun as indirect object.

1. The girl in the picture is I.
2. We saw her at the mall.
3. She handed me the notes from yesterday's science class.
4. You gave them a chance, but they wasted it.
5. The mysterious stranger was he, and I thanked him for the help.

PRETEST Using Pronouns

Write the correct word or phrase from the choices in parentheses.

6. (You and I, You and me, I and you, Me and you) make a good team.
7. Su and (he, him) explored the cave together.
8. The store owner gave (he and I, I and he, him and me, me and him) part-time jobs.
9. (She, Her) and Mrs. Cranston share the garden chores and the vegetables.
10. Mr. Lusalah gave (he and she, him and her, he and her, him and she) several old comic books.
11. (We, Us) newspaper carriers struggle with the heavy Sunday edition.
12. (Clare and I, Clare and me, I and Clare, Me and Clare) took photographs of the race, and (Samantha and they, Samantha and them) developed the pictures in a tiny darkroom.
13. Mom tested Charlie and (she, her) on their spelling words.
14. The most exciting actor was (he, him).
15. The scientist showed Zainab and (they, them) the fossil of a trilobite.

PRETEST Pronouns and Antecedents

Write each personal pronoun and its antecedent. If a pronoun doesn't have a clear antecedent, rewrite the numbered item to make the meaning clear.

16. The people light lamps during one festival to honor the man. They think he is important.
17. Prehistoric food gatherers tied logs together for rafts. Then they fished from them.

18. Eric and Carl met Rocknie and Romeo at the skating rink. They were late.
19. Black Shawl rented a movie. She watched it in the living room.
20. They have strict safety rules at the local swimming pool.

PRETEST Identifying Pronouns

Write each pronoun. Then write possessive, indefinite, reflexive, intensive, interrogative, *or* demonstrative *to identify it.*

21. Grace drew this herself.
22. Whose are these?
23. Has anyone found mine?
24. Ms. Grimes takes her trash to the alley, but several leave theirs in the hallway.
25. The musicians themselves took their instruments to the repair shop.
26. All know the decision about that is yours.
27. Mr. McFadden bought himself a new tractor for his fields.
28. The great horned owl has fourteen bones in its neck.
29. What did the thieves steal?
30. The professional ballet dancers treated themselves to a rare night without a practice.

PRETEST Indefinite Pronouns

Write the subjects and the correct words from the choices in parentheses.

31. Everyone (wonder, wonders) about the accuracy of the story in the newspaper.
32. In my opinion, all of the action movies this summer (are, is) unrealistic.

GRAMMAR/USAGE/MECHANICS

33. Both of the doctors (tell, tells) the nurses about new procedures.
34. This morning everything (have, has) gone wrong.
35. (Do, Does) either of the magicians ask you for assistance?
36. Few of the students (have, has) volunteered yet.
37. All of the sugar (are, is) spilling onto the floor.
38. Why (were, was) none of the long jumpers ready for the event?
39. Anybody in the spelling bee (get, gets) only one chance for a correct spelling.
40. Several of the flooded areas (receive, receives) help from the government.

PRETEST Personal, Reflexive, Intensive, Interrogative, and Demonstrative Pronouns

Write the correct word from the choices in parentheses.

41. The young cowboy drove the cattle (hisself, himself).
42. Esi and (I, myself) learned about Neil Armstrong.
43. (Who, Whom) did the coach choose for the varsity squad?
44. (These, This) is a great day for the outdoor scavenger hunt.
45. Ms. Hammersmith promised Talika and (me, myself) some fruit from her cherry tree.
46. (Whose, Who's) is this?
47. The engineers (theirselves, themselves) examined the bridge.
48. Do (that, those) belong to you?
49. (Whose, Who's) brought refreshments?
50. The crossword puzzle stumped (us, ourselves).

4.1 PERSONAL PRONOUNS

A **pronoun** is a word that takes the place of one or more nouns.

EXAMPLE Max likes books. **He** particularly enjoys novels.

EXAMPLE Max and Irma like books. **They** particularly enjoy novels.

In the first example, the pronoun *He* replaces the noun *Max* as the subject of the sentence. In the second example, *They* replaces *Max and Irma.*

Pronouns that refer to people or things are called **personal pronouns.**

Some personal pronouns are used as the subjects of sentences. Others are used as the objects of verbs.

A **subject pronoun** is used as the subject of a sentence. It may also be used like a predicate noun, in which case it's called a predicate pronoun.

EXAMPLE **I** enjoy a good book in my spare time. **[subject]**

EXAMPLE **We** belong to a book club. **[subject]**

EXAMPLE **She** gave a good book report. **[subject]**

EXAMPLE **It** was about Andrew Jackson. **[subject]**

EXAMPLE **They** especially like adventure stories. **[subject]**

EXAMPLE The most popular author was **he. [predicate pronoun]**

An **object pronoun** may be a direct object or an indirect object.

EXAMPLE The teacher praised **us. [direct object]**

EXAMPLE Tell **me** a story. **[indirect object]**

EXAMPLE The movie frightened **them. [direct object]**

EXAMPLE The class wrote **her** a letter. **[indirect object]**

EXAMPLE The story amuses **you. [direct object]**

EXAMPLE The plot gives **him** an idea. **[indirect object]**

PERSONAL PRONOUNS		
	SINGULAR	**PLURAL**
Subject Pronouns	I you he, she, it	we you they
Object Pronouns	me you him, her, it	us you them

PRACTICE Identifying Personal Pronouns

Write each personal pronoun. Then write one of the following phrases to identify the pronoun: subject pronoun as subject, subject pronoun as predicate pronoun, object pronoun as direct object, object pronoun as indirect object.

1. They awarded her the prize.
2. We drove them to the airport.
3. I fixed him a tuna sandwich.
4. The person in the chicken costume was you!
5. They saw you and him at the mall.
6. He and she found it on the beach.
7. The winner of the essay contest was I.
8. It showed us the location of the treasure.
9. She helped you with the dishes.
10. You are giving me a headache.

4.2 USING PRONOUNS

Use subject pronouns in compound subjects. Use object pronouns in compound objects.

EXAMPLE **He** and Carmen wrote the report. **[not *Him and Carmen*]**

EXAMPLE Tell John and **me** about the report. **[not *John and I*]**

If you're not sure which form of the pronoun to use, read the sentence with only the pronoun as the subject or the object. Your ear will tell you which form is correct.

When the pronoun *I, we, me,* or *us* is part of a compound subject or object, *I, we, me,* or *us* should come last. (It's simply courteous to name yourself or the group of which you are a part last.)

EXAMPLE Lee and **I** played some new tunes. **[not *I and Lee*]**

EXAMPLE Country music interests Lee and **me.** **[not *me and Lee*]**

In formal writing and speech, use a subject pronoun after a linking verb.

EXAMPLE The writer of this report was **she.**

EXAMPLE It is **I.**

A pronoun and a noun may be used together. The form of the pronoun depends on its use in the sentence.

EXAMPLE **We** students read the book. **[*We* is the subject.]**

EXAMPLE The book delighted **us** readers. **[*Us* is a direct object.]**

Some sentences make incomplete comparisons. The form of the pronoun can affect the meaning of such sentences. In any incomplete comparison, use the form of the pronoun that would be correct if the comparison were complete.

EXAMPLE You like pizza better than **I** [like pizza].

EXAMPLE You like pizza better than [you like] **me.**

GRAMMAR/USAGE/MECHANICS

PRACTICE Using Subject and Object Pronouns

Write the correct word or phrase from the choices in parentheses.

1. Kareem will save Mr. Jerome and (we, us) seats in the bleachers.
2. (Jed and I, I and Jed, Me and Jed, Jed and me) fixed the bicycle ourselves.
3. The drama director assigned (we, us) volunteers jobs as ushers.

4. The coach told (Sally and I, I and Sally, me and Sally, Sally and me) the results of the tryouts for the volleyball team.
5. Ziggy and (we, us) took the subway to the zoo.
6. The principal asked Sheryl and (he, him) for help with the middle school handbook.
7. Mrs. Santini sent (she and I, I and she, me and her, her and me) to the office for supplies.
8. The contestants were (they and we, them and we, they and us, them and us).
9. (We, Us) volunteers will meet at the hospital after school.
10. Mrs. Feinstein fixed Isaac and (they, them) a snack.

4.3 PRONOUNS AND ANTECEDENTS

Read the following sentences. Can you tell to whom the pronoun *She* refers?

EXAMPLE Louisa May Alcott wrote a novel about a young woman. **She** had three sisters.

The sentence is not clear because the word *She* could refer to either *Louisa May Alcott* or *a young woman.* Sometimes you must repeat a noun or rewrite a sentence to avoid confusion.

EXAMPLE Louisa May Alcott wrote a novel about a young woman. **The young woman** had three sisters.

The word a pronoun refers to is called its **antecedent.** The word *antecedent* means "going before."

EXAMPLE **Jo March** is the main character in *Little Women.* **She** writes stories. **[*Jo March* is the antecedent of the pronoun *She*.]**

EXAMPLE **Meg, Beth,** and **Amy** are Jo's sisters. Jo writes **them** stories. **[*Meg, Beth,* and *Amy* are the antecedents of *them*.]**

When you use a pronoun, be sure it refers to its antecedent clearly. Be especially careful when you use the pronoun *they.* Read the following sentence.

EXAMPLE **They** have five books by Alcott at the school library.

The meaning of *They* is unclear. The sentence can be improved by rewriting it in the following way.

EXAMPLE The school library has five books by Alcott.

"YOU, Bernie Horowitz? . . . So YOU'RE the 'they' in 'that's what they say'?"

GRAMMAR/USAGE/MECHANICS

When you use pronouns, be sure they agree with their antecedents in **number** (singular or plural) and **gender.** The gender of a noun may be masculine (male), feminine (female), or neuter (referring to things).

EXAMPLE The Marches must face a death in the family. **They** face **it** with courage.

They is plural; it agrees with the plural antecedent *Marches. It* is singular and agrees with the singular antecedent *death.*

GRAMMAR/USAGE/MECHANICS

PRACTICE Identifying Pronouns and Antecedents

Write each personal pronoun and its antecedent. If a pronoun doesn't have a clear antecedent, rewrite the numbered item to make the meaning clear.

1. Ms. Johnson spoke to Mary about the science fair. She was enthusiastic.
2. Jody's grandparents are experts in motorcycle repair. They often talk to Jody about it.
3. They have no books about women in chemistry at the library.
4. Malcolm went to the mall with Jaleel. He needed some new shoes.
5. Myrna collects books about baseball history. She keeps them in a special bookcase.
6. They charge too much for the latest albums at Music Madness.
7. The Lloyds have adopted a boy and a girl. They love him and her equally.
8. In this geography book, they don't have up-to-date maps of Africa.
9. Todd has an expensive new bike. He takes good care of it.
10. The students filled the vases with flowers for the sick. Mrs. Shelby sent them to the nursing center.

4.4 POSSESSIVE PRONOUNS

You often use personal pronouns to replace nouns that are subjects or objects in sentences. You can use pronouns in place of possessive nouns, too.

A **possessive pronoun** is a pronoun that shows who or what has something. A possessive pronoun may take the place of a possessive noun.

Read the following sentences. Notice the possessive nouns and the possessive pronouns that replace them.

EXAMPLE Lisa's class put on a play. **Her** class put on a play.

EXAMPLE The idea was Lisa's. The idea was **hers.**

Possessive pronouns have two forms. One form is used before a noun. The other form is used alone.

GRAMMAR/USAGE/MECHANICS

POSSESSIVE PRONOUNS

	SINGULAR	PLURAL
Used Before Nouns	my your her, his, its	our your their
Used Alone	mine yours hers, his, its	ours yours theirs

Possessive pronouns are not written with apostrophes. Don't confuse the possessive pronoun *its* with the word *it's*. *It's* is a contraction, or shortened form, of *it is* or *it has.*

EXAMPLE **Its** popularity is growing. **[possessive pronoun]**

EXAMPLE **It's** popular with many students. **[contraction of *It is*]**

EXAMPLE **It's** succeeded on the stage. **[contraction of *It has*]**

GRAMMAR/USAGE/MECHANICS

PRACTICE Identifying Possessive Pronouns

Write the possessive pronouns.

1. These are their tickets. Where are ours?
2. This is his equipment. Theirs is in the lab.
3. Did you prefer her performance or his?
4. It's been a pleasure to meet your parents.
5. Is this jacket yours, or is it hers?
6. Will your mother or your dad pick us up after our game?
7. My best friend is staying at our house.
8. The dishwasher has finished its cycle.
9. Where are your coats? Here is mine.
10. Their new house will be smaller than yours.

4.5 INDEFINITE PRONOUNS

An **indefinite pronoun** is a pronoun that does not refer to a particular person, place, or thing.

EXAMPLE **Everybody** thinks about the plot.

Some indefinite pronouns are always singular. Others are always plural. A few may be either singular or plural.

SOME INDEFINITE PRONOUNS

ALWAYS SINGULAR			ALWAYS PLURAL
another	everybody	no one	both
anybody	everyone	nothing	few
anyone	everything	one	many
anything	much	somebody	others
each	neither	someone	several
either	nobody	something	

The indefinite pronouns *all, any, most, none,* and *some* may be singular or plural, depending on the phrase that follows them.

When an indefinite pronoun is used as the subject of a sentence, the verb must agree with it in number.

EXAMPLE **Everyone reads** part of the novel. **[singular]**

EXAMPLE **Several enjoy** it very much. **[plural]**

EXAMPLE **Most** of the story **happens** in England. **[singular]**

EXAMPLE **Most** of the characters **seem** real. **[plural]**

Possessive pronouns often have indefinite pronouns as their antecedents. In such cases, the pronouns must agree in number. Note that in the first example below the words that come between the subject and the verb don't affect the agreement.

EXAMPLE **Each** of the actors memorizes **his** or **her** lines.

EXAMPLE **Many** are enjoying **their** roles in the play.

GRAMMAR/USAGE/MECHANICS

PRACTICE Using Indefinite Pronouns

Write the indefinite pronouns and the correct words from the choices in parentheses.

1. Some of the students (has, have) formed a science club.
2. Some of the food (is, are) cold.
3. Everyone (makes, make) a mistake occasionally.
4. Several of the band members (is, are) suggesting a picnic.
5. Someone left (his or her, their) umbrella in the hall.
6. Most of the voters (wants, want) more information.
7. Both (has, have) asked (his or her, their) parents for permission.
8. Nobody (likes, like) ants in (his or her, their) picnic lunch.
9. Everything in these three cupboards (is, are) dirty.
10. Few (gives, give) (his or her, their) most valuable possessions to charity.

4.6 REFLEXIVE AND INTENSIVE PRONOUNS

A **reflexive pronoun** ends with *-self* or *-selves* and refers to the subject of a sentence. In a sentence with a reflexive pronoun, the action of the verb returns to the subject.

EXAMPLE Yolanda bought **herself** a book on engine repair.
Reflexive Pronoun

Don't use a reflexive pronoun in place of a personal pronoun.

EXAMPLE Yolanda asked Pat and **me** for help. **[not *Pat and myself*]**

EXAMPLE Yolanda and **I** read the book. **[not *Yolanda and myself*]**

An **intensive pronoun** ends with *-self* or *-selves* and is used to draw special attention to a noun or a pronoun already named.

EXAMPLE Yolanda **herself** repaired the engine.
Intensive Pronoun

EXAMPLE Yolanda repaired the engine **herself.**
Intensive Pronoun

Reflexive and intensive pronouns are formed by adding *-self* or *-selves* to certain personal and possessive pronouns.

REFLEXIVE AND INTENSIVE PRONOUNS

SINGULAR	PLURAL
myself	ourselves
yourself	yourselves
himself, herself, itself	themselves

Don't use *hisself* or *theirselves* in place of *himself* and *themselves.*

GRAMMAR/USAGE/MECHANICS

PRACTICE Using Reflexive and Intensive Pronouns

Write the correct word from the choices in parentheses. Then write personal, reflexive, *or* intensive *to identify the word you chose.*

1. Ms. Statler gave Moisha and (me, myself) the good news.
2. The volunteers were proud of (themselves, theirselves).
3. Progress brings (us, ourselves) advantages and disadvantages.
4. Jim repaired the old grandfather clock (himself, hisself).
5. The drama director chose Peyton and (me, myself) for the lead roles.
6. The students (themselves, theirselves) made all the decorations.
7. The twins and (I, myself) prepared the entire meal.
8. We found (us, ourselves) in an awkward situation.
9. The coach (himself, hisself) presented the trophies.
10. I promised (me, myself) a reward for all my hard work.

GRAMMAR/USAGE/MECHANICS

4.7 INTERROGATIVE AND DEMONSTRATIVE PRONOUNS

An **interrogative pronoun** is a pronoun used to introduce an interrogative sentence.

The interrogative pronouns *who* and *whom* refer to people. *Who* is used when the interrogative pronoun is the subject of the sentence. *Whom* is used when the interrogative pronoun is an object.

EXAMPLE **Who** borrowed the book? **[subject]**

EXAMPLE **Whom** did the librarian call? **[direct object]**

Which and *what* refer to things and ideas.

EXAMPLES **Which** is it? **What** interests you?

Whose shows possession.

EXAMPLE I found a copy of the play. **Whose** is it?

Don't confuse *whose* with *who's*. *Who's* is a contraction of *who is* or *who has*.

A **demonstrative pronoun** is a pronoun that points out something.

The demonstrative pronouns are *this, that, these*, and *those*. *This* (singular) and *these* (plural) refer to things nearby. *That* (singular) and *those* (plural) refer to things at a distance.

EXAMPLE **This** is an interesting book. **[singular, nearby]**

EXAMPLE **These** are interesting books. **[plural, nearby]**

EXAMPLE **That** was a good movie. **[singular, at a distance]**

EXAMPLE **Those** were good movies. **[plural, at a distance]**

GRAMMAR/USAGE/MECHANICS

For Better or For Worse® **by Lynn Johnston**

PRACTICE Using Interrogative and Demonstrative Pronouns

Write the correct word from the choices in parentheses.

1. (Who, Whom) left these muddy shoes in the living room?
2. (Who, Whom) did you meet at the mall this afternoon?

3. (Whose, Who's) that bald man with the yellow umbrella?
4. Is (that, those) the most comfortable chair?
5. (Whose, Who's) broken my new camera?
6. (Whose, Who's) looking for me?
7. Do (this, these) make suitable gifts for young men?
8. (Whose, Who's) are the red sneakers with the pink shoelaces?
9. (Who, Whom) have your parents invited for dinner?
10. (Who, Whom) has won the election?

GRAMMAR/USAGE/MECHANICS

PRACTICE Proofreading

Rewrite the following passage, correcting errors in spelling, grammar, and usage. Write legibly to be sure one letter is not mistaken for another. There are ten errors.

Sandra Cisneros

[1]Us students have just read the short stories "Bums in the Attic" and "A Smart Cookie." [2]Both is by Sandra Cisneros. [3]Whom is Sandra Cisneros? [4]She is a Mexican American writer. [5]She writes short stories and poems.

[6]At the age of fifteen, Cisneros moved to a new house. [7]Her and her family moved into a red house in a Puerto Rican neighborhood. [8]There is a simlar house in *The House on Mango Street,* Cisneros's most famous book. [9]It's main character is Esperanza.

[10]Sandra Cisneros is a well-known writer. [11]They probably have her books at your local library. [12]Juan and myself read her short story "Eleven." [13]I enjoyed the story more than him. [14]Esperanza reminded me of my friend Alice. [15]She is a very strong girl.

POSTTEST Personal Pronouns

Write each personal pronoun. Then write one of the following phrases to identify the pronoun: subject pronoun as subject, subject pronoun as predicate pronoun, object pronoun as direct object, object pronoun as indirect object.

1. I told them the news.
2. They saw her and us at the library.
3. You are asking me too many questions.
4. She and he carried it into the garage.
5. The guests of honor at the banquet were we.

GRAMMAR/USAGE/MECHANICS

POSTTEST Using Pronouns

Write the correct word or phrase from the choices in parentheses.

6. Mrs. Sindato and (we, us) students watched the free performance in the park.
7. (You and I, I and you, You and me, Me and you) tasted peaches in Georgia and ate crab in Maryland.
8. The astronomer told (she and he, she and him, her and he, her and him) about the meteor shower.
9. At the construction site, the supervisor gave Greg and (they, them) hammers, saws, and nails.
10. Hariza and (she, her) left the house early in the morning.
11. (Mr. Gilbert and we, We and Mr. Gilbert, Mr. Gilbert and us, Us and Mr. Gilbert) saw a bolt of lightning during the snowstorm.
12. The true winners of the race were (they, them).
13. Mr. Polinski coaches (she and I, I and she, her and me, me and her) in gymnastics.
14. That new adventure film thrilled (we, us) moviegoers.
15. The most enthusiastic band members are (she and I, I and she, her and me, me and her).

POSTTEST Pronouns and Antecedents

Write each personal pronoun and its antecedent. If a pronoun doesn't have a clear antecedent, rewrite the numbered item to make the meaning clear.

16. Many small parts make up a watch. They all fit together and make it work.
17. John and Mary look hungry. Give him or her the rest of the fruit salad.
18. Eagle Plume told Kim the news. She had made the volleyball team.
19. They serve delicious meals at the Chinese Dragon.
20. Shelley lost the tennis match. She was disappointed.

POSTTEST Identifying Pronouns

Write each pronoun. Then write possessive, indefinite, reflexive, intensive, interrogative, *or* demonstrative *to identify it.*

21. Who invented the legend of the Minotaur, a creature half man and half bull?
22. The blue shirts are theirs; the red shirts are ours.
23. Nothing, not even a large body of water, stops the lemming during its self-destructive journey.
24. The Perezes bought that and saved themselves some money.
25. Both appreciated the photo finish, but neither celebrated before the judges' ruling.
26. Yours is a story of courage.
27. The bargain hunter bought herself this and many of the gifts at the sale.
28. The trainer herself rubs down the horse after each of the practices.
29. Which are poisonous snakes?
30. The astronaut cares for his equipment himself.

POSTTEST Indefinite Pronouns

Write the subjects and the correct words from the choices in parentheses.

31. Most of the mountain (are, is) under a watch for forest fires.
32. No one here (know, knows) the difference between stalagmites and stalactites.
33. We stroll along the river; others (walk, walks) to the new video arcade.
34. Somebody in my class (walk, walks) three miles every day.
35. (Are, Is) any of the clouds producing hail?
36. Many of the volcanoes in the Ring of Fire (have, has) erupted.
37. Some of the water in the fire hydrants (have, has) leaked.
38. Most of the old elm trees (have, has) died of disease.
39. (Is, Are) either of the children asking about the trip to the zoo?
40. Much of the activity (were, was) too difficult.

POSTTEST Personal, Reflexive, Intensive, Interrogative, and Demonstrative Pronouns

Write the correct word from the choices in parentheses.

41. Debra and (I, myself) watched the intense chess match.
42. (Whose, Who's) are these?
43. Is (this, these) your only pencil?
44. These spiders spun the enormous webs (themselves, theirselves) in a single hour.
45. (Who, Whom) told you about the danger of the sun's ultraviolet rays?
46. The astronaut gave (me, myself) a piece of moon rock.

47. Are (that, those) Habib's shoes?
48. (Who, Whom) did you ask to the dance?
49. (Whose, Who's) the new student in your math class?
50. The police officer warned (me, myself) about the dangers of jaywalking.

GRAMMAR/USAGE/MECHANICS

Chapter 5

Adjectives

PRETEST Identifying Adjectives

Write each adjective. Beside the adjective, write the noun it modifies.

1. The cougar is a large North American cat.
2. Bill Nye, a wacky scientist, performs goofy experiments on Saturday television.
3. An astronaut suit is a complex piece of scientific equipment with bright lights, a drinking bag, a cooling unit, and other devices.
4. Amahl felt happy about the test results.
5. Wilhelm Roentgen, a German scientist, discovered the amazing capabilities of the invisible X-ray.
6. The Komodo dragon, an endangered lizard, has a poisonous bite.
7. Many voters seemed angry or disappointed with the outcome of the last election.
8. The famous athlete visited the sick children at the local hospital after the big game.

9. Omar Vizquel picked up the ball with one bare hand, tagged second base, and threw out the speedy runner at first base.
10. The kitten was a soft, round ball of silky fur.

PRETEST Articles and Demonstratives

Write the correct word or phrase from the choices in parentheses.

11. (This, This here) dog is my constant companion.
12. (A, An) human can reason, but (a, an) animal cannot.
13. Don't sit in (this, that) chair on (an, the) other side of the room.
14. Is (that, that there) your brother?
15. (This, These) boomerang will return to me.
16. Name (a, the) person with the same first and last initials.
17. Rafael attends (a, an) university in (a, an) small town (a, an) hour from here.
18. Jane took (them, those) aluminum cans to the recycling center.
19. Are (that, those) your shoes on the back porch?
20. Look at (these, those) dark clouds on the horizon.

PRETEST Comparative and Superlative Adjectives

Write the correct comparative or superlative form of the adjective in parentheses.

21. Are wetlands (valuable) than forests?
22. Thomas Edison invented the light bulb, a (reliable) light than the gas light.
23. What is the (tall) plant on earth?
24. From the two pieces of pizza, I chose the (big) one.
25. I think he is the (funny) comedian on television.
26. In this story about a shy dancer, the main character is (lonely) than her sister.

27. There were six watches in the showcase. I bought the (expensive) one.
28. Which dog looks (sad)—the basset hound or the bulldog?
29. Of all my vegetables, the (large) one is my eggplant.
30. What is the (important) step in the process?

PRETEST Irregular Comparative and Superlative Adjectives

Write the correct word or phrase from the choices in parentheses.

31. Of the three children, Buddy wanted the (more, most) attention.
32. Which of the three plans will cause the (less, least) trouble?
33. The (baddest, worst) actor forgot her lines, fell on the stage, and burst into tears.
34. Andreas took (less, least) gravy today than yesterday.
35. My grades in science are (better, more better) than my grades in English.
36. Out of one hundred paintings, the judges found the (better, best) one.
37. The untreated duster picks up (little, less) dust than the treated one.
38. This cold medication tastes (more worse, worse) than that one.
39. Don has (more, most) computer games than Harold.
40. I am feeling (gooder, better) today than yesterday.

5.1 ADJECTIVES

The words we use to describe people, places, and things are called adjectives.

An **adjective** is a word that describes, or modifies, a noun or a pronoun.

Adjectives modify nouns in three ways.

HOW ADJECTIVES MODIFY NOUNS	
WHAT KIND?	We studied **ancient** history.
HOW MANY?	I read **four** chapters.
WHICH ONE?	**That** invention changed history.

Most adjectives come before the nouns they modify. Some adjectives follow linking verbs and modify the noun or pronoun that is the subject of the sentence.

EXAMPLE **Some** architects are **skillful** and **imaginative.**

The adjective *some* precedes the noun *architects*. The adjectives *skillful* and *imaginative* follow the linking verb, *are,* and modify the subject, *architects.* They are called predicate adjectives.

A **predicate adjective** follows a linking verb and modifies the subject of a sentence.

PEANUTS reprinted by permission of United Feature Syndicate, Inc.

Two verb forms are often used as adjectives and predicate adjectives. They are the present participle and the past participle.

EXAMPLE The architect drew a **surprising** design. **[present participle]**

EXAMPLE Visitors seem **impressed.** **[past participle]**

Some adjectives are formed from proper nouns and begin with a capital letter. They are called proper adjectives.

Proper adjectives are adjectives formed from proper nouns.

Some proper adjectives have the same form as the noun. Others are formed by adding an ending to the noun form.

FORMING PROPER ADJECTIVES	
PROPER NOUN	**PROPER ADJECTIVE**
oranges from **Florida**	**Florida** oranges
the history of **America**	**American** history

More than one adjective may modify the same noun.

EXAMPLE **These new frozen** *dinners* are **tasty** and **nutritious.**

These, new, frozen, tasty, and *nutritious* all modify *dinners.*

NOTE Many words that are usually nouns can also be used as adjectives: ***stone*** *wall,* ***band*** *uniform,* ***baseball*** *game.*

PRACTICE Identifying Adjectives

Write each adjective. Beside the adjective, write the noun it modifies.

1. The old green sprinkling can was rusty and dented.
2. Several stories about Spanish explorers are in this book.
3. Lazy people often lead dull lives.
4. Fragrant red roses bloomed beside the babbling brook.
5. Old coins from Roman ruins are valuable.
6. These portraits are familiar to many visitors from Italian cities.
7. Rock bands usually include some guitars.
8. I counted twenty-two mistakes in this composition.
9. French fashions are popular with American women.
10. Three broken dishes lay on the dirty floor.

5.2 ARTICLES AND DEMONSTRATIVES

The words *a, an,* and *the* make up a special group of adjectives called **articles.**

A and *an* are called **indefinite articles** because they refer to one of a general group of people, places, things, or ideas. *A* is used before words beginning with a consonant sound. *An* is used before words beginning with a vowel sound. Don't confuse sounds with spellings. In speaking, you would say *a university* but *an uncle, a hospital* but *an honor.*

EXAMPLES **a** union **a** picture **an** hour **an** easel

The is called the **definite article** because it identifies specific people, places, things, or ideas.

EXAMPLE **The** picture beside **the** fireplace is **the** best one.

The words *this, that, these,* and *those* are called **demonstrative adjectives.** They are used to point out something.

DEMONSTRATIVE ADJECTIVES	
Take **this** umbrella with you.	**That** store is closed.
Take **these** boots too.	**Those** clouds are lovely.

Demonstrative adjectives point out something and modify nouns by answering the question *which one?* or *which ones?*

Use *this* and *that* with singular nouns. Use *these* and *those* with plural nouns. Use *this* and *these* to point out something close to you. Use *that* and *those* to point out something at a distance.

DEMONSTRATIVES

	SINGULAR	PLURAL
NEAR	this	these
FAR	that	those

Demonstratives can be used with nouns or without them. When they're used without nouns, they're called **demonstrative pronouns.**

DEMONSTRATIVE PRONOUNS	
This is mine.	**These** are his.
That is hers.	**Those** are yours.

The words *here* and *there* should not be used with demonstrative adjectives or demonstrative pronouns. The words *this, these, that,* and *those* already point out the locations *here* and *there.*

EXAMPLE Look at **this** photograph. **[not *this here photograph*]**

Don't use the object pronoun *them* in place of the demonstrative adjective *those.*

EXAMPLE I took a photo of **those** buildings. **[not *them buildings*]**

GRAMMAR/USAGE/MECHANICS

PRACTICE Using Articles and Demonstratives

Write the correct word from the choices in parentheses.

1. (A, An) honest person will not tell (a, an) lie.
2. (This, These) are the posters I was telling you about.
3. Do you know (them, those) people across the street?
4. My father has joined (a, an) union.
5. (This, This here) is (a, the) house where I was born.
6. Can you think of (a, the) word with six syllables?
7. (This, These) house is exactly like (these, those) in your neighborhood.
8. (This, That) portrait on (a, the) opposite wall is a picture of my great-grandfather.
9. (A, An) animal has damaged (these, those) shrubs on the far side of the lawn.
10. (That, That there) is (a, an) historic battlefield.

5.3 COMPARATIVE AND SUPERLATIVE ADJECTIVES

The **comparative form** of an adjective compares one person or thing with another.

The **superlative form** of an adjective compares one person or thing with several others.

For most adjectives with one syllable and for some with two syllables, add *-er* to form the comparative and *-est* to form the superlative.

EXAMPLE Is Venezuela **larger** than Peru?

EXAMPLE Is Brazil the **richest** country in South America?

For most adjectives with two or more syllables, form the comparative by using *more* before the adjective. Form the superlative by using *most* before the adjective.

EXAMPLE Is Chile **more mountainous** than Bolivia?

EXAMPLE Was Simón Bolívar South America's **most successful** general?

GRAMMAR/USAGE/MECHANICS

COMPARATIVE AND SUPERLATIVE FORMS

BASE FORM	COMPARATIVE	SUPERLATIVE
small	small**er**	small**est**
big	big**ger**	big**gest**
pretty	pretti**er**	pretti**est**
fabulous	**more** fabulous	**most** fabulous

The words *less* and *least* are used before both short and long adjectives to form the negative comparative and superlative.

NEGATIVE COMPARATIVE AND SUPERLATIVE FORMS	
BASE FORM	The first dancer was **graceful.**
COMPARATIVE	The second dancer was **less graceful** than the first.
SUPERLATIVE	The third dancer was the **least graceful** one.

Don't use *more, most, less,* or *least* before adjectives that already end with *-er* or *-est.* This is called a double comparison.

GRAMMAR/USAGE/MECHANICS

PRACTICE Using Comparative and Superlative Adjectives I

Write the correct comparative or superlative form of the adjective in parentheses.

1. Who has the (easy) job—you or I?
2. This has been the (splendid) vacation of my life!
3. Do you think a screwdriver is (useful) than a hammer?
4. Are Tony's pizzas (spicy) than Gino's pizzas?
5. You're the (wonderful) friend I've ever had!
6. The downtown bus is (slow) than the crosstown bus.
7. This must be the (beautiful) spot in the world!
8. Is your pizza (delicious) than mine?
9. Is this the (short) route to the amusement park?
10. The (old) person in my family is Great-grandma Harris.

PRACTICE Using Comparative and Superlative Adjectives II

Write the correct word or phrase from the choices in parentheses.

1. The baby becomes (curiouser, more curious) every day.
2. Janine is the (more popular, most popular) girl in the seventh grade.
3. Science is my (less favorite, least favorite) subject.

4. Kenji is the (fastest, most fastest) runner on the track team.
5. Emmy is (less talkative, least talkative) than Margaret.
6. You have the (most unusualest, most unusual) dog I've ever seen.
7. This pizza is (less flavorful, least flavorful) than the one we had last weekend.
8. No one is (slower, slowest) than you!
9. This photograph of Mount Rushmore is the (more interesting, most interesting) picture in your entire album.
10. Is your brother Ted (younger, more younger) than your cousin Alisha?

GRAMMAR/USAGE/MECHANICS

5.4 IRREGULAR COMPARATIVE AND SUPERLATIVE ADJECTIVES

The comparative and superlative forms of some adjectives are not formed in the regular way.

EXAMPLE Harriet Tubman believed in a **good** cause.

EXAMPLE She knew that freedom was **better** than slavery.

EXAMPLE The Underground Railroad was the **best** route to freedom.

Better is the comparative form of the adjective *good*. *Best* is the superlative form of *good*.

IRREGULAR COMPARATIVE AND SUPERLATIVE FORMS

BASE FORM	COMPARATIVE	SUPERLATIVE
good, well	better	best
bad	worse	worst
many, much	more	most
little	less	least

Don't use *more* or *most* before irregular adjectives that are already in the comparative or superlative form.

EXAMPLE Tubman felt **better** at the end of the day. **[not *more better*]**

PRACTICE Using Irregular Adjectives

Write the correct word or phrase from the choices in parentheses.

1. My parents pay (much, more) attention to my sister than to me.
2. Of all the employees, Carol Ann has the (less, least) influence with the president.
3. This cough syrup tastes (worse, more worse) than the other one.
4. Which month has the (most, mostest) holidays?
5. Yoko is a (good, gooder) tap dancer.
6. Today is (good, better) than yesterday.
7. My dad's job requires (less, least) physical labor than my mom's job.
8. That was the (baddest, worst) joke I've ever heard!
9. Tobias has (little, most little) sympathy for me.
10. This was my (best, bestest) performance ever!

GRAMMAR/USAGE/MECHANICS

PRACTICE Proofreading

Rewrite the following passage, correcting errors in spelling, capitalization, grammar, and usage. Add any missing punctuation. Write legibly to be sure one letter is not mistaken for another. There are ten errors.

Maya Angelou

[1]Maya Angelou is a author and a poet. [2]Her parents named her Marguerite Johnson. [3]She was born in St. Louis. [4]These city is in Missouri. [5]She had one brother, Bailey. [6]Bailey was oldest than she was. [7]He called Marguerite "Mya Sister," and her nickname became

Maya. [8]She was the goodest student in her eighth-grade class.

[9]Johnson became a dancer and changed her name to Maya Angelou. [10]She worked at the Purple Onion. [11]She was more better than some of the other dancers there. [12]She toured Europe in the african american musical *Porgy and Bess.*

[13]At the age of thirty, Angelou became a writer. [14]She learned from such writers as James Baldwin. [15]Their advice was benificial.

[16]Angelou also worked for civil rights. [17]She met one of the most famousest civil rights leaders, Martin Luther King Jr.

[18]Angelou wrote five books about her life. [19]One of them books is *I Know Why the Caged Bird Sings.* [20]She wrote the poem "On the Pulse of Morning," and she read it at the inauguration of President Clinton. [21]It was surely a honor for her.

GRAMMAR/USAGE/MECHANICS

POSTTEST Identifying Adjectives

Write each adjective. Beside the adjective, write the noun it modifies.

1. During the hot summer, the inventive youth sold large glasses of cold lemonade.
2. This year I learned the names of the nine planets.
3. A disabled vehicle stood at the northwest corner of the busy intersection.
4. Six visitors to the ancient ruins of the Roman Colosseum bought expensive souvenirs.
5. The golden eagle loves these mountainous areas.
6. The first president of the United States was George Washington, a man with a strong reputation for absolute honesty.
7. The hot Mexican chili was spicy and delicious.
8. The French gift of the copper Statue of Liberty stands on tiny Liberty Island.

9. Which wrestler wears the strange outfit with ostrich feathers?
10. An enormous sailing ship appeared against the misty glow of the full moon.

POSTTEST Articles and Demonstratives

Write the correct word or phrase from the choices in parentheses.

11. Is (this, that) your house on the opposite side of the street?
12. Ronald Reagan was (a, an) actor, (a, an) governor, and (a, an) president.
13. Are you preserving (that, that there) flower for (a, an) reason?
14. (This, These) dry weather makes my allergies worse.
15. Mischa received (a, an) honor at (a, the) last awards ceremony.
16. Do you know the name of (these, those) mountains in the distance?
17. In (this, this here) movie, (a, an) meteor hits (a, an, the) earth.
18. May I have some of (that, those) grapes?
19. (A, An) Olympic athlete needs (a, an) one-track mind.
20. (A, An, The) horrid bug is crawling among (them, those) flowers on your desk.

POSTTEST Comparative and Superlative Adjectives

Write the correct comparative or superlative form of the adjective in parentheses.

21. Is a curveball (fast) than a slider?
22. That was the (embarrassing) moment of my life.
23. Stocks are a (risky) investment than a savings account.

24. From the batch of thirty, the chef rejected the two (small) tomatoes.
25. Of the two disc jockeys, we hired the (expensive) one.
26. This has been the (hot) day of the summer.
27. Dreama chose the (sensible) of the two plans.
28. The (large) python in the wild can devour an entire crocodile.
29. Benson gave the (interesting) report in the class.
30. The river is now (high) than ever before.

POSTTEST Irregular Comparative and Superlative Adjectives

Write the correct word or phrase from the choices in parentheses.

31. John Deere made a (gooder, better) plow than others on the market in 1838.
32. Our team's record is (worse, worser) than your team's.
33. Yellowstone suffered (less, least) damage from the fire than other areas of the West.
34. That was the (worse, worst) mistake I've ever made.
35. Do you have a (better, more better) answer?
36. Of all Sean's friends, Don has the (most, mostest) computer games.
37. The exotic birds receive the (most, mostest) attention at the zoo.
38. I spent (more, most) time on the project than you.
39. Of the two travelers, Mei-Ling paid (less, least) attention to the map.
40. This is the (best, most best) day of my life.

Chapter 6

Adverbs

PRETEST Identifying Adverbs

Write each adverb and the word it modifies. Then write whether the modified word is a verb, *an* adjective, *or an* adverb.

1. Susan B. Anthony fought tirelessly for women's voting rights.
2. The women often suffered defeats, but they continued their campaign.
3. In 1919 the Nineteenth Amendment finally gave women the vote.
4. Are women always treated fairly today?
5. We arrived really early for the concert.
6. The kittens were extremely tiny, and we handled them quite gently.
7. I completely admire gymnasts' amazingly complex performances.
8. Have you ever seen that movie anywhere?
9. Beth's handwriting is somewhat sloppy, but she expresses her ideas very well.
10. Do you play soccer here?

PRETEST Comparative and Superlative Adverbs

Write the correct word or phrase from the choices in parentheses.

11. Dad thinks (better, best) of all in peace and quiet.
12. Cars on the German autobahn travel (faster, more faster, fastest, most fastest) than vehicles on American highways.
13. Some students work (more independently, most independently) than others.
14. Of all my students, Sherman works (harder, hardest).
15. You play this game even (worse, worser, worst) than I.
16. Of the six families, which traveled (farther, more farther, farthest, most farthest) to the reunion?
17. Which of these two computer games do you like (better, best)?
18. Who practices (more frequently, most frequently)—Trisha, Moishi, or Teodoro?
19. Does André serve (more rapidly, most rapidly) than Pete?
20. Which of the three babies cries (less, least)?

PRETEST Using Adjectives and Adverbs

Write the correct word from the choices in parentheses.

21. Spiders cause (real, really) fear in some people.
22. I (most, almost) never take a walk after nine o'clock in the evening.
23. Jamaica is a (real, really) good artist.
24. After that enormous dinner, I don't feel (good, well).
25. Your brother (sure, surely) knows a great deal about computers.
26. The volleyball player with the sprained wrist played (bad, badly).

27. I felt (bad, badly) about the loss.
28. (Most, Almost) visitors to the zoo move (slow, slowly) through the exhibits.
29. A surgeon needs keen eyes and (sure, surely) hands.
30. You look (good, well) in that new hairstyle.

PRETEST Correcting Double Negatives

Rewrite each sentence so it correctly expresses a negative idea.

31. Because of a Siberian tiger's colored stripes, you can't scarcely see it in the autumn.
32. Don't never ask me about that mistake again.
33. I wouldn't hardly call a crocodile a good pet!
34. Edwin Land wouldn't never have invented the Polaroid camera without a question from his daughter.
35. Can't I say nothing about the missing suitcase of money?
36. Without luck I couldn't never have caught that line drive.
37. In Red Bird's fifteen years, he hadn't gone nowhere outside the reservation.
38. Doesn't nobody here know about humans' eight wrist bones?
39. The train wreck wasn't no accident.
40. I haven't no homework tonight.

6.1 ADVERBS THAT MODIFY VERBS

Adjectives are words that modify nouns and pronouns. Adverbs are another type of modifier. They modify verbs, adjectives, and other adverbs.

An **adverb** is a word that modifies a verb, an adjective, or another adverb.

WHAT ADVERBS MODIFY	
VERBS	People *handle* old violins **carefully.**
ADJECTIVES	**Very** *old* violins are valuable.
ADVERBS	Orchestras **almost** *always* include violins.

An adverb may tell *how* or *in what manner* an action is done. It may tell *when* or *how often* an action is done. It may also tell *where* or *in what direction* an action is done.

WAYS ADVERBS MODIFY VERBS

ADVERBS TELL	EXAMPLES
HOW	grandly, easily, completely, neatly, gratefully, sadly
WHEN	soon, now, immediately, often, never, usually, early
WHERE	here, there, everywhere, inside, downstairs, above, far

When an adverb modifies an adjective or another adverb, the adverb usually comes before the word it modifies. When an adverb modifies a verb, the adverb can sometimes occupy different positions in a sentence.

POSITION OF ADVERBS MODIFYING VERBS	
BEFORE THE VERB	Guests **often** dine at the White House.
AFTER THE VERB	Guests dine **often** at the White House.
AT THE BEGINNING	**Often** guests dine at the White House.
AT THE END	Guests dine at the White House **often.**

Many adverbs are formed by adding *-ly* to adjectives. However, not all words that end in *-ly* are adverbs. The words *friendly, lively, kindly, lovely,* and *lonely* are usually adjectives. On the other hand, not all adverbs end in *-ly.*

SOME ADVERBS NOT ENDING IN *-LY*			
afterward	everywhere	near	short
already	fast	never	sometimes
always	forever	not	somewhere
anywhere	hard	now	soon
away	here	nowhere	straight
below	home	often	then
even	late	outside	there
ever	long	seldom	well

GRAMMAR/USAGE/MECHANICS

PRACTICE Identifying Adverbs I

Write each adverb. Beside the adverb, write the verb it modifies.

1. Cinderella whisked her broom quickly across the floor.
2. She sighed heavily and stepped outside.
3. Cinderella wished desperately for an invitation to the ball.
4. Her mean stepsisters were already dressing for the event.
5. At the ball, Cinderella danced gracefully with the prince.
6. She left the ball late and arrived home without one of her glass slippers.
7. The prince searched eagerly for the owner of the slipper.
8. Cinderella and the prince lived happily for the rest of their days.
9. The newlyweds traveled everywhere throughout the kingdom.
10. The happy couple seldom invited the mean stepsisters for a visit.

6.2 ADVERBS THAT MODIFY ADJECTIVES AND OTHER ADVERBS

Adverbs are often used to modify adjectives and other adverbs. Notice how adverbs affect the meaning of the adjectives in the following sentences. Most often they tell *how* or *to what extent.*

EXAMPLE Harry Truman used **extremely** direct language.

EXAMPLE He became a **very** popular president.

In the first sentence, the adverb *extremely* modifies the adjective *direct. Extremely* tells to what extent Truman's language was direct. In the second sentence, the adverb *very* modifies the adjective *popular. Very* tells to what extent Truman was popular.

PEANUTS reprinted by permission of United Feature Syndicate, Inc.

In the following sentences, adverbs modify other adverbs.

EXAMPLE Truman entered politics **unusually** late in life.

EXAMPLE He moved through the political ranks **quite** quickly.

In the first sentence, the adverb *unusually* modifies the adverb *late. Unusually* tells how late Truman entered politics. In the second sentence, the adverb *quite* modifies the adverb *quickly. Quite* tells how quickly Truman moved through the ranks.

When an adverb modifies an adjective or another adverb, the adverb almost always comes directly before the word it modifies. On the following page is a list of some adverbs that are often used to modify adjectives and other adverbs.

ADVERBS OFTEN USED TO MODIFY ADJECTIVES AND OTHER ADVERBS			
almost	just	rather	too
barely	nearly	really	totally
extremely	partly	so	unusually
hardly	quite	somewhat	very

GRAMMAR/USAGE/MECHANICS

PRACTICE Identifying Adverbs II

Write each adverb and the word it modifies. Then write whether the modified word is a verb, *an* adjective, *or an* adverb.

1. Anita almost never misses a foul shot.
2. Jason told a very silly joke.
3. That movie was just wonderful!
4. These coins are extremely rare and unusually valuable.
5. My parents nearly always vote on election day.
6. Norma Jean is really shy, but she is quite popular.
7. Harrison ate too fast and felt rather sick.
8. Tessa stacked the dishes somewhat carelessly in the sink.
9. Fred and Ginger glide so smoothly around the dance floor.
10. I have barely enough money for one hamburger, and I am totally hungry!

6.3 COMPARATIVE AND SUPERLATIVE ADVERBS

The **comparative form** of an adverb compares one action with another.

The **superlative form** of an adverb compares one action with several others.

Most short adverbs add *-er* to form the comparative and *-est* to form the superlative.

COMPARING ADVERBS WITH *-ER* AND *-EST*	
COMPARATIVE	The pianist arrived **earlier** than the violinist.
SUPERLATIVE	The drummer arrived **earliest** of all the players.

Long adverbs and a few short ones require the use of *more* or *most.*

COMPARING ADVERBS WITH *MORE* AND *MOST*	
COMPARATIVE	The violinist plays **more often** than the harpist.
SUPERLATIVE	Which musicians play **most often?**

Some adverbs have irregular comparative and superlative forms.

IRREGULAR COMPARATIVE AND SUPERLATIVE FORMS

BASE FORM	COMPARATIVE	SUPERLATIVE
well	better	best
badly	worse	worst
little	less	least
far (distance)	farther	farthest
far (degree)	further	furthest

The words *less* and *least* are used before adverbs to form the negative comparative and superlative.

EXAMPLES I play **less well.** I play **least accurately.**

Don't use *more, most, less,* or *least* before adverbs that already end in *-er* or *-est.*

GRAMMAR/USAGE/MECHANICS

PRACTICE Using Comparative and Superlative Adverbs

Write the correct word or phrase from the choices in parentheses.

1. George finished his work (later, more later) than Stanley.
2. Of all the students, Bonita completed the assignment (more, most) successfully.
3. Which of these two books did you like (better, best)?
4. Eleanor draws (worse, worst) than Elizabeth.
5. Who walks (farther, farthest) to school–Jackson, Emerson, or Theo?
6. Which of the fifteen team members swims (faster, more faster, fastest, most fastest)?
7. Mr. Roberts works (less, least) energetically than his son.
8. Which of your six cousins do you see (more often, more oftener, most often, most oftenest)?
9. Of the three pianists, which one plays (better, best)?
10. Jan does her chores (more, most) cheerfully than her sister.

GRAMMAR/USAGE/MECHANICS

6.4 USING ADJECTIVES AND ADVERBS

Sometimes it's hard to decide whether a sentence needs an adjective or an adverb. Think carefully about how the word is used.

EXAMPLE He was (**careful, carefully**) with the antique clock.

EXAMPLE He worked (**careful, carefully**) on the antique clock.

In the first sentence, the missing word follows a linking verb and modifies the subject, *He.* Therefore, an adjective is needed. *Careful* is the correct choice. In the second sentence, the missing word modifies the verb, *worked.* Thus, an adverb is needed, and *carefully* is the correct choice.

The words *good* and *well* and the words *bad* and *badly* are sometimes confused. *Good* and *bad* are adjectives. Use them before nouns and after linking verbs. *Well* and *badly* are adverbs. Use them to modify verbs. *Well* may also be used as an adjective to mean "healthy": *You look well today.*

TELLING ADJECTIVES FROM ADVERBS

ADJECTIVE	ADVERB
The band sounds **good.**	The band plays **well.**
The band sounds **bad.**	The band plays **badly.**
The soloist is **well.**	The soloist sings **well.**

GRAMMAR/USAGE/MECHANICS

Use these modifiers correctly: *real* and *really, sure* and *surely, most* and *almost. Real* and *sure* are adjectives. *Really, surely,* and *almost* are adverbs. *Most* can be an adjective or an adverb.

TELLING ADJECTIVES FROM ADVERBS

ADJECTIVE	ADVERB
Music is a **real** art.	This music is **really** popular.
A pianist needs **sure** hands.	Piano music is **surely** popular.
Most pianos have eighty-eight keys.	Piano strings **almost** never break.

PRACTICE Using Adjectives and Adverbs

Write the correct word from the choices in parentheses.

1. Proceed (immediate, immediately) to the exit.
2. Stan (most, almost) always takes the garbage out.

3. That chicken sandwich tasted (bad, badly).
4. Those colors look (good, well) on you.
5. Mr. and Mrs. Kim have a (sure, surely) chance for a trophy.
6. Jolene has a (real, really) good sense of humor.
7. Dalila has a (real, really) talent for mathematics.
8. You are (sure, surely) right about that!
9. My little brother reads very (good, well) for his age.
10. The team played (bad, badly) in the first half.

6.5 CORRECTING DOUBLE NEGATIVES

The adverb *not* is a **negative word,** expressing the idea of "no." *Not* often appears in a short form as part of a contraction. When *not* is part of a contraction, as in the words in the chart below, *n't* is an adverb.

CONTRACTIONS WITH *NOT*		
are not = aren't	does not = doesn't	should not = shouldn't
cannot = can't	had not = hadn't	was not = wasn't
could not = couldn't	has not = hasn't	were not = weren't
did not = didn't	have not = haven't	will not = won't
do not = don't	is not = isn't	would not = wouldn't

In all but two of these words, the apostrophe replaces the *o* in *not.* In *can't* both an *n* and the *o* are omitted. *Will not* becomes *won't.*

Other negative words are listed in the following chart. Each negative word has several opposites. These are **affirmative words,** or words that show the idea of "yes."

SOME NEGATIVE AND AFFIRMATIVE WORDS	
NEGATIVE	**AFFIRMATIVE**
never, scarcely, hardly, barely	always, ever
nobody	anybody, everybody, somebody
no, none	all, any, one, some
no one	anyone, everyone, one, someone
nothing	anything, something
nowhere	anywhere, somewhere

Don't use two negative words to express the same idea. This is called a **double negative.** Only one negative word is necessary to express a negative idea. You can correct a double negative by removing one of the negative words or by replacing one of the negative words with an affirmative word.

EXAMPLE **INCORRECT** I **don't** have **no** homework.

EXAMPLE **CORRECT** I have **no** homework.

EXAMPLE **CORRECT** I **don't** have **any** homework.

PRACTICE Expressing Negative Ideas

Rewrite each sentence so it correctly expresses a negative idea.

1. George Washington wouldn't never tell a lie.
2. Wasn't nobody in the auditorium?
3. There isn't a better school nowhere than this one.
4. Mr. Perez couldn't find nothing wrong with the electrical system.
5. None of this stuff doesn't belong in the living room.

6. We can't tell you nothing about the surprise.
7. No one doesn't never go to the wrestling matches.
8. There weren't no eggs in the refrigerator.
9. Didn't you never see a real circus before?
10. I haven't no money for lunch.

PRACTICE Proofreading

Rewrite the following passage, correcting errors in spelling, grammar, and usage. Write legibly to be sure one letter is not mistaken for another. There are ten errors.

Langston Hughes

[1]Langston Hughes was real popular in his time. [2]He wrote really good. [3]Hughes's father moved to Mexico. [4]Hughes was only one year old at the time. [5]His mother didn't never go with him. [6]She stayed behind in the United States, and Hughes lived with his grandmother in Kansas.

[7]At the age of five, Hughes went to a libary with his mother. [8]He fell deep in love with books. [9]At Central High School in Cleveland, Ohio, he wrote poems and edited the school yearbook. [10]He also ran more faster than many athletes in his class. [11]His school won a city championship in track.

[12]At the age of eighteen, Hughes wrote "The Negro Speaks of Rivers" on a train to Mexico. [13]He crossed the Mississippi River and wrote the poem quick on the back of an envelope. [14]Students most always read this poem by Hughes.

[15]Hughes included jazz and blues rhythms in his poetry more oftener than many other poets. [16]With his poetry, novels, and plays, Hughes sure became one of the most important writers of his day.

POSTTEST Identifying Adverbs

Write each adverb and the word it modifies. Then write whether the modified word is a verb, *an* adjective, *or an* adverb.

1. I occasionally read books about the Egyptian pyramids.
2. These enormous monuments rise grandly from the sands.
3. Outside they almost always look very simple.
4. In one horror movie, an Egyptian mummy came to life and extremely quickly terrified an entire city.
5. Sometimes nature accidentally produces a mummy.
6. Two hikers in the Alps found a partially frozen body.
7. Someone had died there between 3350 and 3300 B.C.
8. The baseball season will soon end.
9. Today will be partly sunny, but it will be too cold for a picnic.
10. A rather chilly wind blew quite fiercely through the trees.

GRAMMAR/USAGE/MECHANICS

POSTTEST Comparative and Superlative Adverbs

Write the correct word or phrase from the choices in parentheses.

11. Which of those two Disney movies did you like (better, best)?
12. I studied (less, least) for this test than for the last one.
13. Which of the five instruments measured the distance (more exactly, most exactly)?
14. This new modem connects me to the Internet (faster, more faster, fastest, most fastest) than the old one.
15. Hetty plays the violin (worse, worst) than anyone else in the orchestra.
16. I eat hot dogs (more frequently, most frequently) than hamburgers.
17. Of all the test-takers, Ashley left the room (later, latest).
18. My dog eats (more often, most often, more oftener, most oftenest) than my cat.

19. Which of the students in your class travels (farther, farthest) to school?
20. Of the six girls, which one arrived (earlier, earliest) for the interview?

POSTTEST Using Adjectives and Adverbs

Write the correct word from the choices in parentheses.

21. The crash between the car and the bicycle damaged the bicycle (bad, badly).
22. Corey (most, almost) always finishes his homework.
23. Are you (sure, surely) about that answer?
24. That fried chicken (sure, surely) smells (good, well).
25. Dionne finished her chores (quick, quickly).
26. How (good, well) do you swim half a mile?
27. Is that a (real, really) diamond?
28. (Most, Almost) children want a pet of some kind.
29. Do you feel (bad, badly) about the broken promise?
30. This new can opener works (real, really) (good, well).

POSTTEST Correcting Double Negatives

Rewrite each sentence so it correctly expresses a negative idea.

31. There isn't nothing wrong with Monica's brother.
32. Maddie hadn't barely touched her food.
33. We didn't never expect the movie's sad ending.
34. There wasn't no one in the room.
35. I hadn't no knowledge of Kwanza until African American culture week.
36. Wasn't nobody listening to the weather reports?
37. Kevin couldn't take nobody with him to the audition.
38. Akiba wouldn't hardly do a thing like that.
39. The stray dog wasn't nowhere near the trash cans.
40. People in the space program won't never forget the tragedy of the space shuttle *Challenger.*

Chapter 7

Prepositions, Conjunctions, and Interjections

PRETEST Prepositions and Prepositional Phrases

Write each prepositional phrase. Underline the preposition and circle the object of the preposition. Then write the word the prepositional phrase modifies. Finally, write adjective *or* adverb *to tell how the prepositional phrase is used.*

1. The flowers along the fence look very pretty.
2. Just wait until tomorrow.
3. Emilio left the house without his jacket.
4. Have you read this letter from your cousin?
5. Are you busy for lunch?
6. During the last month, I have read ten books.
7. Have you read any books by S. E. Hinton?
8. Mitzi began her homework late in the afternoon.

9. Drive across the bridge and through the town.
10. Please put the clothes on your bureau into the washing machine.

PRETEST Pronouns as Objects of Prepositions

Write the correct word or phrase from the choices in parentheses.

11. Mr. Borelli made these costumes for Kiki and (she, her).
12. Give your money for the theater tickets to Mr. Corso or (they, them).
13. Please move your car around this van and (we, us).
14. To (who, whom) am I speaking?
15. Without Mudiwa and (he, him), we don't have a full team.
16. Except for Ms. Sandoval and (we, us), no one seems pleased by the announcement.
17. Cassy will sit between you and (I, me).
18. Across from (who, whom) did you sit?
19. Michael Jordan walked onto the court in front of Charlotte and (they, them).
20. Above (he and she, him and her, he and her, him and she) hung the family's portrait.

PRETEST Conjunctions

Write each conjunction. Then write compound subject, compound object, compound predicate, *or* compound sentence *to tell what parts the conjunction joins.*

21. The chemist or the geologist knows the answer.
22. My friend has a pager, but I don't want one.
23. Neither Michael Jordan nor Shaquille O'Neal is my favorite basketball player.
24. Mark handed my twin sister and me birthday cards.
25. Either a book or a game makes a good gift for John or Tonya.

26. In 1683 Anton van Leeuwenhoek first saw bacteria with a microscope, and in 1864 Louis Pasteur killed bacteria in milk.
27. I went to the library but forgot my library card.
28. Both Luke and Leah arrived late and left early.
29. We hiked or sat in the sun all day.
30. I admire both the suspension bridge and the covered bridge.

PRETEST Making Compound Subjects and Verbs Agree

Write the correct word from the choices in parentheses.

31. (Does, Do) men or women have more automobile accidents?
32. Andrea and Cliff (works, work) at the library.
33. Neither Hannah nor her sisters (has, have) met your cousin.
34. Either carrots or corn (accompanies, accompany) the pork chops on this menu.
35. (Is, Are) the Eiffel Tower or the Statue of Liberty taller than the Empire State Building?
36. Either the boat or the van (fits, fit) in the garage.
37. Both gas and electricity (provides, provide) fuel.
38. Neither the students nor the teacher (has, have) seen this film.
39. Neither the dog nor the cat (sleeps, sleep) outdoors.
40. Two uniformed guards and a fierce dog (guards, guard) the gate of the mansion.

PRETEST Conjunctive Adverbs

Write each sentence. Underline the conjunctive adverb. Add appropriate punctuation.

41. Grass cuttings contain nutrients for your lawn furthermore short clippings break down fast.

42. The Fukuyamas have a large garden consequently they eat many fresh vegetables.
43. You should stop now besides the report is not due until next week.
44. Put away all your sports equipment likewise put away your other toys.
45. France won the World Cup Brazil however was second.

GRAMMAR/USAGE/MECHANICS

7.1 PREPOSITIONS AND PREPOSITIONAL PHRASES

A **preposition** is a word that relates a noun or a pronoun to another word in a sentence.

EXAMPLE The boy **near** the window is French.

The word *near* is a preposition. It shows the relationship between the noun *window* and the word *boy.*

COMMON PREPOSITIONS				
aboard	at	down	off	to
about	before	during	on	toward
above	behind	except	onto	under
across	below	for	opposite	underneath
after	beneath	from	out	until
against	beside	in	outside	up
along	besides	inside	over	upon
among	between	into	past	with
around	beyond	like	since	within
as	but (except)	near	through	without
	by	of	throughout	

A preposition may consist of more than one word.

EXAMPLE Yasmin will visit Trinidad **instead of** Jamaica.

SOME PREPOSITIONS OF MORE THAN ONE WORD			
according to	aside from	in front of	instead of
across from	because of	in place of	on account of
along with	except for	in spite of	on top of

A **prepositional phrase** is a group of words that begins with a preposition and ends with a noun or a pronoun, which is called the **object of the preposition.**

EXAMPLE Hang the painting **outside the new auditorium.**

A preposition may have a compound object.

EXAMPLE Between the **chair** and the **table** was a window.

GRAMMAR/USAGE/MECHANICS

PRACTICE Identifying Prepositional Phrases

Write each prepositional phrase. Underline the preposition and draw a circle around the object of the preposition.

1. Under the books on the desk, you will find an envelope with your name on it.
2. The driver of the sleigh stopped in the woods near the lake for a few minutes.
3. Since last week, we have planted flowers along the fence and behind the house.
4. Until yesterday I had never been inside the museum without my parents.
5. Go down the street to the corner and turn left at the light.
6. After today Ms. Peters will arrive by bus at the stop across the street from the school.

7. The stranger walked past the post office and into the bank.
8. Will you sit beside me during the period before lunch?
9. The coach postponed the match between the Tigers and the Bears because of rain.
10. Today we go over the river and through the woods to Grandmother's house in a car instead of an old-fashioned buggy.

7.2 PRONOUNS AS OBJECTS OF PREPOSITIONS

GRAMMAR/USAGE/MECHANICS

When a pronoun is the object of a preposition, use an object pronoun, not a subject pronoun.

EXAMPLE Dan handed the tickets to Natalie.

EXAMPLE Dan handed the tickets to **her.**

In the example, the object pronoun *her* replaces *Natalie* as the object of the preposition *to.*

A preposition may have a compound object: two or more nouns, two or more pronouns, or a combination of nouns and pronouns. Use object pronouns in compound objects.

EXAMPLE I borrowed the suitcase from Ivan and Vera.

EXAMPLE I borrowed the suitcase from Ivan and **her.**

EXAMPLE I borrowed the suitcase from **him** and Vera.

EXAMPLE I borrowed the suitcase from **him** and **her.**

Object pronouns are used in the second, third, and fourth sentences. In the second sentence, *Ivan and her* is the compound object of the preposition *from.* In the third sentence, *him and Vera* is the compound object of the preposition *from.* In the fourth sentence, *him and her* is the compound object of the preposition *from.*

If you're not sure whether to use a subject pronoun or an object pronoun, read the sentence aloud with only the pronoun.

EXAMPLE I borrowed the suitcase from **her.**

EXAMPLE I borrowed the suitcase from **him.**

Who is a subject pronoun. *Whom* is an object pronoun.

EXAMPLE **Who** lent you the suitcase?

EXAMPLE From **whom** did you borrow the suitcase?

DILBERT reprinted by permission of United Feature Syndicate, Inc.

GRAMMAR/USAGE/MECHANICS

PRACTICE Using Pronouns as Objects of Prepositions

Write the correct word or phrase from the choices in parentheses.

1. To (who, whom) did you give the message?
2. Sit between Tasha and (I, me).
3. Were you pointing to (they or we, they or us, them or us, them or we)?
4. The twins and their brother played against Keith and (we, us).
5. We will go to the movies without Kim and (she, her).
6. Did you buy that hot dog for (he or I, he or me, him or me, him or I)?
7. The principal hurried down the hall toward Mr. Corso and (we, us).
8. For Jerry and (she, her), math is easy.
9. Six cheerleaders were sitting near my mom and (I, me) at the restaurant.
10. We stood in line behind Miss O'Neill and (he, him) at the theater.

GRAMMAR/USAGE/MECHANICS

7.3 PREPOSITIONAL PHRASES AS ADJECTIVES AND ADVERBS

A prepositional phrase is an **adjective phrase** when it modifies, or describes, a noun or a pronoun.

EXAMPLE The servers **at the new restaurant** are courteous.

EXAMPLE The atmosphere includes photographs **from old movies.**

In the first sentence, the prepositional phrase *at the new restaurant* modifies the subject of the sentence, *servers.* In the second sentence, the prepositional phrase *from old movies* modifies the direct object, *photographs.*

Notice that, unlike most adjectives, an adjective phrase usually comes after the word it modifies.

A prepositional phrase is an **adverb phrase** when it modifies a verb, an adjective, or another adverb.

ADVERB PHRASES

USE	EXAMPLES
Modifies a Verb	The servers *dress* **like movie characters.**
Modifies an Adjective	The restaurant is *popular* **with young people.**
Modifies an Adverb	The restaurant opens *early* **in the morning.**

Most adverb phrases tell *when, where,* or *how* an action takes place. More than one prepositional phrase may modify the same word.

HOW ADVERB PHRASES MODIFY VERBS	
WHEN?	Many people eat a light meal **during the lunch hour.**
WHERE?	Some eat lunch **on the covered patio.**
HOW?	Others eat their meals **in a hurry.**

PRACTICE Identifying Adjective and Adverb Phrases

Write each prepositional phrase. Then write the word it modifies. Finally, write adjective *or* adverb *to tell how it's used.*

1. How many countries lie on the equator?
2. I read a book about Martin Luther King Jr.
3. The patient sipped water through a straw.
4. The flowers along the fence are daffodils.
5. This game is perfect for a rainy day.
6. The day before yesterday was my birthday.
7. My great-grandparents came from Germany.
8. I like movies with action.
9. The luncheon will begin at noon.
10. The young man chose his career early in life.

7.4 TELLING PREPOSITIONS AND ADVERBS APART

Sometimes it can be difficult to tell whether a particular word is being used as a preposition or as an adverb. Both prepositions and adverbs can answer the questions *where?* and *when?* The chart below shows fifteen words that can be used as either prepositions or adverbs. Whether any one of these words is a preposition or an adverb depends on its use in a particular sentence.

SOME WORDS THAT CAN BE USED AS PREPOSITIONS OR ADVERBS		
about	below	out
above	down	outside
around	in	over
before	inside	through
behind	near	up

If you have trouble deciding whether a word is being used as a preposition or as an adverb, look at the other words in the sentence. If the word is followed closely by a noun or a pronoun, the word is probably a preposition, and the noun or pronoun is the object of the preposition.

EXAMPLE We ate our lunch **outside** the **library.**

EXAMPLE We walked **around** the **park** for an hour.

In the first example, *outside* is followed closely by the noun *library. Outside* is a preposition, and *library* is the object of the preposition. In the second example, *around* is a preposition, and *park* is the object of the preposition.

If the word is not followed closely by a noun or a pronoun, the word is probably an adverb.

EXAMPLE We ate our lunch **outside.**

EXAMPLE We walked **around** for an hour.

In the first sentence, *outside* answers the question *where?* but is not followed by a noun or a pronoun. In this sentence, *outside* is an adverb. In the second sentence, *around* is an adverb. *For an hour* is a prepositional phrase.

PRACTICE Identifying Prepositions and Adverbs

Write preposition *or* adverb *to identify each underlined word.*

1. A flock of geese flew over.
2. The cow jumped over the moon.
3. The boy hid behind a tree.
4. Zack fell behind in the race.
5. The detective entered the room and looked around.
6. He walked around the library several times.
7. From the top of the tower, we looked down.
8. Come inside and get warm.
9. Six impossible things happened before breakfast.
10. Don't stand near the door.

7.5 CONJUNCTIONS

A **coordinating conjunction** is a word used to connect compound parts of a sentence. *And, but, or, nor,* and *for* are coordinating conjunctions. *So* and *yet* are also sometimes used as coordinating conjunctions.

USING COORDINATING CONJUNCTIONS TO FORM COMPOUNDS	
COMPOUND SUBJECT	Allison **and** Rosita have lived in Mexico City.
COMPOUND OBJECTS	Give your suitcases **and** packages to Ben **or** Bill.
COMPOUND PREDICATE	Tourists shop **or** relax on the beaches.
COMPOUND SENTENCE	Tillie shopped every day, **but** we toured the city.

GRAMMAR/USAGE/MECHANICS

To make the relationship between words or groups of words especially strong, use correlative conjunctions.

Correlative conjunctions are pairs of words used to connect compound parts of a sentence. Correlative conjunctions include *both . . . and, either . . . or, neither . . . nor,* and *not only . . . but also.*

EXAMPLE Examples of great architecture exist in **both** New York **and** Paris.

EXAMPLE **Neither** Luis **nor** I have visited those cities.

When a compound subject is joined by *and,* the subject is usually plural. The verb must agree with the plural subject.

EXAMPLE Winnie **and** Sumi **are** in Madrid this week.

When a compound subject is joined by *or* or *nor,* the verb must agree with the nearer subject.

EXAMPLE **Neither** Rhondelle **nor** the twins **speak** Spanish.

EXAMPLE **Neither** the twins **nor** Rhondelle **speaks** Spanish.

GRAMMAR/USAGE/MECHANICS

PRACTICE Identifying Conjunctions and Compounds

Write each conjunction. Then write compound subject, compound object, compound predicate, *or* compound sentence *to tell what parts the conjunction joins.*

1. Tom plays soccer, but his sister prefers softball.
2. Either Mrs. James or her husband will bring both the food and the flowers.
3. Neither the assistants nor the head coach teaches any classes.
4. I brought my raincoat but left my umbrella at home.
5. Midori will deliver the books or the old magazines to the hospital or the nursing center.
6. Give either Mrs. Rio or Ms. Stern my thanks for their help with the costumes and the scenery.
7. Enrique and Marisa told the twins and me a good joke.
8. Neither Stan nor his brothers have time for the job, and Ms. Hancock will not hire either Scott or Seth.
9. My sister will take her driver's test tomorrow or wait until next week.
10. Not only the mayor but also the council members will borrow a van or rent a car, but the students will walk to the parade site.

PRACTICE Making Compound Subjects and Verbs Agree

Write the correct word from the choices in parentheses.

1. Ted and his father (repairs, repair) motorcycles.
2. Neither the band nor sports (takes, take) all my extra time.
3. Either the teacher or her aide (prepares, prepare) the daily attendance report.
4. Neither potato chips nor candy (is, are) good for your health.

5. Either curtains or draperies (offers, offer) an attractive window treatment.
6. Neither Bubba nor Jethro (has, have) time for athletics in the summer.
7. Either my mom or my sisters (helps, help) me with my homework.
8. Either two chairs or a sofa (is, are) suitable for a small room.
9. Both biology and botany (is, are) life sciences.
10. Neither the Joneses nor the Hillmans (lives, live) on this street.

7.6 CONJUNCTIVE ADVERBS

You can use a special kind of adverb instead of a conjunction to join the simple sentences in a compound sentence. This special kind of adverb is called a **conjunctive adverb.**

EXAMPLE Many Asians use chopsticks, but some use forks.

EXAMPLE Many Asians use chopsticks; **however,** some use forks.

A conjunctive adverb, such as *however,* is usually stronger and more exact than a coordinating conjunction like *and* or *but.*

USING CONJUNCTIVE ADVERBS	
TO REPLACE *AND*	besides, furthermore, moreover
TO REPLACE *BUT*	however, nevertheless, still
TO STATE A RESULT	consequently, therefore, thus
TO STATE EQUALITY	equally, likewise, similarly

A **conjunctive adverb** may be used to join the simple sentences in a compound sentence.

When two simple sentences are joined with a conjunctive adverb, use a semicolon at the end of the first sentence. Place a comma after a conjunctive adverb that begins the second part of a compound sentence. If a conjunctive adverb is used in the middle of a simple sentence, set it off with commas.

EXAMPLE The school cafeteria sometimes serves Chinese food; **however,** these meals are not very tasty.

EXAMPLE The school cafeteria sometimes serves Chinese food; these meals**,** **however,** are not very tasty.

GRAMMAR/USAGE/MECHANICS

PRACTICE Identifying Conjunctive Adverbs

Write each sentence. Underline the conjunctive adverb. Add appropriate punctuation.

1. I forgot my lunch furthermore I have no money.
2. There is no train service from here to Biloxi a bus however leaves here at noon.
3. I have no talent for the piano still I do my best.
4. Harry is hoping for a career in the United States Marine Corps Michael likewise will join the armed forces.
5. Morgan gave the best campaign speech consequently she was elected.
6. Mr. Caruso is a great teacher besides he has a wonderful sense of humor.
7. The islands of the Caribbean have a tropical climate nevertheless pleasant ocean breezes cool the beaches of these islands.
8. Rick is a fine guitarist he has moreover written several original compositions.
9. The new restaurant had few customers thus it closed in a few months.
10. The crime was committed in a locked room the detective was therefore puzzled for a solution.

7.7 INTERJECTIONS

You can express emotions in short exclamations that aren't complete sentences. These exclamations are called interjections.

An **interjection** is a word or group of words that expresses emotion. It has no grammatical connection to other words in a sentence.

Interjections are used to express emotion, such as surprise or disbelief. They're also used to attract attention.

SOME COMMON INTERJECTIONS			
aha	great	my	ouch
alas	ha	no	well
gee	hey	oh	wow
good grief	hooray	oops	yes

GRAMMAR/USAGE/MECHANICS

An interjection that expresses strong emotion may stand alone. It begins with a capital letter and ends with an exclamation point.

EXAMPLE **Good grief!** My favorite restaurant has closed.

When an interjection expresses mild feeling, it is written as part of the sentence. In that case, the interjection is set off with commas.

EXAMPLE **Oh, well,** I'll just eat at home.

NOTE Most words may be more than one part of speech. A word's part of speech depends on its use in a sentence.

EXAMPLE A duck has soft **down** on its body. **[noun]**

EXAMPLE The hungry boy **downed** the hamburger in three bites. **[verb]**

EXAMPLE Libby felt **down** all day. **[adjective]**

EXAMPLE The baby often falls **down.** **[adverb]**

EXAMPLE A car drove **down** the street. **[preposition]**

EXAMPLE **"Down!"** I shouted to the dog. **[interjection]**

PRACTICE Writing Sentences with Interjections

Write ten sentences, using a different interjection with each. Punctuate correctly.

GRAMMAR/USAGE/MECHANICS

PRACTICE Proofreading

Rewrite the following passage, correcting errors in spelling, capitalization, grammar, and usage. Add any missing punctuation. Write legibly to be sure one letter is not mistaken for another. There are ten errors.

Amy Tan

[1]Amy Tan is the author of *The Joy Luck Club* and *The Kitchen God's Wife.* [2]About who does she write? [3]She writes about Chinese American women.

[4]Amy Tan was born on Febuary 19, 1952. [5]At the age of fifteen, Tan moved to Europe. [6]She attended high school in Switzerland; however she was unhappy there. [7]She returned to the United States and studied English in college.

[8]Tan became a successful business writer nevertheless, she was dissatisfied with her career. [9]For a change, she took jazz piano lessons; furthermore she joined a group of writers. [10]She remembered stories about her mother. [11]Tan wrote about she and other women.

[12]Tan is a popular writer, and her husband is a tax attorney. [13]Both she and her husband lives in California and New York.

[14]Tan is my favorite author. [15]Her stories appeal to my cousin and I. [16]Either Mom or my aunt discuss the stories with us. [17]Maybe our teacher will assign more of Tan's stories. [18]Great

POSTTEST Prepositions and Prepositional Phrases

Write each prepositional phrase. Underline the preposition and circle the object of the preposition. Then write the word the prepositional phrase modifies. Finally, write adjective *or* adverb *to tell how the prepositional phrase is used.*

1. Inside the dark and gloomy room, Lucy saw only the dim outlines of the bulky furniture.
2. Jacob kicked the ball down the field and between the goalposts.
3. Aboard the ship, many passengers without life jackets were frantic.
4. Our guests arrived late in the evening.
5. The library near the school will show an educational film on Sunday afternoon.
6. The park behind the library will be suitable for our picnic.
7. On account of rain, the umpire canceled the game.
8. The bakery across the street makes delicious sweet rolls.
9. I started this book about King Arthur at eight and finished it around midnight.
10. The cyclists rode past the barn, over the hill, through the trees, and along the stream.

GRAMMAR/USAGE/MECHANICS

POSTTEST Pronouns as Objects of Prepositions

Write the correct word from the choices in parentheses.

11. Did you eat lunch with Jorge and (they, them)?
12. The shiny black limousine drove slowly toward Kevin and (I, me).
13. Besides Hawa and (she, her), who screamed at the scary scene in the movie?
14. Mrs. Chang waved at the girls and (he, him).
15. Behind (who, whom) did you wait?
16. Did you hear the good news about Jeff and (they, them)?
17. Nothing stood between the barking dog and (we, us).
18. Against (who, whom) will you play in the tournament?

19. Mr. Alionzo hurried past Lorenzo and (I, me) on his way to the parking lot.
20. No one was in the room but (she, her) and her sister.

POSTTEST Conjunctions

Write each conjunction. Then write compound subject, compound object, compound predicate, *or* compound sentence *to tell what parts the conjunction joins.*

21. The doctor examined the patient, and the nurse took notes.
22. Neither Mom nor Dad enjoys television cartoons, but we children watch them faithfully.
23. Both Carla and Luisa dry flowers or press them between the pages of a book.
24. We wanted neither the spinach nor the zucchini, but our mother fed them to us.
25. Francis Scott Key wrote "The Star-Spangled Banner" in 1814, and the song became our national anthem in 1931.
26. Is the galaxy or the universe larger?
27. Did you find either the Nile River or the Amazon River on the map?
28. Muwanee will play the part of the judge or the mayor.
29. The students walk to school or take a bus.
30. Give either your aunt or your uncle those free passes.

POSTTEST Making Compound Subjects and Verbs Agree

Write the correct word from the choices in parentheses.

31. Neither a paper clip nor these postage stamps (weighs, weigh) much.
32. Neither these dimes nor this quarter (starts, start) the coin-operated washing machine.

33. Bill Nye and my science teacher (conducts, conduct) science experiments on television.
34. Either the captain or the sailors (helps, help) the passengers.
35. Either the spider exhibits or the snake house (gives, give) me a scare.
36. Both the turtle and the tortoise (has, have) shells of bony plates.
37. Either Amy or Ilom (rides, ride) the snowboard.
38. (Does, Do) a lion or a hyena hunt at night?
39. Neither Mark nor his father (wants, want) these old bicycle tires.
40. You or the twins (deserves, deserve) a merit badge.

POSTTEST Conjunctive Adverbs

Write each sentence. Underline the conjunctive adverb. Add appropriate punctuation.

41. Most farmers use machines at harvest time nevertheless some Amish farmers follow older traditions.
42. Fresh vegetables from your own garden taste delicious furthermore they're good for you.
43. Amelia Earhart flew successfully across the Atlantic in 1932 thus she won America's respect.
44. Niagara Falls touches New York likewise it touches Ontario, Canada.
45. Beavers dam waterways with their homes wolves however shelter in caves or dig dens.

Chapter 8

Clauses and Complex Sentences

PRETEST Simple, Compound, and Complex Sentences

Write simple, compound, *or* complex *to identify each sentence.*

1. The dollar is the basic unit of money in both the United States and Canada.
2. People in Jordan use the dinar when they buy things.
3. A Zambian buys goods with the kwacha, but a Brazilian buys them with the cruzeiro.
4. If you visit Mexico, convert your dollars into pesos.
5. A traveler visits a banker or a librarian for information on foreign money.
6. In 1700 B.C., people in the country of Lydia, which occupied the site of present-day Turkey, used the first coins as money.

7. A Dutch coin with the head of a lion traveled to the United States in 1620.
8. Did you know that George Washington began the first United States mint?
9. Silver was scarce, and Washington gave the mint some of his silver dishes.
10. Washington's portrait appears on a one-dollar bill; Abraham Lincoln appears on a penny and a five-dollar bill.

PRETEST Adjective, Adverb, and Noun Clauses

Identify each italicized clause by writing adjective, adverb, *or* noun.

11. *How plants grow* will be our next topic of study.
12. Dad became angry *when he discovered the truth.*
13. Trains *that carry passengers* are becoming rare.
14. We promised *whoever found our dog* a reward.
15. The student *whose essay won first prize* is Beverly Ching.
16. *Before I had finished the assignment,* the bell rang.
17. The story "Basketball Blues," *which I read on Saturday,* is very funny.
18. Lurlene was hurrying *because she was late.*
19. No one knows *what the future will bring.*
20. The committee will award a silver trophy to *whoever designs the best plan.*
21. My brother, *who is captain of the football team,* will attend college in the fall.
22. Everyone rose *as the judge entered the courtroom.*
23. The counselor *whom I saw yesterday* gave me some good advice.
24. The truth is *that some people don't like sports.*
25. *If you submit your order by June 30,* you'll receive a free computer game.

8.1 SENTENCES AND CLAUSES

A **sentence** is a group of words that has a subject and a predicate and expresses a complete thought.

A **simple sentence** has one complete subject and one complete predicate.

The **complete subject** names whom or what the sentence is about. The **complete predicate** tells what the subject does or has. Sometimes the complete predicate tells what the subject is or is like. The complete subject or the complete predicate or both may be compound.

COMPLETE SUBJECT	COMPLETE PREDICATE
People	travel.
Neither automobiles nor airplanes	are completely safe.
Travelers	meet new people and see new sights.
Trains and buses	carry passengers and transport goods.

A **compound sentence** contains two or more simple sentences. Each simple sentence is called a main clause.

A **main clause** has a subject and a predicate and can stand alone as a sentence.

Main clauses can be connected by a comma and a conjunction, by a semicolon, or by a semicolon and a conjunctive adverb. The conjunctive adverb is followed by a comma. In the following examples, each main clause is in black. The connecting elements are in blue type.

EXAMPLE Many people live in cities, **but** others build houses in the suburbs. **[comma and coordinating conjunction]**

EXAMPLE Most people travel to their jobs; others work at home. **[semicolon]**

EXAMPLE Companies relocate to the suburbs; **therefore,** more people leave the city. **[semicolon and conjunctive adverb]**

GRAMMAR/USAGE/MECHANICS

PRACTICE Identifying and Punctuating Simple and Compound Sentences

Write each sentence. Underline each main clause. Add commas or semicolons where they're needed. Write simple *or* compound *to identify the sentence.*

1. The Falcons and the Red Hawks played yesterday and today both teams are exhausted.
2. The young boy survived alone in the wilderness.
3. Gordon joined the photography club but Marty and Manny had other plans.
4. The twins play in the band and sing in the chorus.
5. Mr. Jonquil planted tulips and daffodils his wife planted pumpkins and watermelons.
6. Dad and the girls washed the car and cleaned the garage.
7. The ideas in your composition are good however your handwriting is sloppy.
8. The house had a fresh coat of paint furthermore the yard looked clean and tidy.
9. Both Yoko and her mother enjoy nature walks in the fall.
10. Mrs. Gardenia washes her clothes by hand or her daughter takes them to a laundry.

GRAMMAR/USAGE/MECHANICS

8.2 COMPLEX SENTENCES

A **main clause** has a subject and a predicate and can stand alone as a sentence. Some sentences have a main clause and a subordinate clause.

A **subordinate clause** is a group of words that has a subject and a predicate but does not express a complete thought and cannot stand alone as a sentence. A subordinate clause is always combined with a main clause in a sentence.

A **complex sentence** has one main clause and one or more subordinate clauses.

In each complex sentence that follows, the subordinate clause is in blue type.

EXAMPLE Mariah, **who moved here from Montana,** is very popular.

EXAMPLE **Since Mariah moved to Springfield,** she has made many new friends.

EXAMPLE Everyone says **that Mariah is friendly.**

Subordinate clauses can function in three ways: as adjectives, as adverbs, or as nouns. In the examples, the first sentence has an adjective clause that modifies the noun *Mariah.* The second sentence has an adverb clause that modifies the verb *has made.* The third sentence has a noun clause that is the direct object of the verb *says.* Adjective, adverb, and noun clauses are used in the same ways one-word adjectives, adverbs, and nouns are used.

NOTE A **compound-complex sentence** has two or more main clauses and one or more subordinate clauses.

GRAMMAR/USAGE/MECHANICS

PRACTICE Identifying Simple and Complex Sentences

Write each sentence. Underline each main clause once and each subordinate clause twice. Write simple *or* complex *to identify the sentence.*

1. I spoke before I thought.
2. After several weeks had passed, I wrote another letter to the mayor.
3. Mark and his best friend, Tony, work in the stables at Kingston Park.
4. We finished the job before noon.
5. Zeena dreamed that she was a colonist on Mars.
6. This book, which I read in a single evening, is hilarious.
7. After the movie, we stopped for a snack at Hamburger Heaven.

8. I like math because it's easy for me.
9. When we met, Connor pretended that he had never seen me before.
10. The baby, who has curly red hair, laughs if you tickle her.

8.3 ADJECTIVE CLAUSES

An **adjective clause** is a subordinate clause that modifies a noun or a pronoun in the main clause of a complex sentence.

EXAMPLE The Aqua-Lung, **which divers strap on,** holds oxygen.

EXAMPLE The divers breathe through a tube **that attaches to the tank.**

Each subordinate clause in blue type is an adjective clause that adds information about a noun in the main clause. An adjective clause is usually introduced by a relative pronoun. The relative pronoun *that* may refer to people or things. *Which* refers only to things.

RELATIVE PRONOUNS				
that	which	who	whom	whose

An adjective clause can also begin with *where* or *when.*

EXAMPLE Divers search for reefs **where much sea life exists.**

EXAMPLE Herb remembers the day **when he had his first diving experience.**

A relative pronoun that begins an adjective clause is often the subject of the clause.

EXAMPLE Some divers prefer equipment **that is lightweight.**

EXAMPLE Willa is a new diver **who is taking lessons.**

In the first sentence, *that* is the subject of the adjective clause. In the second sentence, *who* is the subject of the adjective clause.

GRAMMAR/USAGE/MECHANICS

PRACTICE Identifying Adjective Clauses

Write each adjective clause. Underline the subject of the adjective clause. Then write the word the adjective clause modifies.

1. I read a story that reminded me of you.
2. Tom Farmer, whose calf won a blue ribbon at the state fair, has been in 4-H for three years.
3. Is this the log cabin where Abraham Lincoln once lived?
4. The shoes that Carrie wants are somewhat expensive.
5. This computer, which is our newest model, has a reasonable price.
6. There are times when I don't like my brother.
7. We often visit my great-grandmother, who is eighty-six.
8. My cousin, whom you met yesterday, will move here permanently in June.
9. The boy who is standing beside Tammy is Nathan's brother.
10. The girls' basketball team, which has won the state championship five times, is the pride and joy of the school district.

GRAMMAR/USAGE/MECHANICS

"He appears to have eaten some homework."

8.4 ESSENTIAL AND NONESSENTIAL CLAUSES

Read the example sentence. Is the adjective clause in blue type needed to make the meaning of the sentence clear?

EXAMPLE The girl **who is standing beside the coach** is our best swimmer.

The adjective clause in blue type is essential to the meaning of the sentence. The clause tells *which* girl is the best swimmer.

An **essential clause** is a clause that is necessary to make the meaning of a sentence clear. Don't use commas to set off essential clauses.

Now look at the adjective clause in this sentence.

EXAMPLE Janice, **who is standing beside the coach,** is our best swimmer.

In the example, the adjective clause is set off with commas. The clause is nonessential, or not necessary to identify which swimmer the writer means. The clause simply gives additional information about the noun it modifies.

A **nonessential clause** is a clause that is not necessary to make the meaning of a sentence clear. Use commas to set off nonessential clauses.

In this book, adjective clauses that begin with *that* are always essential, and adjective clauses that begin with *which* are always nonessential.

EXAMPLE Were you at the meet **that** our team won yesterday? **[essential]**

EXAMPLE That meet, **which** began late, ended after dark. **[nonessential]**

GRAMMAR/USAGE/MECHANICS

GRAMMAR/USAGE/MECHANICS

PRACTICE Identifying and Punctuating Adjective Clauses

Write each sentence. Underline the adjective clause. Add commas where they're needed. Write essential *or* non-essential *to identify each adjective clause.*

1. I like movies that have happy endings.
2. Jeff Brush whose sculpture was selected by the judges has won a scholarship to art camp.
3. This is the house where James Thurber lived as a child.
4. The ships that dock here are foreign vessels.
5. This photograph which I found in a trunk in the attic shows my great-grandmother as a girl.
6. That was the summer when I met my best friend.
7. Chris often discusses problems with her mother who is remarkably understanding.
8. Sada's aunt Carla whom I interviewed last week gave me some interesting information about Sacramento history.
9. The person who delivered the package was wearing a brown uniform and a baseball cap.
10. The White House which is located at 1600 Pennsylvania Avenue is the home of the president and his family.

8.5 ADVERB CLAUSES

An **adverb clause** is a subordinate clause that often modifies the verb in the main clause of a complex sentence.

An adverb clause tells *how, when, where, why,* or *under what conditions* the action occurs.

EXAMPLE **After we won the meet,** we shook hands with our opponents.

EXAMPLE We won the meet **because we practiced hard.**

In the first sentence, the adverb clause *After we won the meet* modifies the verb *shook.* The adverb clause tells *when* we shook hands. In the second sentence, the adverb clause *because we practiced hard* modifies the verb *won.* The adverb clause tells *why* we won the meet.

An adverb clause is introduced by a subordinating conjunction. A subordinating conjunction signals that a clause is a subordinate clause and cannot stand alone.

SUBORDINATING CONJUNCTIONS			
after	because	though	whenever
although	before	till	where
as	if	unless	whereas
as if	since	until	wherever
as though	than	when	while

Use a comma after an adverb clause that begins a sentence. You usually don't use a comma before an adverb clause that comes at the end of a sentence.

NOTE Adverb clauses can also modify adjectives and adverbs.

PRACTICE Identifying Adverb Clauses

Write each adverb clause. Underline the subordinating conjunction. Then write the verb the adverb clause modifies.

1. I will feel grateful if you will work with me on this project.
2. Although the detective had investigated the case for a year, he had found no other evidence.
3. I think of you whenever I hear that song.
4. As the sun sets over Honolulu, our plane departs for home.

5. When you're smiling, the whole world smiles with you.
6. Do nothing till you hear from me.
7. Since you went away, we have missed your happy disposition.
8. Three people called while you were sleeping.
9. Unless everyone cooperates, we will make no progress.
10. I failed the test because I did not study.

GRAMMAR/USAGE/MECHANICS

8.6 NOUN CLAUSES

A **noun clause** is a subordinate clause used as a noun.

Notice how the subject in blue type in the following sentence can be replaced by a clause.

EXAMPLE **A hockey player** wears protective equipment.

EXAMPLE **Whoever plays hockey** wears protective equipment.

The clause in blue type, like the words it replaces, is the subject of the sentence. Because this kind of clause acts as a noun, it's called a noun clause.

You can use a noun clause in the same ways you use a noun—as a subject, a direct object, an indirect object, an object of a preposition, and a predicate noun. In most sentences containing noun clauses, you can replace the noun clause with the word *it,* and the sentence will still make sense.

HOW NOUN CLAUSES ARE USED	
SUBJECT	**Whoever plays hockey** wears protective equipment.
DIRECT OBJECT	Suzi knows **that ice hockey is a rough game.**
INDIRECT OBJECT	She tells **whoever will listen** her opinions.
OBJECT OF A PREPOSITION	Victory goes to **whoever makes more goals.**
PREDICATE NOUN	This rink is **where the teams play.**

Here are some words that can introduce noun clauses.

WORDS THAT INTRODUCE NOUN CLAUSES		
how, however	when	who, whom
if	where	whoever, whomever
that	whether	whose
what, whatever	which, whichever	why

EXAMPLE **Whichever you choose** will look fine.

EXAMPLE **What I wonder** is **why she said that.**

EXAMPLE I don't know **who left this package here.**

EXAMPLE Ask the teacher **if this is the right answer.**

EXAMPLE Promise **whoever calls first** a special bonus.

EXAMPLE He worried about **what he had done.**

GRAMMAR/USAGE/MECHANICS

PRACTICE Identifying Noun Clauses

Write each noun clause. Then write subject, direct object, indirect object, object of a preposition, *or* predicate noun *to tell how the noun clause is used.*

1. The judges have promised whoever wins the essay contest a trip to Washington, D.C.
2. Tell us how you will achieve your goal.
3. What he said made no sense.
4. Pay attention to whatever the coach tells you.
5. This cave is where Johnson found the lost treasure of Timbaloo.
6. I don't know whether I passed the test.
7. The result of the argument was that the two women never spoke to each other again.
8. Give these free pamphlets to whomever you meet.
9. When they will return is still a mystery.
10. I understand why you did that.

PRACTICE Proofreading

Rewrite the following passage, correcting errors in spelling, capitalization, grammar, and usage. Add any missing punctuation. Write legibly to be sure one letter is not mistaken for another. There are ten errors.

Alice Walker

[1]Alice Walker who was the youngest of eight children grew up in Eatonton, Georgia. [2]When she was eight years old she injured her face. [3]She was embarassed because her face was scarred. [4]She spent much time alone. [5]She read many novels and poems and she wrote poems. [6]She was a clever student consequently, she finished first in her high school class. [7]She attended Spelman College which is in Atlanta, Georgia. [8]She also attended Sarah Lawrence College in New York. [9]While she was a student she traveled to Africa.

[10]After she graduated from college Walker became a writer. [11]She wrote an essay that won *The American Scholar* essay contest. [12]*The Color Purple* which won the Pulitzer Prize in 1983 and *The Temple of My Familiar* are two of her novels. [13]Walker has written essays and reviews for *Ms.* magazine which contains articles about women's concerns.

POSTTEST Simple, Compound, and Complex Sentences

Write simple, compound, *or* complex *to identify each sentence.*

1. Ida Tarbell and Jacob Riis were two American writers who exposed social problems.

2. Ida Tarbell attacked John D. Rockefeller's control of the oil industry, and Jacob Riis criticized conditions in urban slums.

3. Although John D. Rockefeller was a heartless businessman, he gave away over 520 million dollars after his retirement.
4. Streets in cities were unbelievably dirty, and the street lighting was bad.
5. Many houses had no running water; tall buildings had no fire escapes.
6. Fire was a constant threat because most buildings were wooden and had little space between them.
7. Riis believed that such conditions were unhealthy and unsafe.
8. Jane Addams established a famous settlement house in Chicago in 1889.
9. Settlement houses provided neighborhood people with hot meals and educational and cultural activities.
10. Many people made suggestions for improvements in cities, but progress was slow.

GRAMMAR/USAGE/MECHANICS

POSTTEST Adjective, Adverb, and Noun Clauses

Identify each italicized clause by writing adjective, adverb, *or* noun.

11. Lashawnda takes the downtown bus *when she visits Betty.*
12. *After Owanah finished her homework,* she called her friend Jessica.
13. Brian worked on his English assignment *until the bell rang for lunch.*
14. Please tell me *how you did that trick.*
15. People *who live in the country* enjoy cleaner air.
16. Please sit *wherever you wish.*
17. Miguel's father shows Miguel's trophies to *whoever visits.*
18. A thesaurus, *which is a book of synonyms,* is a helpful tool for writers.
19. The problem is *that you won't cooperate.*

20. This is the spot *where the pirates found the buried treasure.*

21. *What you see before you* is my science project.

22. We're taking the flight *that leaves at 7:35 A.M.*

23. The doctor *whom Grandmother consulted* treated her kindly.

24. Amanda will give *whoever races from Milton Middle School* tough competition.

25. *Before we moved into this house,* we lived in an apartment.

Chapter 9

Verbals

PRETEST Verbal Phrases

Identify each italicized phrase by writing participial, gerund, *or* infinitive.

1. The whole family enjoys *camping in the wilderness.*
2. Many people don't like *to speak before large groups.*
3. Are automobiles *made in Japan* better than American cars?
4. *To make a mistake* is human.
5. *Making craft items from seashells* is Miriam's hobby.
6. *Stepping onto the moon,* Neil Armstrong made his famous speech.
7. He was charged with *disturbing the peace.*
8. *To become a famous actor* is Marilyn's dream.
9. *Invented by Alexander Graham Bell in 1876,* the telephone revolutionized communication.
10. The team's mission was *to rescue the space travelers.*
11. *Pitching a perfect game* is a rare achievement.
12. The Gianellis increased the value of their home by *remodeling their kitchen.*
13. Jake offered *to help me.*
14. *To build a new stadium* will cost 55 million dollars.
15. The author's latest book, *written in just six weeks,* has become a best-seller.

16. The Underground Railroad assisted many African Americans *fleeing cruel masters in the South.*
17. I have finally stopped *worrying about the problem.*
18. Our job is *to build a better mousetrap.*
19. Wood *treated with chemicals* is suitable for decks and other outdoor structures.
20. Today I learned *to throw a curveball.*
21. *Lowering my voice,* I responded to Wendy's question.
22. I promise *to clean the garage on Saturday.*
23. *Designing computer programs* requires much technical knowledge.
24. The young woman *dancing with the prince* is Cinderella.
25. Jing-Mei thanked me for *helping her.*

9.1 PARTICIPLES AND PARTICIPIAL PHRASES

A present participle is formed by adding *-ing* to a verb. A past participle is usually formed by adding *-d* or *-ed* to a verb. A participle can act as the main verb in a verb phrase or as an adjective to modify a noun or a pronoun.

EXAMPLE Erik is **taking** piano lessons. **[present participle used as main verb in a verb phrase]**

EXAMPLE His talent has **impressed** his teacher. **[past participle used as main verb in a verb phrase]**

EXAMPLE His **playing** skill improves daily. **[present participle used as adjective modifying *skill*]**

EXAMPLE He practices at home on a **rented** piano. **[past participle used as adjective modifying *piano*]**

A participle that is used as an adjective may be modified by a single adverb or by a prepositional phrase. It may also have a direct object.

EXAMPLE **Sitting quietly,** Erik loses himself in the music.

EXAMPLE **Sitting at the piano,** Erik loses himself in the music.

EXAMPLE **Playing the piano,** Erik loses himself in the music.

A **participial phrase** is a group of words that includes a participle and other words that complete its meaning.

A participial phrase that begins a sentence is always set off with a comma. Participial phrases in other places in a sentence may or may not need commas. If the phrase is necessary to identify the modified word, it is an essential phrase and should not be set off with commas. If the phrase simply gives additional information about the modified word, it is a nonessential phrase. Use commas to set off nonessential phrases.

EXAMPLE The musician **seated at the piano** is Erik. **[essential]**

EXAMPLE Erik, **dreaming of fame,** sits at the piano. **[nonessential]**

EXAMPLE **Dreaming of fame,** Erik sits at the piano. **[nonessential]**

An essential participial phrase must follow the noun it modifies. A nonessential participial phrase can appear before or after the word it modifies. Place the phrase as close as possible to the modified word to make the meaning of the sentence clear.

GRAMMAR/USAGE/MECHANICS

PRACTICE Identifying Participles

Write each participle. Then write main verb *or* adjective *to tell how the participle is used.*

1. Juan Escobeda has just moved to Taylorville from Puerto Rico.
2. Stay away from that deserted building.
3. Who is watching the baby?
4. Mr. and Mrs. Ford are shopping for a new car.
5. I am delivering meals to disabled shut-ins.
6. Mitsuko had entered the diving competition with high hopes.
7. The glaring lights of the bus station shone down on the stranded travelers.

8. Alicia's amazing writing skills have gained her many awards.
9. Mervin and Leroy were looking for you.
10. A battered old sprinkling can was standing on the porch.

PRACTICE Identifying Participial Phrases

Write each sentence. Underline the participial phrase once. Draw two lines under the word the participial phrase modifies. Add commas where they're needed.

1. The sculpture painted bright red gave the park a weird appearance.
2. Lingering at the door Bobbi Jo waited for her friend.
3. The price tag attached to the silk shirt read "$69.95."
4. Nurse Primrose opening the door to the examining room gave the patient a cheery smile.
5. Attacked by a wild boar the warrior bravely defended himself.
6. The boy peering through the window is my cousin Ned.
7. On the table were several packages wrapped in bright paper and tied with ribbons and bows.
8. Dressed in clown costumes the band marched onto the field.
9. Norm Spendall is the producer financing the movie.
10. Placing a comma after the participial phrase Jasmine finished the assignment.

9.2 GERUNDS AND GERUND PHRASES

When a verb form ending in *-ing* is used as a noun, it's called a gerund.

EXAMPLE The **skating** rink is near my house. **[adjective]**

EXAMPLE **Skating** is a favorite winter pastime in my neighborhood. **[noun, gerund]**

A **gerund** is a verb form that ends in *-ing* and is used as a noun.

Like other nouns, a gerund may be used as a subject, a predicate noun, a direct object, or the object of a preposition.

EXAMPLE **Exercising** builds strength and endurance. **[subject]**

EXAMPLE My favorite activity is **exercising.** **[predicate noun]**

EXAMPLE Some people enjoy **exercising.** **[direct object]**

EXAMPLE What are the benefits of **exercising?** **[object of a preposition]**

A gerund may be modified by a single adverb or by a prepositional phrase. It may also have a direct object.

EXAMPLE **Exercising daily** is a good habit.

EXAMPLE Many people enjoy **exercising on a bike.**

EXAMPLE Tell me something about **exercising the body.**

A **gerund phrase** is a group of words that includes a gerund and other words that complete its meaning.

You can identify the three uses of *-ing* verb forms if you remember that a present participle can serve as part of a verb phrase, as an adjective, and as a noun.

EXAMPLE The young people are **bicycling** in the country. **[main verb]**

EXAMPLE The **bicycling** club travels long distances. **[adjective]**

EXAMPLE **Bicycling** is good exercise. **[noun, gerund]**

GRAMMAR/USAGE/MECHANICS

PRACTICE Identifying Gerunds and Participles

Write main verb, adjective, *or* gerund *to identify each underlined word.*

1. My favorite sport is swimming.
2. Everyone was swimming in the lake.
3. We all jumped into the swimming pool.
4. Few people enjoy ironing.

5. A <u>growing</u> child needs care, love, and attention.
6. John is <u>working</u> for his brother.
7. Those in the lifeboats helplessly watched the <u>sinking</u> ship.
8. Rosalind is <u>earning</u> money by <u>tutoring</u>.
9. I am <u>living</u> with my uncle Ralph and my aunt Susan.
10. <u>Studying</u> is a <u>learning</u> experience.

PRACTICE **Identifying Gerund Phrases**

Write each gerund phrase. Then write subject, predicate noun, direct object, *or* object of a preposition *to tell how it's used.*

1. I read a book about climbing Mount Everest.
2. Many people avoid speaking before large groups.
3. Her greatest talent was playing the flute.
4. After the first five minutes, I stopped listening to the speaker.
5. I exhausted myself by walking ten miles.
6. Becoming a medical doctor requires many years of education.
7. Poison ivy causes itching of the affected area.
8. Succeeding in school depends on hard work.
9. What are the advantages of living in Alaska?
10. Playing first base will be a real stretch for me.

9.3 INFINITIVES AND INFINITIVE PHRASES

Another verb form that may be used as a noun is an infinitive.

EXAMPLE **To write** is Alice's ambition.

EXAMPLE Alice wants **to write.**

An **infinitive** is formed with the word *to* and the base form of a verb. Infinitives are often used as nouns in sentences.

How can you tell if the word *to* is a preposition or part of an infinitive? If the word *to* comes immediately before a verb, it's part of an infinitive.

EXAMPLE Alice liked **to write.** **[infinitive]**

EXAMPLE She sent a story **to a magazine.** **[prepositional phrase]**

In the first sentence, the words in blue type work together as a noun to name *what* Alice liked. In the second sentence, the words in blue type are a prepositional phrase used as an adverb to tell *where* she sent a story.

Because infinitives are used as nouns, they can be subjects, predicate nouns, and direct objects.

EXAMPLE **To write** was Alice's ambition. **[subject]**

EXAMPLE Alice's ambition was **to write.** **[predicate noun]**

EXAMPLE Alice liked **to write.** **[direct object]**

An infinitive may be modified by a single adverb or by a prepositional phrase. It may also have a direct object.

EXAMPLE **To write well** was Alice's ambition.

EXAMPLE Alice's ambition was **to write for fame and money.**

EXAMPLE Alice wanted **to write a great novel.**

An **infinitive phrase** is a group of words that includes an infinitive and other words that complete its meaning.

GRAMMAR/USAGE/MECHANICS

PRACTICE Identifying Infinitives and Prepositional Phrases

Write infinitive phrase *or* prepositional phrase *to identify each underlined group of words.*

1. Margo's goal was <u>to become a ballerina</u>.
2. I rode my bike <u>to the library</u>.
3. This shirt fits me <u>to perfection</u>.
4. <u>To criticize others</u> seems unkind.
5. I hate <u>to clean my room</u>.

6. James traveled <u>to Arizona</u> with his aunt Carla.
7. Please go <u>to the grocery</u> for a gallon of skim milk.
8. <u>To improve your grades</u> will take a great deal of work.
9. The cat likes <u>to look out the window</u>.
10. The road <u>to Mayberry</u> passes through Junebug.

PRACTICE Identifying Infinitive Phrases

Write each infinitive phrase. Then write subject, predicate noun, *or* direct object *to tell how it's used.*

1. Morton refused to help us.
2. Remember to brush your teeth.
3. To play the piano well requires practice.
4. Linda's decision was to sell her bicycle.
5. Robby learned to repair motorcycles.
6. My intention is to read one hundred books this year.
7. The baby began to cry loudly.
8. To sit in the sun on a spring day feels wonderful.
9. Don't forget to take out the garbage.
10. To blame others for your problems doesn't solve them.

GRAMMAR/USAGE/MECHANICS

PRACTICE Proofreading

Rewrite the following passage, correcting errors in spelling and adding missing punctuation. Write legibly to be sure one letter is not mistaken for another. There are ten errors.

Nikki Giovanni

[1]Growing up in Cincinnati Nikki Giovanni loved books. [2]She attended Fisk University. [3]Giovanni dissatisfied with the school was unhappy there. [4]Rebelling against the rules she ran home to her grandmother. [5]She later returned to Fisk and edited a school magazine. [6]Interested in civil rights she became politically active. [7]Taking

part in a writers' workshop she learned from a famous author. [8]Giovanni receiving honors graduated in 1967.

[9]After her graduation, Giovanni organized a black arts festival. [10]The festival held in Cincinnati celebrated African American arts and culture.

[11]Giovanni published *Spin a Soft Black Song* in 1971. [12]It was a book of childern's poems. [13]More poems for young people appeared in *Vacation Time: Poems for Children* published in 1980. [14]The book published in 1971 was her first book of children's poems.

[15]Many people recogized Giovanni's talent. [16]The album recorded in 1971 made her even more famous. [17]It is called *Truth Is on Its Way*. [18]Anyone having Giovanni's talent and ambition will always succeed.

GRAMMAR/USAGE/MECHANICS

POSTTEST Verbal Phrases

Identify each italicized phrase by writing participial, gerund, *or* infinitive.

1. *Eating strawberries* gives me hives.
2. *Waving to his family,* Charlie boarded the plane.
3. A soldier's duty is *to obey orders.*
4. I tried *to tell her the truth.*
5. The two women *playing tennis* are my mother and my aunt Virginia.
6. Meteorologists practice *forecasting the weather.*
7. Terri earned money by *walking her neighbor's dog.*
8. On one corner was a vacant lot *surrounded by a high fence.*
9. *To lose a friend* is painful.
10. My father likes *to sing in the shower.*
11. There lay the priceless vase, *shattered into a million pieces.*
12. Don't make any decision without *talking to your parents first.*
13. *Designed by James Hoban,* the White House has been the home of presidents since 1800.

14. *To walk to the nearest library* takes twenty minutes.

15. Jerry's suggestion for the class project was *to perform a musical show at the retirement home.*

16. Oscar, *winking at his brother,* slipped the rubber spider onto his sister's plate.

17. *Smoking cigarettes* is bad for your health.

18. Children *raised in poverty* are poor candidates for success in later life.

19. Harry and Sally refused *to join us for dinner.*

20. Who is the person *wearing the Superman costume*?

21. After *meeting with the counselor,* I decided *to take algebra next year.*

22. Aunt Cora has begun *studying art history.*

23. *To become an outstanding athlete* demands devotion and hard work.

24. My plan is *to join the Peace Corps.*

25. Chan enjoys *playing in the band.*

Chapter 10

Subject-Verb Agreement

PRETEST Subject-Verb Agreement

Write the correct verb from the choices in parentheses.

1. The class (wants, want) to enter their photographs in the contest.
2. The author and illustrator (is, are) Kwesi Malloum.
3. Meteorologists (studies, study) weather patterns.
4. *The Wind in the Willows* (is, are) my younger brother's favorite book.
5. Mathematics (is, are) difficult for me.
6. Those blue jays or that cardinal (eats, eat) the old bread.
7. In the alley behind the building (is, are) three dumpsters.
8. A brook (gurgles, gurgle) through the leafy forest.
9. Everyone (takes, take) an interest in the tournament.
10. The children (is, are) watching a cartoon.
11. Jamake (seems, seem) happy at his new school.
12. The farms of Nebraska (produces, produce) millions of bushels of grain.

13. Both Wayne Gretzky and Cammi Granato (deserves, deserve) respect for their playing ability.
14. Few (chooses, choose) spinach as their favorite vegetable.
15. These special scissors (cuts, cut) through metal.
16. They (listens, listen) to music in the evening.
17. A book of riddles (lies, lie) on the desk.
18. (Does, Do) robins migrate south for the winter?
19. Neither our congresswoman nor our two senators ever (votes, vote) for higher taxes.
20. Any of these sweaters (looks, look) good with jeans.
21. Here (is, are) three coins from ancient Rome.
22. Some of this clothing (is, are) going to the homeless shelter.
23. Three months (passes, pass) during summer vacation.
24. Some of the students (wants, want) more study time.
25. The Johnsons or their son (drives, drive) the car to the shop for repairs.

10.1 MAKING SUBJECTS AND VERBS AGREE

The basic idea of subject-verb agreement is a simple one: A singular subject requires a singular verb, and a plural subject requires a plural verb. The subject and its verb are said to *agree in number.*

Notice that in the present tense the singular form of the verb usually ends in *-s* or *-es.*

SUBJECT-VERB AGREEMENT WITH NOUNS AS SUBJECTS

SINGULAR	PLURAL
A **botanist studies** plant life.	**Botanists study** plant life.
A **plant requires** care.	**Plants require** care.

A verb must also agree with a subject that is a pronoun. Look at the chart that follows. Notice how the verb changes. In the present tense, the *-s* ending is used with the subject pronouns *he, she,* and *it.*

SUBJECT-VERB AGREEMENT WITH PRONOUNS AS SUBJECTS	
SINGULAR	**PLURAL**
I **work.**	We **work.**
You **work.**	You **work.**
He, she, *or* it **works.**	They **work.**

The irregular verbs *be, have,* and *do* can be main verbs or helping verbs. These verbs must agree with the subject whether they're main verbs or helping verbs.

EXAMPLES I **am** a botanist. He **is** a botanist. They **are** botanists. **[main verbs]**

EXAMPLES She **is** working. You **are** studying. **[helping verbs]**

EXAMPLES I **have** a job. She **has** a career. **[main verbs]**

EXAMPLES He **has** planted a tree. They **have** planted trees. **[helping verbs]**

EXAMPLES He **does** well. They **do** the job. **[main verbs]**

EXAMPLES It **does** sound good. We **do** work hard. **[helping verbs]**

PRACTICE Making Subjects and Verbs Agree I

Write the subject. Then write the correct verb from the choices in parentheses.

1. Forest fires (destroys, destroy) millions of trees each year.
2. He (is, are) reading about space travel.

GRAMMAR/USAGE/MECHANICS

3. The river (flows, flow) past the old cabin.
4. You (has, have) forgotten your homework again!
5. They (is, are) students at another school.
6. The children (shares, share) their toys.
7. I (does, do) my homework faithfully.
8. Janelle (does, do) play in the band.
9. Your idea (makes, make) sense to me.
10. She (has, have) a stamp collection.

10.2 PROBLEMS IN LOCATING THE SUBJECT

Making a verb agree with its subject is easy when the verb directly follows the subject. Sometimes, however, a prepositional phrase comes between the subject and the verb.

EXAMPLE This **book** of Mark Twain's stories **appeals** to people of all ages.

EXAMPLE **Stories** by Washington Irving **are** also popular.

In the first sentence, *of Mark Twain's stories* is a prepositional phrase. The singular verb *appeals* agrees with the singular subject, *book,* not with the plural noun *stories,* which is the object of the preposition *of.* In the second sentence, *by Washington Irving* is a prepositional phrase. The plural verb *are* agrees with the plural subject, *Stories,* not with the singular noun *Washington Irving,* which is the object of the preposition *by.*

An **inverted sentence** is a sentence in which the subject follows the verb.

Inverted sentences often begin with a prepositional phrase. Don't mistake the object of the preposition for the subject of the sentence.

EXAMPLE Across the ocean **sail millions** of immigrants.

In inverted sentences beginning with *Here* or *There*, look for the subject after the verb. *Here* or *there* is never the subject of a sentence.

EXAMPLE Here **is** a **picture** of my grandparents.

EXAMPLE There **are** many **immigrants** among my ancestors.

By rearranging the sentence so the subject comes first, you can see the agreement between the subject and the verb.

EXAMPLE **Millions** of immigrants **sail** across the ocean.

EXAMPLE A **picture** of my grandparents **is** here.

EXAMPLE Many **immigrants are** there among my ancestors.

In some interrogative sentences, a helping verb comes before the subject. Look for the subject between the helping verb and the main verb.

EXAMPLE **Do** these **stories interest** you?

You can check the subject-verb agreement by making the sentence declarative.

EXAMPLE These **stories do interest** you.

PRACTICE Making Subjects and Verbs Agree II

Write the subject. Then write the correct verb from the choices in parentheses.

1. Among the shrubs (was, were) a tiny kitten.
2. (Has, Have) rabbits destroyed your garden this summer?
3. Here (is, are) the garden chairs for your party.
4. (Is, Are) the eighth-graders organizing the school picnic?
5. The fangs of a rattlesnake (carries, carry) poison to its prey.
6. (Does, Do) marigolds bloom in the spring?
7. There (is, are) your classmate across the street.
8. A nest of hornets (was, were) in the barn.

9. From the roof of the porch (hangs, hang) several baskets of geraniums.
10. Apartments in this neighborhood (is, are) inexpensive.

10.3 COLLECTIVE NOUNS AND OTHER SPECIAL SUBJECTS

A **collective noun** names a group.

Collective nouns follow special agreement rules. A collective noun has a singular meaning when it names a group that acts as a unit. A collective noun has a plural meaning when it refers to the members of the group acting as individuals. The meaning helps you decide whether to use the singular or plural form of the verb.

EXAMPLE The **audience sits** in silence. **[a unit, singular]**

EXAMPLE The **audience sit** on chairs and pillows. **[individuals, plural]**

Certain nouns, such as *news* and *mathematics,* end in *s* but require singular verbs. Other nouns that end in *s* and name one thing, such as *scissors* and *binoculars,* require plural verbs.

EXAMPLE **News is** important to everyone. **[singular]**

EXAMPLE The **scissors are** in the top drawer. **[plural]**

SPECIAL NOUNS THAT END IN *S*

SINGULAR		PLURAL	
civics	physics	binoculars	scissors
Los Angeles	United Nations	jeans	sunglasses
mathematics	United States	pants	trousers
news		pliers	tweezers

GRAMMAR/USAGE/MECHANICS

A subject that refers to an amount as a single unit is singular. A subject that refers to a number of individual units is plural.

EXAMPLE **Ten years seems** a long time. **[single unit]**

EXAMPLE **Ten years pass** quickly. **[individual units]**

EXAMPLE **Three dollars is** the admission price. **[single unit]**

EXAMPLE **Three dollars are** on the table. **[individual units]**

The title of a book or a work of art is always singular, even if a noun in the title is plural.

EXAMPLE ***Snow White and the Seven Dwarfs*** **is** a good Disney movie.

EXAMPLE ***The Last of the Mohicans*** **was** written by James Fenimore Cooper.

GRAMMAR/USAGE/MECHANICS

PRACTICE Making Subjects and Verbs Agree III

Write the subject. Then write the correct verb from the choices in parentheses.

1. Ten minutes (is, are) a long time to a two-year-old.
2. Where (is, are) your sunglasses?
3. *Across Five Aprils* (tells, tell) the story of a family with sons on opposite sides in the Civil War.
4. The committee (is, are) studying the plan for the new lunchroom.
5. The orchestra (tunes, tune) their instruments.
6. *The Five Little Peppers* (was, were) once a popular series for young readers.
7. Ten dollars (was, were) scattered across the top of the bureau.
8. Every morning the family (goes, go) their separate ways to work or school.
9. Mathematics (is, are) fascinating to some students.
10. The jury (has, have) announced its verdict.

10.4 INDEFINITE PRONOUNS AS SUBJECTS

An **indefinite pronoun** is a pronoun that does not refer to a particular person, place, or thing.

Some indefinite pronouns are singular. Others are plural. When an indefinite pronoun is used as a subject, the verb must agree in number with the pronoun.

SOME INDEFINITE PRONOUNS

	SINGULAR		PLURAL
another	everybody	no one	both
anybody	everyone	nothing	few
anyone	everything	one	many
anything	much	somebody	others
each	neither	someone	several
either	nobody	something	

GRAMMAR/USAGE/MECHANICS

The indefinite pronouns *all, any, most, none,* and *some* may be singular or plural, depending on the phrase that follows.

EXAMPLE **Most** of the forest **lies** to the east. **[singular]**

EXAMPLE **Most** of these scientists **study** forest growth. **[plural]**

Often a prepositional phrase follows an indefinite pronoun that can be either singular or plural. To decide whether the pronoun is singular or plural, look at the object of the preposition. In the first sentence, *most* refers to *forest.* Because *forest* is singular, *most* must be considered as a single unit. In the second sentence, *most* refers to *scientists.* Because *scientists* is plural, *most* should be considered as individual units.

PRACTICE Making Subjects and Verbs Agree IV

Write the subject. Then write the correct verb from the choices in parentheses.

1. Everyone (shares, share) the work.
2. Some of the responsibility (was, were) yours.
3. Both (wishes, wish) to help with the scenery.
4. Most of the workers (has, have) left the building.
5. Neither of the girls (likes, like) chocolate pudding.
6. Few (has, have) time for other activities.
7. Any of this clothing (is, are) ready for the volunteers.
8. Something (is, are) wrong with the television set.
9. All of our supporters (was, were) cheering from the stands.
10. None of the weather report (has, have) changed since this morning.

GRAMMAR/USAGE/MECHANICS

10.5 AGREEMENT WITH COMPOUND SUBJECTS

A **compound subject** contains two or more simple subjects that have the same verb.

Compound subjects may require a singular or a plural verb, depending on how the subjects are joined. When two or more subjects are joined by *and* or by the correlative conjunction *both . . . and,* the plural form of the verb should be used.

EXAMPLE New York, Denver, **and** London **have** smog.

EXAMPLE **Both** automobiles **and** factories **contribute** to smog.

Sometimes *and* is used to join two words that are part of one unit or refer to a single person or thing. In these cases, the subject is singular. In the following example, *captain* and *leader* refer to the same person. Therefore, the singular form of the verb is used.

EXAMPLE The captain **and** leader of the team **is** Ms. Cho.

When two or more subjects are joined by *or* or by the correlative conjunction *either . . . or* or *neither . . . nor,* the verb agrees with the subject that is closer to it.

EXAMPLE The cities **or** the state **responds** to pollution complaints.

EXAMPLE **Either** smoke **or** gases **cause** the smog.

In the first sentence, *responds* is singular because the closer subject, *state,* is singular. In the second sentence, *gases* is the closer subject. The verb is plural because the closer subject is plural.

GRAMMAR/USAGE/MECHANICS

PRACTICE Making Subjects and Verbs Agree V

Write the complete subject. Then write the correct verb from the choices in parentheses.

1. Ravi and his brother (is, are) participating in the science competition.
2. Neither Beth nor her sisters (has, have) studied Spanish.
3. Both the teachers and the principal (attends, attend) the school dances.
4. Either violins or a piano (plays, play) during dinner.
5. Washington, Jefferson, and Lincoln (is, are) three of our greatest presidents.
6. Our math teacher and softball coach (is, are) Ms. Fiorella.
7. Either the groom or his parents (provides, provide) the rehearsal dinner.
8. The suspect or his lawyer (answers, answer) questions.
9. Neither family responsibilities nor illness (has, have) kept Mrs. Portero from her job as a mail carrier.
10. Gloves and a hat (was, were) once important parts of a woman's costume.

PRACTICE Proofreading

Rewrite the following passage, correcting the errors in subject-verb agreement. Write legibly to be sure one letter is not mistaken for another. There are ten errors.

Mark Twain

[1]Does Mark Twain's stories appeal to today's readers? [2]Yes, books by Mark Twain is still popular today. [3]There is two very famous books by Twain. [4]They are called *The Adventures of Huckleberry Finn* and *The Adventures of Tom Sawyer.* [5]The United States are the setting of these books. [6]*The Adventures of Huckleberry Finn* are great. [7]Both Huck and Jim is characters in the story. [8]The main character and my favorite character are Huck. [9]Down the Mississippi sails Huck and Jim.

[10]Each year, the school drama club choose a story. [11]Then students perform the story as a play. [12]This year, the members chose *The Adventures of Huckleberry Finn.* [13]There is an admittance charge. [14]Five dollars are the price of the show.

GRAMMAR/USAGE/MECHANICS

POSTTEST Subject-Verb Agreement

Write the correct verb from the choices in parentheses.

1. Those jeans (is, are) too tight.
2. Everybody (donates, donate) something for the bake sale.
3. The news (is, are) good.
4. One of the girls usually (brings, bring) refreshments.
5. Two weeks (is, are) the length of the soccer camp.
6. Both the ostrich and the kangaroo (travels, travel) at high speeds.
7. The team (poses, pose) for its photograph.
8. The best trumpet player and soloist (is, are) Daniel.
9. Most appliances in your home (has, have) serial numbers.

10. I (finds, find) serial numbers on many of our appliances.

11. Trina, Soraya, and Kwami (is, are) playing a board game on the porch.

12. Either her grandparents or her father (stays, stay) with the children.

13. He (sees, see) something strange through the window.

14. There (is, are) thirteen stars, thirteen stripes, thirteen arrows, thirteen olive leaves, and thirteen levels to the pyramid on a dollar bill.

15. Most of the country (has, have) a temperate climate.

16. Most of the band members (has, have) their own instruments.

17. In the corner of the garden (grows, grow) tomatoes.

18. (Does, Do) those comedians seem funny to you?

19. Disney's *101 Dalmatians* (is, are) the children's favorite animated film.

20. Many (suffers, suffer) in hot weather.

21. How many people (has, have) visited the space exhibit?

22. The audience (scatters, scatter) toward the exits at the end of the show.

23. One mountain in the Cascades (is, are) Mount Shasta.

24. A cat or a dog (makes, make) a good pet.

25. Neither Lorna nor her sisters (plays, play) a musical instrument.

Chapter 11

Diagraming Sentences

PRETEST Diagraming Sentences

Diagram each sentence.

1. Máire smiled.
2. Joe is winning.
3. Did Rachel sing?
4. Stop!
5. Mail this letter.
6. Mr. Avila promised me a job.
7. Heidi sent Tim several postcards.
8. Outside the fierce wind howled viciously.
9. Your very delicious Irish stew disappeared so fast.

10. The door behind you leads to the kitchen.
11. My brother is growing taller.
12. That old bike looks a wreck.
13. Colds and the flu travel around school during winter.
14. These machines are slow but reliable.
15. The First Amendment protects freedom of speech, and the Thirteenth Amendment abolished slavery.
16. Jason wrote a letter to the president, but he received no reply.
17. Students who damage their books will pay a fine.
18. Before Ms. Sumi became a teacher, she was a flight attendant.
19. What I need is a new computer.
20. I do not know why Thai Tong missed the meeting.
21. Gabriel delivers hot meals to whoever needs them.
22. The wallet found in the victim's pocket contained no identification.
23. Smiling happily, Gina accepted the award.
24. Helping at the food drive took only two hours.
25. Mom likes to sing in the shower.

11.1 DIAGRAMING SIMPLE SUBJECTS AND SIMPLE PREDICATES

The basic parts of a sentence are the subject and the predicate. To diagram a sentence, first draw a horizontal line. Then draw a vertical line that crosses the horizontal line.

To the left of the vertical line, write the simple subject. To the right of the vertical line, write the simple predicate. Use capital letters as they appear in the sentence, but don't include punctuation.

EXAMPLE **People are working.**

People | are working

In a diagram, the positions of the subject and the predicate always remain the same.

EXAMPLE **Caravans rumbled** across the prairie.

Caravans	rumbled

EXAMPLE Across the prairie **rumbled caravans.**

caravans	rumbled

PRACTICE **Diagraming Simple Subjects and Simple Predicates**

Diagram the simple subject and the simple predicate.

1. Horns blare.
2. Overhead circled the vultures.
3. The boy seems nervous.
4. Jaleela will plan the party.
5. Several people were waiting patiently.
6. They have eaten the birthday cake.
7. Cody is writing his report.
8. I dozed restlessly.
9. The sailboat had sprung a leak.
10. You have finished the job.

11.2 DIAGRAMING THE FOUR KINDS OF SENTENCES

Study the diagrams of the simple subject and the simple predicate for the four kinds of sentences. Recall that in an interrogative sentence the subject often comes between the two parts of a verb phrase. In an imperative sentence, the simple subject is the understood *you.*

Notice that the positions of the simple subject and the simple predicate in a sentence diagram are always the same, regardless of the word order in the original sentence.

DECLARATIVE

EXAMPLE **People write** letters.

People | write

INTERROGATIVE

EXAMPLE **Do** many **people write** letters?

people | Do write

IMPERATIVE

EXAMPLE **Write** a letter.

(you) | Write

EXCLAMATORY

EXAMPLE What interesting letters **you write!**

you | write

GRAMMAR/USAGE/MECHANICS

PRACTICE Diagraming the Four Kinds of Sentences

Diagram the simple subject and the simple predicate.

1. Does the sun rise in the east?
2. Whales are mammals.
3. Send me a postcard.
4. The warm rain fell silently.
5. The detective has solved the mystery.
6. How happy I am today!
7. Is your mother's car blue?
8. Hand me that magazine.
9. Have you seen my camera?
10. How funny you look in that costume!

11.3 DIAGRAMING DIRECT AND INDIRECT OBJECTS

A direct object is part of the predicate. In a sentence diagram, write the direct object to the right of the verb. Draw a vertical line to separate the verb from the direct object. This vertical line, however, does *not* cross the horizontal line.

EXAMPLE People invent **machines.**

People | invent | machines

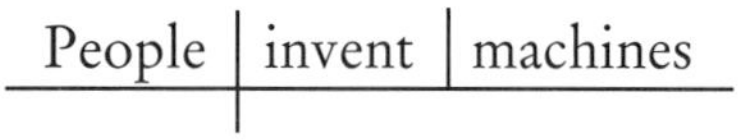

EXAMPLE Students use **computers.**

Students | use | computers

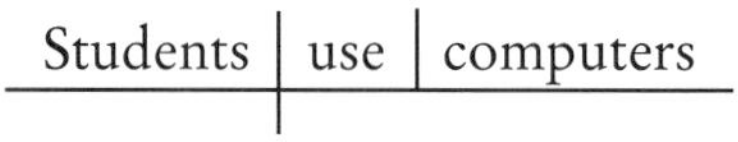

An indirect object is also part of the predicate. It usually tells to whom or for whom the action of a verb is done. An indirect object always comes before a direct object in a sentence. In a sentence diagram, write an indirect object on a horizontal line below and to the right of the verb. Join it to the verb with a slanted line.

EXAMPLE Rosa gave the **dog** a bone.

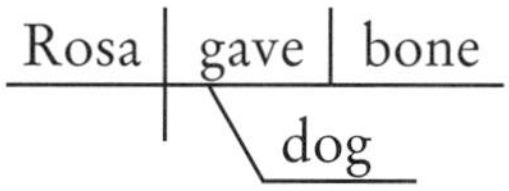

Rosa | gave | bone
\ dog

PRACTICE Diagraming Direct and Indirect Objects

Diagram the simple subject, the simple predicate, and the direct object. Diagram the indirect object if the sentence has one.

1. Jamie brought his father the newspaper.
2. The mechanic fixed the truck.
3. Ms. Lawson teaches health.
4. She assigns the students special projects.
5. Carol played the class a tune on her harmonica.

GRAMMAR/USAGE/MECHANICS

6. The ship hit an iceberg.
7. Mr. Yamamoto is giving Lenora piano lessons.
8. The mayor has written Jonas a letter.
9. Each student will recite a poem.
10. This job will offer you many opportunities.

11.4 DIAGRAMING ADJECTIVES, ADVERBS, AND PREPOSITIONAL PHRASES

In a diagram, write adjectives and adverbs on slanted lines beneath the words they modify.

EXAMPLE **Elena's strange** dream faded **quickly.**

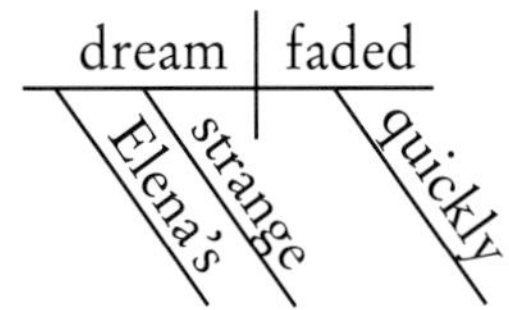

EXAMPLE **The very old** tree produced **incredibly delicious** apples **rather slowly.**

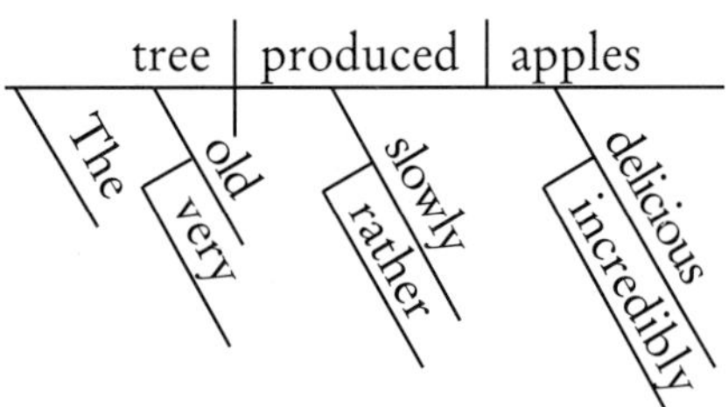

A prepositional phrase can be either an adjective phrase or an adverb phrase. Study the diagram for prepositional phrases.

EXAMPLE A woman **in a pink hat** was sitting **beside me.**

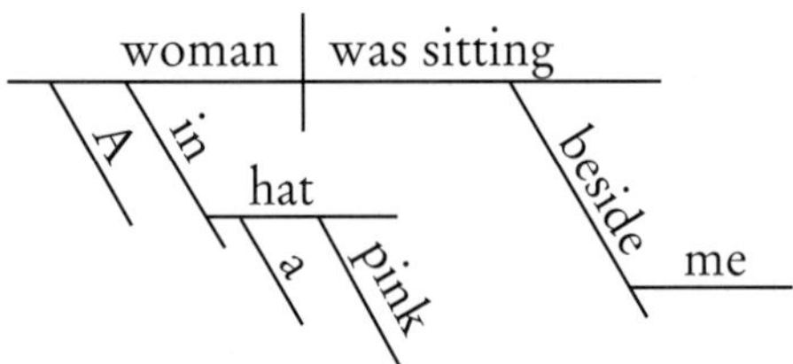

GRAMMAR/USAGE/MECHANICS

Luann

by Greg Evans

PRACTICE Diagraming Adjectives, Adverbs, and Prepositional Phrases

Diagram each sentence.

1. Several students were eating their lunch on the patio.
2. Petula's first performance in the play showed great talent.
3. This extremely expensive automobile has many extraordinary features.
4. A nasty storm attacked the coast of Florida yesterday.
5. Harry's mother was playing the old piano rather quietly.
6. Those very dark colors fade too quickly in the sun.
7. Now we shall see an unusually spectacular trapeze act.
8. The thoughtful girl bought her older brother an orange sweatshirt today.
9. These especially fragile Hawaiian flowers almost never grow outdoors here.
10. My grandma served the entire family a really delicious Thanksgiving dinner with pumpkin pie for dessert.

11.5 DIAGRAMING PREDICATE NOUNS AND PREDICATE ADJECTIVES

In a sentence diagram, a direct object follows the verb.

EXAMPLE People use telephones.

People | use | telephones

To diagram a sentence with a predicate noun, write the predicate noun to the right of the linking verb. Draw a slanted line to separate the verb from the predicate noun.

EXAMPLE Telephones are useful **instruments.**

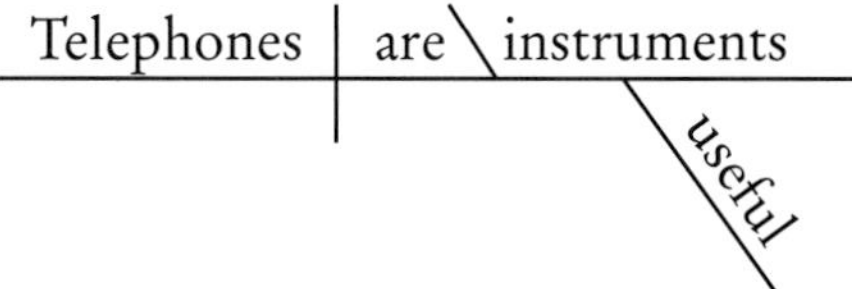

Diagram a predicate adjective in the same way.

EXAMPLE Telephones are **useful.**

Telephones | are \ useful

PRACTICE Diagraming Predicate Nouns and Predicate Adjectives

Diagram each sentence.

1. You sound cheerful today.
2. The twins have become excellent pianists.
3. This soup tastes too salty.
4. Your room looks a mess.
5. The baby is growing fatter.
6. Everyone feels blue sometimes.
7. The attic was a marvelous hideaway.

8. Your meals always smell quite delicious.
9. Rover seems a gentle dog.
10. The swimmer's hair turned green.

11.6 DIAGRAMING COMPOUND SENTENCE PARTS

Coordinating conjunctions such as *and, but,* and *or* are used to join compound parts: words, phrases, or sentences. To diagram compound parts of a sentence, write the second part of the compound below the first. Write the coordinating conjunction on a dotted line connecting the two parts.

GRAMMAR/USAGE/MECHANICS

COMPOUND SUBJECT

EXAMPLE **Gas and oil** heat homes.

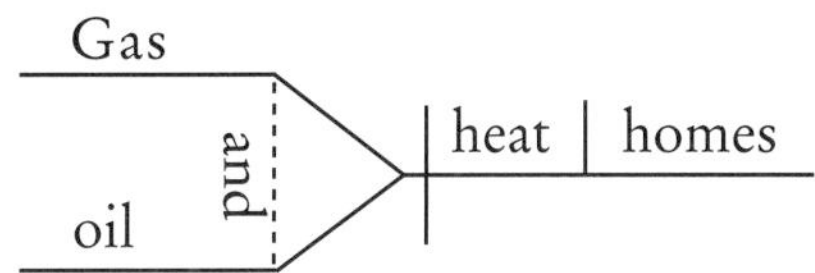

COMPOUND PREDICATE

EXAMPLE Babies **eat and sleep.**

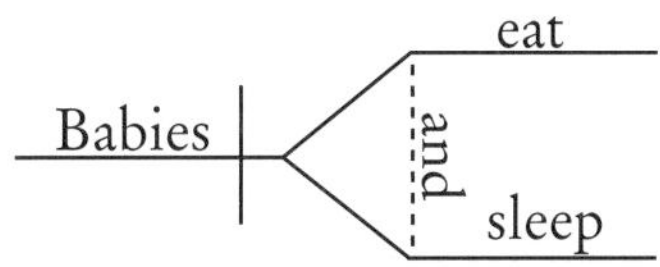

COMPOUND DIRECT OBJECT

EXAMPLE The bakery serves **sandwiches and beverages.**

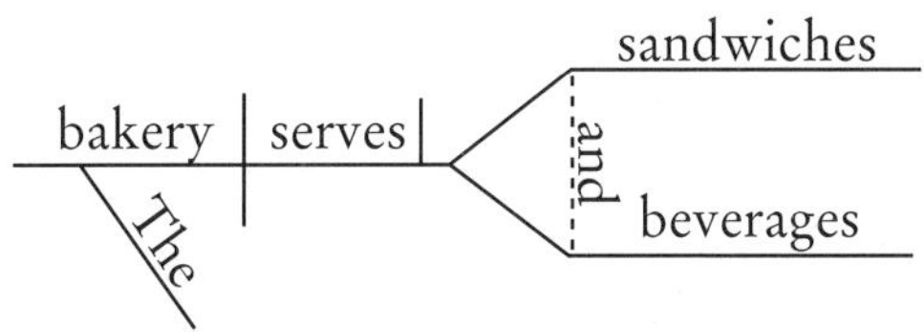

COMPOUND PREDICATE NOUN OR PREDICATE ADJECTIVE

EXAMPLE Dogs are **loyal and friendly.**

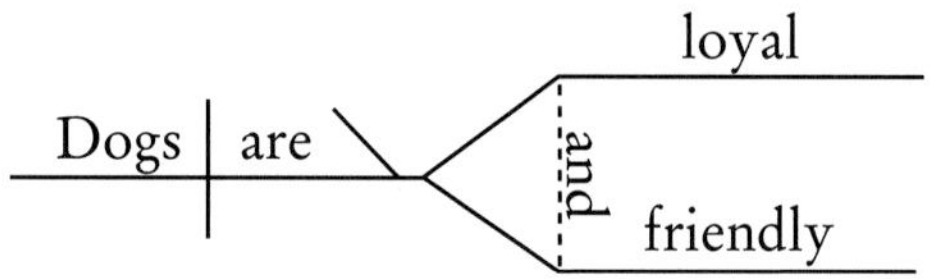

PRACTICE Diagraming Compound Sentence Parts

Diagram each sentence.

1. Shoes and socks littered the floor.
2. The engine coughed and sputtered.
3. Mr. Margolis grows tomatoes and cucumbers.
4. Tamako or Tyrone will be our representative.
5. These cars seem reliable but expensive.
6. Do you want peas or corn?
7. I tried but failed.
8. Ms. Diaz has been a coach and a teacher.
9. Give me your coat and your hat.
10. The big bad wolf huffed and puffed.

11.7 DIAGRAMING COMPOUND SENTENCES

To diagram a compound sentence, diagram each main clause separately. If the main clauses are connected by a semicolon, use a vertical dotted line to connect the verbs of the clauses. If the main clauses are connected by a conjunction such as *and, but,* or *or,* write the conjunction on a solid horizontal line and connect it to the verb in each clause with a dotted line.

EXAMPLE James practices football after school, **and** on Saturdays he helps his parents at their restaurant.

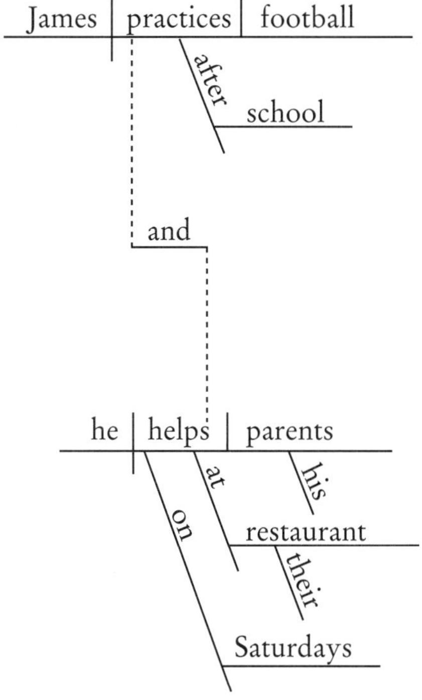

GRAMMAR/USAGE/MECHANICS

PRACTICE Diagraming Compound Sentences

Diagram each sentence.

1. Dad will grill hamburgers, or Mom will fry chicken.
2. Lori plays the saxophone, and Maggie plays the trombone.
3. I looked everywhere, but the letter had vanished.
4. Delaware was the first state; Hawaii was the fiftieth state.
5. Tami called the restaurant, but the line was busy.
6. Alaska is the largest state; Rhode Island is the smallest state.
7. The plane landed safely, and the passengers sighed with relief.
8. The band will play a few numbers, or the chorus will sing several songs.

9. The sun shone brightly; a gentle breeze stirred the leaves.
10. Johnson ran the ball into the end zone, and the fans poured onto the field.

11.8 DIAGRAMING COMPLEX SENTENCES WITH ADJECTIVE AND ADVERB CLAUSES

To diagram a sentence with an adjective clause, write the adjective clause below the main clause. Draw a dotted line between the relative pronoun in the adjective clause and the word the adjective clause modifies in the main clause. Position the relative pronoun according to its use in its own clause. In the first example, *who* is the subject of the verb *complete.* In the second example, *that* is the direct object of the verb *watched.*

ADJECTIVE CLAUSE

EXAMPLE Students **who complete their assignments** will surely succeed.

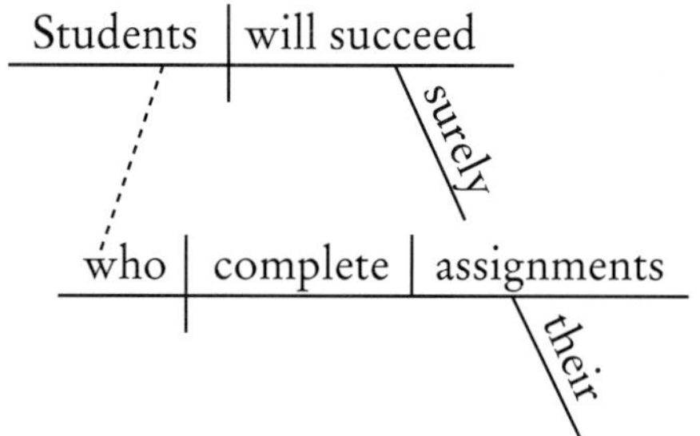

EXAMPLE The movie **that we watched** was very funny.

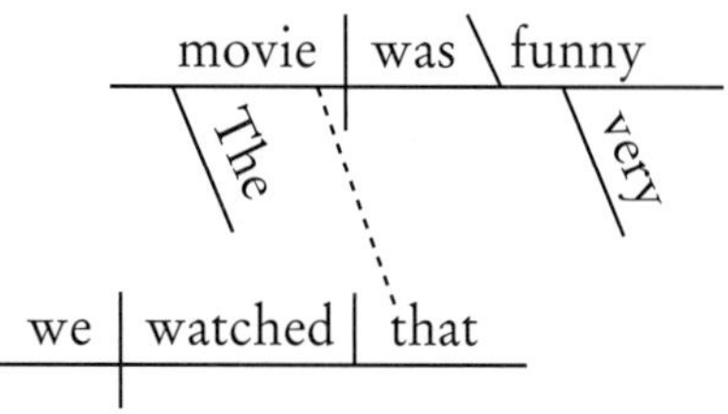

Diagram an adverb clause below the main clause. Draw a dotted line between the verb in the adverb clause and the word the adverb clause modifies in the main clause. Then write the subordinating conjunction on the dotted connecting line.

ADVERB CLAUSE

EXAMPLE **If you complete your assignments,** you will surely succeed.

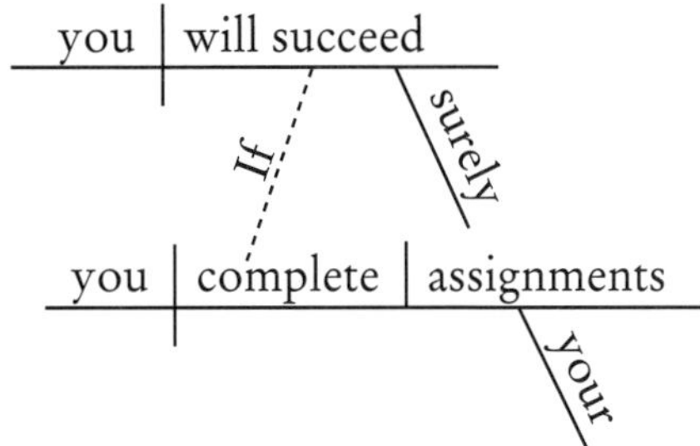

PRACTICE Diagraming Complex Sentences with Adjective and Adverb Clauses

Diagram each sentence.

1. A clause that modifies a noun is an adjective clause.
2. The bridge, which spans the river, carries heavy traffic.
3. Meet Ms. Rodriguez, who has just returned from Mexico.
4. My sister, whom you have met, is taking ballet lessons.
5. The person whose bicycle you are using is my cousin.
6. I read a magazine while I waited.
7. After the rain stopped, we played tennis.
8. I finished my homework before the show began.
9. When the package arrived, I put it in the kitchen.
10. I will pay you a dollar if you will help me.

11.9 DIAGRAMING NOUN CLAUSES

Noun clauses can be used in sentences as subjects, direct objects, indirect objects, objects of prepositions, and predicate nouns. In the following example, the noun clause is the subject.

NOUN CLAUSE AS SUBJECT

EXAMPLE **What she told us** was the simple truth.

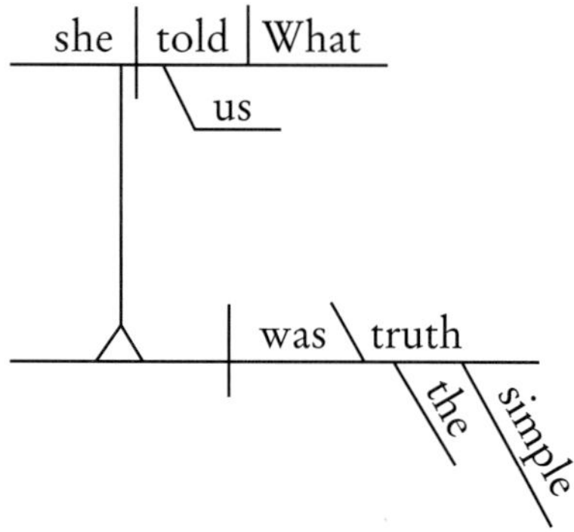

Notice that the clause is written on a "stilt" placed on the base line where the subject usually appears. The word that introduces a noun clause is diagramed according to its use within its own clause. In the noun clause in the example, the word *What* is the direct object. If the word that introduces the noun clause isn't really part of either the noun clause or the main clause, write the word on its own line.

NOUN CLAUSE AS DIRECT OBJECT

EXAMPLE Terry knows **that good grades are important.**

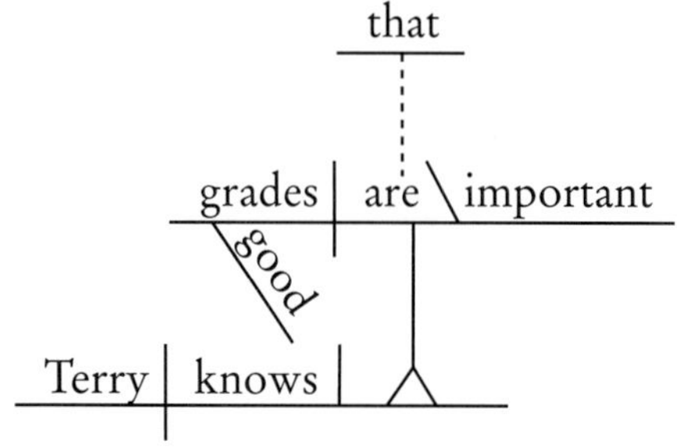

NOUN CLAUSE AS INDIRECT OBJECT

EXAMPLE Tell **whomever you see** the news.

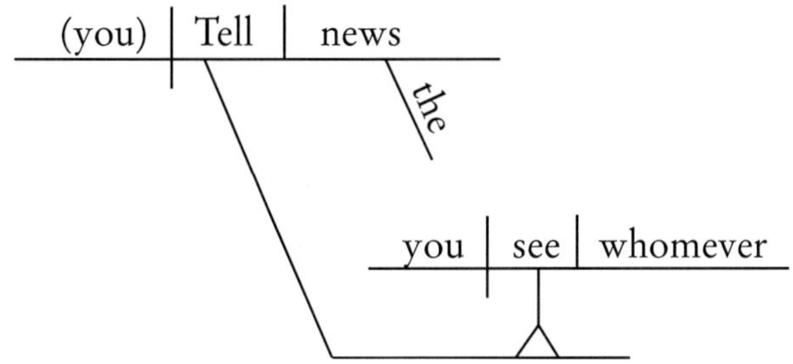

NOUN CLAUSE AS OBJECT OF A PREPOSITION

EXAMPLE This is an example of **what I mean.**

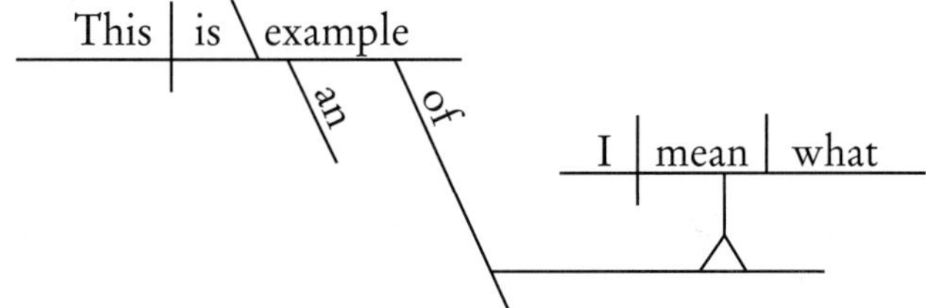

NOUN CLAUSE AS PREDICATE NOUN

EXAMPLE The result was **that nobody believed me.**

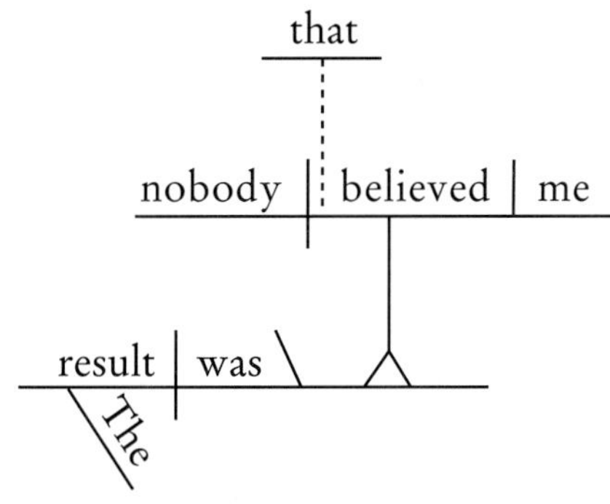

GRAMMAR/USAGE/MECHANICS

PRACTICE Diagraming Noun Clauses

Diagram each sentence.

1. The committee will award whoever gets the highest score a scholarship.
2. I do not understand how you did that.
3. What you are suggesting makes perfect sense.
4. Will you support me in whatever I decide?
5. This house is where James Thurber lived as a boy.
6. Nobody ever knows when Sunny is blue.
7. The outcome of the vote was that the proposal was defeated.
8. Get the name of whomever you interview.
9. Who will provide the entertainment is a secret.
10. Tell me why Edgar Allan Poe is a great writer.

GRAMMAR/USAGE/MECHANICS

11.10 DIAGRAMING VERBALS

To diagram a participle or a participial phrase, draw a line that descends diagonally from the word the participle modifies and then extend it to the right horizontally. Write the participle along the angle, as shown.

EXAMPLE The birds, **singing merrily,** splashed in the birdbath.

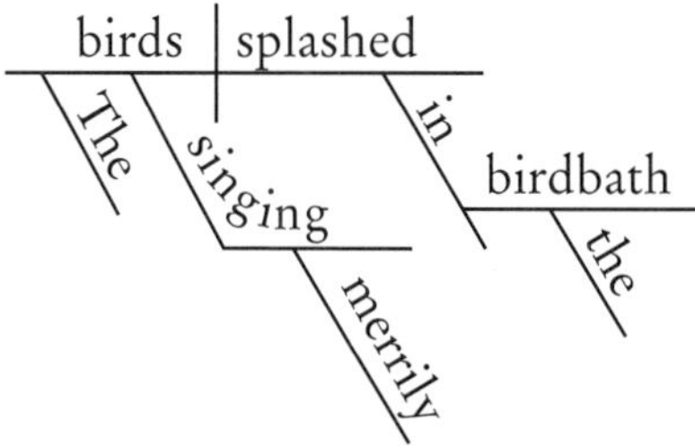

To diagram a gerund or a gerund phrase, make a "stilt," located according to the role of the gerund. (A gerund can be a subject, a direct object, or the object of a preposition.) Then write the gerund on a "step" above the stilt, as shown at the top of the next page.

EXAMPLE **Building new nests** is another job for the returning birds.

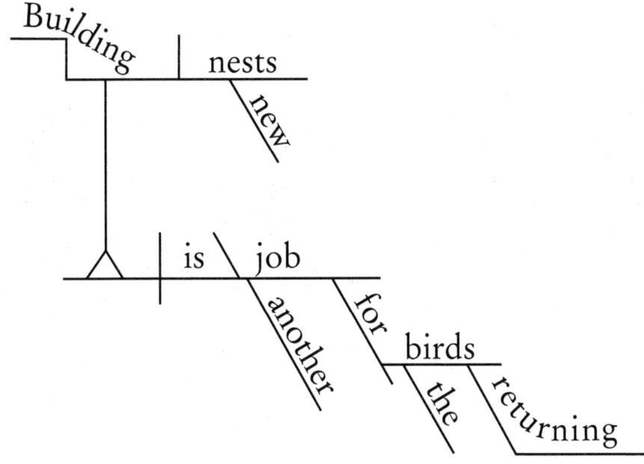

To diagram an infinitive or an infinitive phrase that is used as a noun, make a "stilt" in the appropriate position. Then diagram the phrase as you would a prepositional phrase.

EXAMPLE The purpose of a microscope is **to magnify objects.**

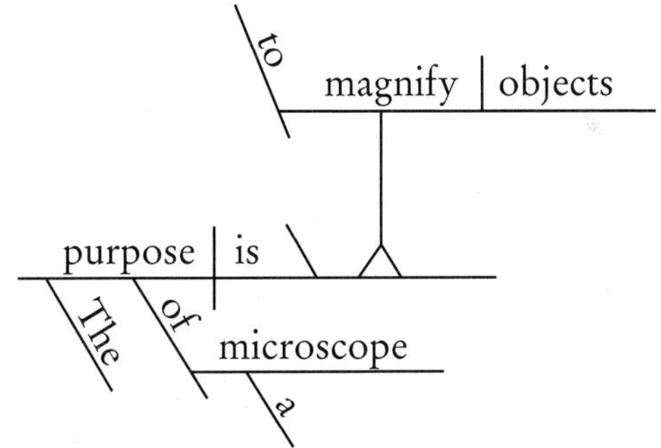

GRAMMAR/USAGE/MECHANICS

PRACTICE Diagraming Verbals

Diagram each sentence.

1. I replaced the broken vase.
2. Grabbing the baton, Tony sprinted down the track.
3. The twittering birds woke me at five.
4. I found a note written in code.

5. Building new roads improves the flow of traffic.
6. Stop giving the children candy.
7. This is our equipment for hiking in the mountains.
8. To own their own home is the dream of many young couples.
9. The aim of the club is to beautify the community.
10. Dad promised to take us to the movies.

POSTTEST Diagraming Sentences

Diagram each sentence.

1. Officers salute.
2. Children were playing.
3. Hide!
4. Does Theresa remember?
5. Accept my apology.
6. Lucinda gave us some advice.
7. The pitcher tossed the batter the ball.
8. The graceful antelope narrowly escaped the lion.
9. That rather silly movie contains several completely unbelievable scenes.
10. A table with a lace cover stood between the two windows.
11. This tea tastes very bitter.
12. The old wooden bridge is a tourist spot.
13. A dog or a cat makes a good pet.
14. Roberto is the coach and a great player.
15. Astronauts lose some muscle in a weightless atmosphere, and their hearts work less.
16. Fires in Yellowstone National Park destroy many trees, but new growth restores the forests.
17. The fire that killed the trees warmed the water in the streams.
18. When fire runs through Yellowstone again, nature will recover.
19. What you think is important to me.

20. Samantha is whom we chose.

21. Tell me how you make these delicious meatballs.

22. The kittens, born yesterday, have not yet opened their eyes.

23. The woman standing in the doorway is Ms. Benson.

24. Mr. Bernstein enjoys teaching science.

25. To find a new route to the East was Columbus's goal.

Chapter 12

Capitalization

PRETEST Capitalization

Write each sentence. Use capital letters correctly.

1. we toured an oil tanker in the harbor.
2. "this oil tanker is so big," said Little Deer, the tour guide, "that three football fields could fit on its deck."
3. Harry asked, "how can i learn more about these ships?"
4. "pay attention," said Little Deer. "then try the Internet or your local library."
5. One of the girls said That she had seen underwater oil pipelines.
6. These salmon swim against the current of kenai river in alaska to return to the place they were born.
7. In 1853 a chef, george crum, invented the potato chip after a customer complained about his thick, soggy fried potatoes.
8. My cousin richard visited mammoth cave in kentucky during the summer.

9. The dentist, dr. truong, spoke with mrs. hampton about her toothache and recommended brite toothpaste.
10. I wonder if ducktown, tennessee, has a mallard avenue or a wood duck drive.
11. "Did we catch the illness in time, doctor?" asked the nurse.
12. Why did you send your cards to north pole, colorado, during december?
13. hector gonzalez jr. works at the gift shop in the statue of liberty on liberty island in new york.
14. my mother drinks a cup of french roast coffee every saturday morning.
15. At the airport, I helped mother and aunt fran with their luggage.
16. On memorial day, i spoke spanish with raul's many relatives.
17. If you move to north dakota, will you miss eastern tennessee?
18. The tacoma narrows bridge collapsed not long after it opened.
19. On sunday i read a story called "all for one" by a young canadian writer named monty preston.
20. On his tour, president clinton visited new england, the west coast, and the south in four days.
21. which groups were fighting in the war of 1812, world war II, and the american revolution?
22. This summer dr. wilson will read *roll of thunder, hear my cry* to his children and watch *my side of the mountain* with them.
23. In the autumn, we will travel from new mexico to maine with grandmother.
24. The librarian recommends the books of british author c. s. lewis, who wrote *the chronicles of narnia.*
25. Lauren buys computer games at a store called explosions and collisions.

12.1 CAPITALIZING SENTENCES, QUOTATIONS, AND LETTER PARTS

A capital letter marks the beginning of a sentence. A capital letter also marks the beginning of a direct quotation and the salutation and the closing of a letter.

RULE 1 Capitalize the first word of every sentence.

EXAMPLE Many people worked for the independence of the colonies.

GRAMMAR/USAGE/MECHANICS

RULE 2 Capitalize the first word of a direct quotation that is a complete sentence. A direct quotation gives a speaker's exact words.

EXAMPLE Travis said, "One of those people was Paul Revere."

RULE 3 When a direct quotation is interrupted by explanatory words, such as *she said,* don't begin the second part of the direct quotation with a capital letter.

EXAMPLE "I read a famous poem," said Kim, "about Paul Revere."

When the second part of a direct quotation is a new sentence, put a period after the explanatory words and begin the second part of the quotation with a capital letter.

EXAMPLE "I know that poem," said Sarah. "My class read it last week."

RULE 4 Don't capitalize an indirect quotation. An indirect quotation does not repeat a person's exact words and should not be enclosed in quotation marks. An indirect quotation is often introduced by the word *that.*

EXAMPLE The teacher said the poem was written by Longfellow.

EXAMPLE The teacher said **that** the poem was written by Longfellow.

RULE 5 Capitalize the first word in the salutation and the closing of a letter. Capitalize the title and the name of the person addressed.

EXAMPLES **D**ear **M**rs. **A**damson, **S**incerely yours,

EXAMPLES **M**y dear **A**bigail, **W**ith love,

NOTE Usually, the first word in each line of a poem is capitalized, but many modern poets don't follow this style. When you copy a poem, use the style of the original version.

GRAMMAR/USAGE/MECHANICS

PRACTICE Capitalizing Sentences, Quotations, and Letter Parts

Write each sentence. Use capital letters correctly. If a sentence is already correct, write correct.

1. sombreros are hats with wide brims.
2. Lucy asked, "when does spring begin?"
3. "Spring begins," answered Suki, "About March 21."
4. "your reports are due tomorrow," said Ms. Perez. "there will be no other homework tonight."
5. Madison told me that He had tried out for the play.
6. Butter and cheese are made from milk.
7. Percy said, "my report will be about dairy farming."
8. "My parents are dairy farmers," said Ginny. "they could give you some information."
9. "I've never been to Germany," said Hildy, "but all my grandparents were born there."
10. *Rewrite each salutation or closing that is incorrect.*
a. Dear Mom and Dad,
b. my dear Ms. Murphy,
c. Best Wishes,
d. your Friend,

12.2 CAPITALIZING NAMES AND TITLES OF PEOPLE

RULE 1 Capitalize the names of people and the initials that stand for their names.

EXAMPLES Clark Kent Susan B. Anthony E. C. Stanton

RULE 2 Capitalize a title or an abbreviation of a title when it comes before a person's name.

EXAMPLES President Wilson Dr. Martin Luther King Ms. Ruiz

Capitalize a title when it's used instead of a name.

EXAMPLE "Has the enemy surrendered, General?" asked the colonel.

Don't capitalize a title that follows a name or one that is used as a common noun.

EXAMPLE Woodrow Wilson, president of the United States during World War I, supported cooperation among nations.

EXAMPLE Who was Wilson's vice president?

RULE 3 Capitalize the names and abbreviations of academic degrees that follow a name. Capitalize *Jr.* and *Sr.*

EXAMPLES M. Katayama, M.D. Janis Stein, Ph.D. Otis Ames Jr.

RULE 4 Capitalize words that show family relationships when they're used as titles or as substitutes for names.

EXAMPLE Last year Father and Aunt Beth traveled to several western states.

Don't capitalize words that show family relationships when they follow possessive nouns or pronouns.

EXAMPLE Jo's uncle took photographs. My aunt Mary framed them.

RULE 5 Always capitalize the pronoun *I*.

EXAMPLE American history is the subject **I** like best.

PRACTICE **Capitalizing Names and Titles of People**

Write each sentence. Use capital letters correctly. If a sentence is already correct, write correct.

1. A favorite author for young people is robert louis stevenson.
2. My father's boss is j. d. bailey.
3. Do you know who dr. jonas salk is?
4. "Will i be all right, doctor?" asked lynn.
5. "The doctor will see you now," said the nurse.
6. The guest speaker was alma prado, ph.d.
7. My mom and sid's aunt suzi are good friends.
8. Last week grandpa meyer and aunt rachel opened their own restaurant.
9. Sometimes i'm not sure if i should speak up or keep quiet.
10. Do you know the story of captain john smith and pocahontas?

GRAMMAR/USAGE/MECHANICS

12.3 CAPITALIZING NAMES OF PLACES

The names of specific places are proper nouns and should be capitalized. Don't capitalize articles and short prepositions that are part of geographical names.

RULE 1 Capitalize the names of cities, counties, states, countries, and continents.

EXAMPLES	San Diego	Cook County	North Carolina
	Japan	Mexico	Europe

RULE 2 Capitalize the names of bodies of water and other geographical features.

EXAMPLES Lake Michigan, Gulf of Mexico, Pacific Ocean, Mojave Desert, Napa Valley, Rocky Mountains

RULE 3 Capitalize the names of sections of a country.

EXAMPLES the Sun Belt, New England, the Great Plains

RULE 4 Capitalize direction words when they name a particular section of a country.

EXAMPLES the South, the West Coast, the Northeast

Don't capitalize direction words used in other ways.

EXAMPLES southern California, northerly winds, Kansas is west of Missouri.

RULE 5 Capitalize the names of streets and highways.

EXAMPLES Main Street, Route 66, Pennsylvania Turnpike

RULE 6 Capitalize the names of particular buildings, bridges, monuments, and other structures.

EXAMPLES the White House, Golden Gate Bridge, Lincoln Memorial, the Rose Bowl

GRAMMAR/USAGE/MECHANICS

PRACTICE Capitalizing Names of Places

Write each sentence. Use capital letters correctly.

1. Is mount mcKinley the highest mountain in north america?
2. Is mexico south of the united states of america?
3. Is helena the capital of montana?
4. Is kansas city located in the great plains?
5. Is seattle the largest city in the northwest?
6. Does route 40 cross southern ohio?

7. Are the empire state building and the brooklyn bridge in new york city?
8. Which is smaller, lake erie or lake ontario?
9. Did pioneers travel west to reach the pacific ocean?
10. Is the cotton bowl in the south?

12.4 CAPITALIZING OTHER PROPER NOUNS AND ADJECTIVES

Many nouns besides the names of people and places are proper nouns and should be capitalized. Adjectives formed from proper nouns are called proper adjectives and should also be capitalized.

RULE 1 Capitalize all important words in the names of clubs, organizations, businesses, institutions, and political parties.

EXAMPLES **G**irl **S**couts of **A**merica | **A**merican **R**ed **C**ross | **M**icrosoft **C**orporation | **S**mithsonian **I**nstitution | **U**niversity of **N**ebraska | **R**epublican **P**arty

RULE 2 Capitalize brand names but not the nouns following them.

EXAMPLES **D**ownhome soup | **L**ull-a-bye diapers | **K**runcho crackers

RULE 3 Capitalize all important words in the names of particular historical events, time periods, and documents.

EXAMPLES **R**evolutionary **W**ar | **I**ron **A**ge | **G**ettysburg **A**ddress

RULE 4 Capitalize the names of days of the week, months of the year, and holidays. Don't capitalize the names of the seasons.

EXAMPLES **S**unday | **A**pril | **T**hanksgiving **D**ay | spring

GRAMMAR/USAGE/MECHANICS

RULE 5 Capitalize the first word and the last word in the titles of books, chapters, plays, short stories, poems, essays, articles, movies, television series and programs, songs, magazines, and newspapers. Capitalize all other words except articles, coordinating conjunctions, and prepositions of fewer than five letters. Don't capitalize the word *the* before the title of a magazine or newspaper.

EXAMPLES *A Wrinkle in Time* "Mammals and Their Young" "The Lady or the Tiger?" "The Truth About Dragons" "Over the Rainbow" *Seventeen*

GRAMMAR/USAGE/MECHANICS

RULE 6 Capitalize the names of languages, nationalities, and ethnic groups.

EXAMPLES English Japanese Native Americans

RULE 7 Capitalize proper adjectives. A proper adjective is an adjective formed from a proper noun.

EXAMPLES African American voters Mexican art a Broadway musical Appalachian families

NOTE Capitalize the names of religions and the people who practice them. Capitalize the names of holy days, sacred writings, and deities.

EXAMPLES Islam Muslims Easter the Bible Allah

NOTE Capitalize the names of trains, ships, airplanes, and spacecraft.

EXAMPLES the Orient Express *Titanic* *Spirit of St. Louis* *Voyager 2*

NOTE Don't capitalize the names of school subjects, except for proper nouns and adjectives and course names followed by a number.

EXAMPLES language arts geography earth science American history French Algebra 1

PRACTICE Capitalizing Other Proper Nouns and Adjectives

Write each sentence. Use capital letters correctly.

1. Several republican candidates will speak at yale university in october.
2. Many american automobile manufacturers once felt threatened by japanese carmakers like honda.
3. My dad uses gleemo car wax on his ford truck every saturday.
4. Did Thomas Jefferson write the declaration of independence or the gettysburg address?
5. Do you know anyone who served in world war II?
6. Every thanksgiving day, we sing "over the river and through the woods" on our way to Grandma's.
7. I plan to study french in the fall.
8. A famous work of american literature is *the last of the mohicans.*
9. The united nations had 184 members as of august 1994.
10. My favorite movie about aliens is *e.t.*

GRAMMAR/USAGE/MECHANICS

PRACTICE Proofreading

Rewrite the following letter, correcting errors in capitalization and spelling. Write legibly to be sure one letter is not mistaken for another. There are ten errors.

1dear Ms. Simpson,

2I highly reccomend a book. 3It is called *the call of the wild.* 4The author of the book is named Jack london.

5Have you heard of Jack London? 6He was born in san francisco. 7Flora Wellman was his Mother. 8His stepfather, John London, had fought in the civil war.

[9]At the age of twenty-one, London spent one Winter in the Klondike. [10]He found many story ideas there.

[11]London wrote novels, short stories, and essays. [12]Sometimes he wrote for fifteen hours each day. [13]He said, "at times, I forgot to eat."

[14]Best wishes,
[15]Fred Ramírez jr.

POSTTEST Capitalization

GRAMMAR/USAGE/MECHANICS

Write each sentence. Use capital letters correctly.

1. does miss america use reel kleen soap?
2. Kyosha asked, "when does winter begin?"
3. "Winter begins," answered Benny, "About december 21."
4. "meet in the band room at three o'clock," said the band director. "we will practice for an hour."
5. "do you support the bill, congresswoman?" asked the reporter for *people's news and views of washington.*
6. She presented the trophy to harriet klein, president of national motors company, for her design of the new zephyr automobile.
7. Pioneers settled the west, but they took the land from such tribes as the sioux, the cherokee, and the comanche.
8. Every saturday I mow the grass for grandpa.
9. Celia told me that She is looking for a summer job.
10. How do you celebrate new year's day?
11. On friday night, i sang "on top of old smoky" in the school play.
12. Is the phone call for neil sindato jr. or neil sindato sr.?
13. In the spring, aunt mary and uncle ken visited the appalachian mountains to gather wildflowers.
14. Head east on kettering avenue, turn right onto odette drive, and stop at 3692.
15. The outlaw jesse w. james fought for the south during the civil war.

16. We ate at a chinese restaurant with dr. montez.

17. To cross the east river in new york, drive along the brooklyn bridge, which opened in may 1883 and is still in use.

18. The speaker, d. c. madison, ph.d., talked to our history class about the declaration of independence.

19. Does your mother or your uncle fred vote for the republican candidates?

20. During the winter, i use sofskin hand cream.

21. troops from the girl scouts and the boy scouts visited mammoth site museum in hot springs, south dakota, where they examined the bones of mammoths from the ice age.

22. the bostonian architecture reminds me of the buildings i saw in providence, rhode island.

23. How many presidents have come from the midwest?

24. We must choose between *the eagle of the ninth,* by rosemary sutcliff, and *the cry of the crow,* by jean craighead george.

25. Please tell me which sports these teams play: the miami dolphins, the baltimore orioles, and the houston comets.

Chapter 13

Punctuation

PRETEST Commas, Semicolons, Colons, and End Punctuation

Write each sentence. Add commas, semicolons, colons, and end punctuation where needed.

1. Hey Where are you going in such a hurry
2. Yes Ted I *do* like green vegetables
3. "The post office is down the street around the corner and past the library" said Felicia.
4. After a month in the country we felt happy and content
5. The dog was barking and the baby was crying
6. On the side opposite the stands were full
7. Do you listen to music while you do your homework
8. Whenever I mow the lawn my allergies bother me

9. Ms. Workman said "Potato chips too have a high fat content."
10. Send your application to Lydia Chekhov Ph.D. 1212 Patterson Drive Yakima WA 98901
11. Leaving the others behind Suzy and Jaime headed down the trail that led to the lake
12. Bring the following a jar with a lid a rubber band a pencil and a notebook
13. Mrs. Lawson our band director has been ill however Mr. Ito has done a fine job in her place
14. The Murphys lived in Flagstaff Arizona from June 1 1998 to May 1999
15. My aunt Morgan who has just arrived for a visit brought her luggage her dog and her cat we were not expecting the dog and the cat

PRETEST Quotation Marks, Italics, and Apostrophes

Write each sentence. Add quotation marks, underlining (for italics), apostrophes, and other punctuation marks where they're needed. If the sentence is already correct, write correct.

16. Today said Mr. Papaleonardos we will talk about seven amazing things that people built before 1700
17. Its anybodys guess how long it took to build the Great Wall of China he added.
18. Who built the wall asked Tsuruji. Its important for me to know
19. Many students reports will tell more about the walls construction replied the teacher.
20. Theres some information from Time magazine in Chriss report.
21. If youre interested in U.S. history, read the article Recollecting the Presidents in the magazine Smithsonian.

22. Are these books and papers yours or hers?
23. Did you say I cant wait for school to begin
24. The boys basketball team won only half its games.
25. Did you ask me if these dolls and trucks are the childrens toys said Susan.

PRETEST Hyphens, Dashes, Parentheses, and Numbers

Write each sentence. Add hyphens, dashes, and parentheses where they're needed. Use the correct form for each number. If the sentence is already correct, write correct.

26. The leaves of poison ivy *Toxicodendron radicans* in Latin grow in clusters of 3.
27. This fast food restaurant serves thirty three kinds of well done hamburgers.
28. Two thirds of the information in this report is not up to date; search the Internet for up to date information.
29. My great aunt, an ex salesperson, said that one hundred sixty million people bought the cheaper jacket.
30. The baby was born on the first day of the month about four o'clock in the morning; he weighed seven pounds and was twenty-one inches long.
31. Only sixty people have read this book, but 111 people have read that one.
32. On May 16th at four forty five P.M., I tried to return the sweater to the store located at One Two Two Newbury Drive.
33. Mary Ann and Josh they're our neighbors' children often visit my parents.
34. 245 people attended the free performance on 5th Avenue.
35. In the survey of students, forty-nine percent were against wearing school uniforms, and fifty-one percent favored wearing uniforms.

13.1 USING END PUNCTUATION

RULE 1 Use a period at the end of a declarative sentence. A declarative sentence makes a statement.

EXAMPLE Tractors perform many jobs on a farm.

EXAMPLE I worked on a farm during the summer.

RULE 2 Use a period at the end of an imperative sentence. An imperative sentence gives a command or makes a request.

EXAMPLE Turn the key. **[command]**

EXAMPLE Please start the motor. **[request]**

RULE 3 Use a question mark at the end of an interrogative sentence. An interrogative sentence asks a question.

EXAMPLE Who built the first tractor?

EXAMPLE Did you know that?

RULE 4 Use an exclamation point at the end of an exclamatory sentence. An exclamatory sentence expresses strong feeling.

EXAMPLE How powerful your tractor is!

EXAMPLE What a loud noise it makes!

RULE 5 Use an exclamation point after a strong interjection. An interjection is a word or group of words that expresses emotion.

EXAMPLES	Wow!	Whew!	My goodness!	Ouch!
	Yippee!	Hi!	Hey!	Oops!

GRAMMAR/USAGE/MECHANICS

PRACTICE Using End Punctuation

Write each sentence. Add the correct end punctuation. Then write declarative, imperative, interrogative, exclamatory, *or* interjection *to show the reason for the end mark you chose.*

1. The announcement was a surprise to the entire class
2. Wow Did you see that elephant in the middle of Main Street
3. Show me a sample of your very best handwriting
4. My goodness How smart you are
5. Have you cleaned your room yet
6. What a funny story that was
7. The president asked his fellow citizens for their support
8. Turn off the lights and put out the cat
9. A pale moon shone down on the silent castle
10. Who will be on your volleyball team

13.2 USING COMMAS I

When you use commas to *separate* items, you place a comma between items. When you use commas to *set off* an item, you place a comma before and after the item. Of course, you never place a comma at the beginning or the end of a sentence.

RULE 1 Separate three or more words, phrases, or clauses in a series.

EXAMPLE Cars, buses, and trucks clog city streets. **[words]**

EXAMPLE Beside the fence, on the porch, or outside the back door is a good place for that potted plant. **[phrases]**

EXAMPLE Call me before you leave town, while you're in Florida, or after you return home. **[clauses]**

RULE 2 Set off an introductory word such as *yes, no,* or *well.*

EXAMPLE Yes, we enjoyed your performance in the play.

EXAMPLE No, you didn't sing off key.

RULE 3 Set off names used in direct address.

EXAMPLE Claire, have you ever traveled on a ship?

EXAMPLE I traveled to Alaska, Mr. Hess, on a cruise ship.

EXAMPLE Did you enjoy your trip down the Ohio River, Dale?

RULE 4 Set off two or more prepositional phrases at the beginning of a sentence. Set off a single long prepositional phrase at the beginning of a sentence.

EXAMPLE In the fall of 1998, Frank Jordan ran for mayor. **[two prepositional phrases–*In the fall* and *of 1998*]**

EXAMPLE Beneath a dozen fluttering red and blue banners, he made his campaign speech. **[one long prepositional phrase–*Beneath a dozen fluttering red and blue banners*]**

You need not set off a single short prepositional phrase, but it's not wrong to do so.

EXAMPLE In 1998 Frank Jordan ran for mayor. **[one short prepositional phrase–*In 1998*]**

RULE 5 Set off participles and participial phrases at the beginning of a sentence.

EXAMPLE Talking, we lost track of the time.

EXAMPLE Talking on the telephone, we lost track of the time.

Set off a participial phrase that is not essential to the meaning of a sentence.

EXAMPLE The band, marching in formation, moves down the field.

EXAMPLE Independence Day, celebrated on July 4, is a national holiday.

RULE 6 Set off words that interrupt the flow of thought in a sentence.

EXAMPLE Politicians, of course, sometimes forget their campaign promises after the election.

RULE 7 Use a comma after a conjunctive adverb, such as *however, moreover, furthermore, nevertheless,* or *therefore.*

EXAMPLE The school district is growing; therefore, taxes will rise.

RULE 8 Set off an appositive that is not essential to the meaning of a sentence.

EXAMPLE The *Titanic*, a luxury liner, sank on its first voyage. **[The appositive, *a luxury liner*, is not essential.]**

PRACTICE Using Commas I

Write the following sentences. Add commas where they're needed.

1. Strolling through the mall Amy spotted her aunt Marge outside the bookstore.
2. Jim Wong our best pitcher has injured his arm; furthermore Rocky Solo our best hitter has the flu.
3. In the heat of the moment Mother I lost my temper.
4. That home run by the way was Rocky's twenty-fifth of the season.
5. The children ran out the door across the lawn and into the woods behind the house.
6. The puppy wrapped in an old blue bath towel shivered in my arms.
7. Are you going to the Toads concert Ali?
8. Yes Dad I will do my homework clean my room and wash the dishes while you're gone.

9. For many years after the war there was bad feeling between the two nations; nevertheless they maintained courteous public relations.
10. Among the green blue and yellow lawn chairs the baby sat in her stroller.

13.3 USING COMMAS II

RULE 9 Use a comma before a coordinating conjunction (*and, but, or, nor,* or *for*) that connects the two parts of a compound sentence.

EXAMPLE Steve opened the door, and the dog ran out.

EXAMPLE Mari called her best friend, but no one answered.

EXAMPLE They will raise money, or they will donate their time.

RULE 10 Set off an adverb clause at the beginning of a sentence. An adverb clause begins with a subordinating conjunction, such as *after, although, as, because, before, if, since, though, unless, until, when, whenever, where, wherever,* or *while.*

EXAMPLE Whenever I feel afraid, I whistle a happy tune.

Usually, an adverb clause that falls at the end of a sentence is not set off.

EXAMPLE I whistle a happy tune whenever I feel afraid.

RULE 11 Set off a nonessential adjective clause. A nonessential adjective clause simply gives additional information and is not necessary to the meaning of a sentence. An adjective clause usually begins with a relative pronoun, such as *who, whom, whose, which,* or *that.*

EXAMPLE My house, which has green shutters, is at the corner of Elm and Maple.

Don't set off an essential adjective clause. An essential adjective clause is necessary to the meaning of a sentence.

EXAMPLE The house that has green shutters is at the corner of Elm and Maple.

GRAMMAR/USAGE/MECHANICS

PRACTICE **Using Commas II**

Write each sentence. Add commas where they're needed. If a sentence needs no commas, write correct.

1. Will your dad drive us to the museum or shall we take a bus?
2. After I had scraped the mud from my shoes I went indoors.
3. The principal entered the room and the students became silent.
4. Jamaica Hightower who will be sixteen soon is learning to drive.
5. I have already read the book that you chose for your report.
6. Please don't leave until I'm ready.
7. Although the sun was shining the air was cold.
8. I took my umbrella with me for it was raining hard.
9. Margarine has less animal fat but butter tastes better.
10. The dingo which is a wild dog is a native of Australia.

13.4 USING COMMAS III

RULE 12 In a date, set off the year when it's used with both the month and the day. Don't use a comma if only the month and the year are given.

EXAMPLE The ship struck an iceberg on April 14, 1912, and sank early the next morning.

EXAMPLE The ship sank in April 1912 on its first voyage.

RULE 13 Set off the name of a state or a country when it's used after the name of a city. Set off the name of a city when it's used after a street address. Don't use a comma after the state if it's followed by a ZIP code.

EXAMPLE The ship was sailing from Southampton, England, to New York City.

EXAMPLE You can write to Leeza at 15 College Court, Stanford, CA 94305.

RULE 14 Set off an abbreviated title or degree following a person's name.

EXAMPLE Michelle Nakamura, Ph.D., will be the graduation speaker.

EXAMPLE Letisha Davis, M.D., is our family physician.

RULE 15 Set off *too* when it's used in the middle of a sentence and means "also." Don't set off *too* at the end of a sentence.

EXAMPLE Parents, too, will attend the ceremony.

EXAMPLE Parents will attend the ceremony too.

RULE 16 Set off a direct quotation.

EXAMPLE Mom asked, "Have you finished your homework?"

EXAMPLE "I did it," I replied, "in study hall."

EXAMPLE "Tell me what you learned," said Mom.

RULE 17 Use a comma after the salutation of a friendly letter and after the closing of both a friendly letter and a business letter.

EXAMPLES Dear Dad, Your loving daughter, Yours truly,

RULE 18 Use a comma to prevent misreading.

EXAMPLE Instead of two, five teachers made the trip.

EXAMPLE In the field below, the brook gurgled merrily.

GRAMMAR/USAGE/MECHANICS

PRACTICE Using Commas III

Write each sentence. Add commas where they're needed.

1. "Mrs. Roberts" I told Mom "is moving to Atlanta Georgia in June."
2. Sweet potatoes too are high in vitamin C.
3. An assassination in Sarajevo Bosnia-Herzegovina in June 1914 set the stage for World War I.
4. "Gettysburg Pennsylvania was the scene of a major battle of the Civil War" said Serena.

5. The Carters left Los Angeles California on Thursday and arrived in Orlando Florida a week later.
6. Sam Lee Ph.D. has written a book on the environment of the Everglades.
7. John commented "Robert E. Lee surrendered at Appomattox Virginia on April 9 1865 to Ulysses S. Grant."
8. The address on the envelope was 1234 Oak Street Houston TX 77032.
9. Soon after they immigrated to the United States.
10. *Write the following message, adding commas where needed.*

    Dear Aunt Julia

    Thanks for the book. Camp is great. Scott too is enjoying himself.

    Your nephew
    David

GRAMMAR/USAGE/MECHANICS

13.5 USING SEMICOLONS AND COLONS

RULE 1 Use a semicolon to join the main clauses of a compound sentence if they're not joined by a conjunction such as *and, but, or, nor,* or *for.*

EXAMPLE The electric car was once the most popular car in the United States; people liked electric cars because they were clean and quiet.

RULE 2 Use a semicolon to join the main clauses of a compound sentence if they're long and if they already contain commas. Use a semicolon even if the clauses are joined by a coordinating conjunction such as *and, but, or, nor,* or *for.*

EXAMPLE Before the invention of the automobile, people rode horses, bicycles, or streetcars for short distances; and they used horse-drawn carriages, trains, or boats for longer trips.

RULE 3 Use a semicolon to separate main clauses joined by a conjunctive adverb, such as *consequently, furthermore, however, moreover, nevertheless,* or *therefore.*

EXAMPLE I started my homework immediately after school; consequently, I finished before dinner.

RULE 4 Use a colon to introduce a list of items that ends a sentence. Use a word or a phrase such as *these, the following,* or *as follows* before the list.

EXAMPLE I'll need **these** supplies for my project: newspapers, flour, water, string, and paint.

EXAMPLE I participate in **the following** sports: softball, tennis, basketball, and swimming.

Don't use a colon immediately after a verb or a preposition.

EXAMPLE My subjects **include** reading, math, home economics, and language arts.

EXAMPLE I sent messages **to** Grandma, Aunt Rita, and Julie.

RULE 5 Use a colon to separate the hour and the minutes when you use numerals to write the time of day.

EXAMPLE The train left the station at 10:17 A.M. and arrived in the city at 12:33 P.M.

RULE 6 Use a colon after the salutation of a business letter.

EXAMPLES Dear Professor Sanchez: Dear Editor in Chief:

PRACTICE Using Semicolons and Colons

Write each sentence. Add semicolons and colons where they're needed. If a sentence is already correct, write correct.

1. Night fell the moon rose.
2. Please do not bring any of these items to the test site radios, pagers, food, beverages.

GRAMMAR/USAGE/MECHANICS

3. The three travelers looked at the object in amazement they had never seen anything like it.
4. It was 312 P.M. when I looked at the clock.
5. I have received pamphlets from Camp Lookout, Camp Dawn, and the Camp in the Pines however, I have not yet made my selection.
6. During the last two years, our family has traveled to Oregon, Washington, Idaho, and Montana and in the next three months, we will see California, Arizona, and New Mexico.
7. The departure time for our flight is 1117 A.M. the plane will land in Houston at 104 P.M.
8. My favorite teams are the Bulls, the Cubs, and the Bears.
9. In the nineteenth century, Henry Wadsworth Longfellow was a popular poet, a professor at Harvard University, and a loving husband and his works include *Evangeline, The Courtship of Miles Standish, The Song of Hiawatha,* and "Paul Revere's Ride."
10. *Write the following business letter, adding necessary punctuation.*

    Dear Mr. Barnes

    Please send me information about the following computer programs Games for Brains, Computer Construction, and Explorers in Space.

    Yours truly,
Shana O'Neill

13.6 USING QUOTATION MARKS AND ITALICS

RULE 1 Use quotation marks to enclose a direct quotation.

EXAMPLE "Please return these books to the library," said Ms. Chu.

RULE 2 Use quotation marks to enclose each part of an interrupted quotation.

EXAMPLE "Spiders," explained Sean, "have eight legs."

RULE 3 Use commas to set off an explanatory phrase, such as *he said,* from the quotation itself. Place commas inside closing quotation marks.

EXAMPLE "Spiders," explained Sean, "have eight legs."

RULE 4 Place a period inside closing quotation marks.

EXAMPLE Toby said, "My aunt Susan received her degree in June."

RULE 5 Place a question mark or an exclamation point inside closing quotation marks if it's part of the quotation.

EXAMPLE Yoko asked, "Have you ever visited Florida?"

Place a question mark or an exclamation point outside closing quotation marks if it's part of the entire sentence but not part of the quotation.

EXAMPLE Did Jerry say, "Spiders have ten legs"?

When both a sentence and the direct quotation at the end of the sentence are questions (or exclamations), use only one question mark (or exclamation point). Place the mark inside the closing quotation marks.

EXAMPLE Did Yoko ask, "Have you ever visited Florida?"

NOTE When you're writing conversation, begin a new paragraph each time the speaker changes.

EXAMPLE

"You're kidding!" I exclaimed. "That sounds unbelievable. Did she really say that?"

"Indeed she did," Kara insisted.

RULE 6 Enclose in quotation marks titles of short stories, essays, poems, songs, articles, book chapters, and single television shows that are part of a series.

EXAMPLES "Charles" **[short story]** "Jingle Bells" **[song]**

RULE 7 Use italics or underlining for titles of books, plays, movies, television series, magazines, newspapers, works of art, music albums, and long musical compositions. Also use italics or underlining for the names of ships, airplanes, and spacecraft. Don't italicize or underline the word *the* before the title of a magazine or newspaper.

EXAMPLE *The Adventures of Tom Sawyer* **[book]**

EXAMPLE The Monsters Are Due on Maple Street **[play]**

EXAMPLE *The Hunchback of Notre Dame* **[movie]**

EXAMPLE Sesame Street **[television series]**

EXAMPLE *Cricket* **[magazine]**

EXAMPLE the New York Times **[newspaper]**

EXAMPLE the *Mona Lisa* **[painting]**

EXAMPLE The Best of Reba McEntire **[music album]**

EXAMPLE *Rhapsody in Blue* **[long musical composition]**

EXAMPLE Titanic **[ship]**

EXAMPLE the *Spirit of St. Louis* **[airplane]**

EXAMPLE Friendship 7 **[spacecraft]**

PRACTICE Using Quotation Marks, Italics, and Other Punctuation

Write each sentence. Add quotation marks, underlining (for italics), and other punctuation marks where they're needed.

1. For my book report said Samantha I will read Treasure Island, by Robert Louis Stevenson
2. Then Jeff played Deep in the Heart of Texas on the piano.
3. What a hilarious story that was exclaimed Trixie.
4. Doesn't the magazine National Geographic have some fine nature photographs asked Dean.
5. I am writing in my journal Zelda told her brother.
6. That movie said Susan was very funny
7. I have never seen it Todd replied.
8. Did Angel say I have never heard of that movie
9. Running Deer said This is the place of the high waters
10. Rita called her essay The Perfect Sandwich

13.7 USING APOSTROPHES

RULE 1 Use an apostrophe and *s ('s)* to form the possessive of a singular noun.

EXAMPLES girl + **'s** = girl**'s** James + **'s** = James**'s**

RULE 2 Use an apostrophe and *s ('s)* to form the possessive of a plural noun that does not end in *s*.

EXAMPLES men + **'s** = men**'s** geese + **'s** = geese**'s**

RULE 3 Use an apostrophe alone to form the possessive of a plural noun that ends in *s*.

EXAMPLES boys + **'** = boys**'** judges + **'** = judges**'**

RULE 4 Use an apostrophe and *s ('s)* to form the possessive of an indefinite pronoun, such as *everyone, everybody, anyone, no one,* or *nobody.*

EXAMPLES anybody + **'s** = anybody**'s** someone + **'s** = someone**'s**

Don't use an apostrophe in the possessive personal pronouns *ours, yours, his, hers, its,* and *theirs.*

EXAMPLES That car is **ours.** Is that cat **yours**?
The bird flapped **its** wings. These skates are **hers.**

GRAMMAR/USAGE/MECHANICS

RULE 5 Use an apostrophe to replace letters that are omitted in a contraction.

EXAMPLES it is = it's you are = you're
I will = I'll is not = isn't

PRACTICE Using Apostrophes

Write each sentence. Add apostrophes where they're needed. If the sentence is already correct, write correct.

1. The girls chorus and the boys glee club will sing at the nursing center on Saturday.
2. Ill tell Debbies father the news.
3. Someones history book is in the teachers workroom.
4. The dog put its head on my knee.
5. The childrens party will begin at one at our house.
6. Shell put everyones reports on the bulletin board.
7. The cars engine sputtered, and its frame shook.
8. That bicycle isnt yours.
9. Its a quarter to three, and nobodys parents have arrived to collect their children.
10. Youre in charge of the luncheon for the womens political club.

13.8 USING HYPHENS, DASHES, AND PARENTHESES

RULE 1 Use a hyphen to divide a word at the end of a line. Divide words only between syllables.

EXAMPLE With her husband, Pierre, Marie Sklodowska Curie dis-covered radium and polonium.

RULE 2 Use a hyphen in compound numbers.

EXAMPLES **thirty-two** pianos **sixty-five** experiments

RULE 3 Use a hyphen in fractions expressed in words.

EXAMPLE Add **one-half** cup of butter or margarine.

EXAMPLE **Three-fourths** of the students sing in the chorus.

RULE 4 Use a hyphen or hyphens in certain compound nouns. Check a dictionary for the correct way to write a compound noun.

EXAMPLES great-aunt brother-in-law attorney-at-law
editor in chief vice president

RULE 5 Use a hyphen in a compound modifier when it comes before the word it modifies.

EXAMPLES Fido is a **well-trained** dog. The dog is **well trained.**

RULE 6 Use a hyphen after the prefixes *all-*, *ex-*, and *self-*. Use a hyphen to separate any prefix from a word that begins with a capital letter.

EXAMPLES all-powerful ex-president
self-educated trans-Atlantic

RULE 7 Use dashes to set off a sudden break or change in thought or speech.

EXAMPLE Billy Adams—he lives next door—is our team manager.

RULE 8 Use parentheses to set off words that define or explain a word.

EXAMPLE Simulators (devices that produce the conditions of space flight) are used in flight training for the space program.

PRACTICE **Using Hyphens, Dashes, and Parentheses**

Write each sentence. Add hyphens, dashes, and parentheses where they're needed.

1. I have collected twenty seven glass bottles and fifty three plastic ones.
2. Two tenths is the same as one fifth.
3. One of the twins I forget which one has won the citizenship award for self improvement.
4. Their property consists of one half acre 21,780 square feet.
5. Susie's brother in law he's our next door neighbor is my science teacher.
6. The Joneses have well behaved children.
7. Use three fourths cup of sugar and one fourth cup of butter.
8. Those seventh grade students are really well liked.
9. Arachnids spiders, scorpions, mites, and ticks are frightening to some people.
10. Kyle's great grandfather was born in Ireland eighty one years ago; he was an all American football player in college.

13.9 USING ABBREVIATIONS

RULE 1 Use the abbreviations *Mr., Mrs., Ms.,* and *Dr.* before a person's name. Abbreviate professional or academic degrees that follow a person's name. Abbreviate *Junior* as *Jr.* and *Senior* as *Sr.* when they follow a person's name.

EXAMPLES **Mr.** Ed Hall **Dr.** Ann Chu Juan Diaz, **Ph.D.**
Ava Danko, **D.D.S.** Amos Finley **Jr.**

RULE 2 Use capital letters and no periods for abbreviations that are pronounced letter by letter or as words. Exceptions are *U.S.* and Washington, *D.C.*, which should have periods.

EXAMPLES **MVP** most valuable player **EST** eastern standard time
NASA National Aeronautics and Space Administration

RULE 3 Use the abbreviations *A.M.* (*ante meridiem,* "before noon") and *P.M.* (*post meridiem,* "after noon") with times. For dates use *B.C.* (before Christ) and, sometimes, *A.D.* (*anno Domini*, "in the year of the Lord," after Christ).

EXAMPLES 6:22 **A.M.** 4:12 **P.M.** 33 **B.C.** **A.D.** 476

RULE 4 Abbreviate days and months only in charts and lists.

EXAMPLES **Mon.** **Wed.** **Thur.** **Jan.** **Apr.** **Aug.** **Nov.**

RULE 5 In scientific writing, abbreviate units of measure. Use periods with abbreviations of U.S. units but not with abbreviations of metric units.

EXAMPLES inch(es) **in.** foot (feet) **ft.** gram(s) **g** liter(s) **l**

RULE 6 In addressing envelopes, abbreviate words that refer to streets. Spell out these words everywhere else.

EXAMPLES **St.** (Street) **Ave.** (Avenue) **Rd.** (Road)
I live at the corner of Elm **Street** and Maple **Road.**

RULE 7 In addressing envelopes, use the two-letter postal abbreviations for states. Spell out state names everywhere else.

EXAMPLES Texas **TX** Florida **FL** California **CA**
My cousin lives in Chicago, **Illinois.**

GRAMMAR/USAGE/MECHANICS

RULE 8 When an abbreviation with a period falls at the end of a sentence, don't add another period. Add a question mark if the sentence is interrogative; add an exclamation point if the sentence is exclamatory.

EXAMPLE I just met Francis X. Colavito Jr.

EXAMPLE Have you met Francis X. Colavito Jr.?

For more information about abbreviations, see pages 56–61 in Part One, Ready Reference.

PRACTICE Using Abbreviations

Write the abbreviation for each item described.

1. the day after Tuesday
2. fourteen minutes after two in the afternoon
3. the title used with the name of an unmarried woman
4. United States
5. Scott Avenue
6. the state of Florida in an address on an envelope
7. the title used before the name of a person who has a medical degree
8. the month before May
9. inches
10. the phrase *before Christ* when it is used with a date

13.10 WRITING NUMBERS

In charts and tables, always write numbers as figures. In ordinary sentences, you sometimes spell out numbers and sometimes write them as numerals.

RULE 1 Spell out numbers you can write in one or two words. If the number is greater than 999,999, see Rule 4.

EXAMPLE There are **twenty-six** students in the class.

EXAMPLE The arena holds **fifty-five hundred** people.

RULE 2 Use numerals for numbers of more than two words.

EXAMPLE The distance between the two cities is **150** miles.

RULE 3 Spell out any number that begins a sentence or reword the sentence so it doesn't begin with a number.

EXAMPLE **Four thousand two hundred eighty-three** fans attended the game.

EXAMPLE Attendance at the game was **4,283.**

RULE 4 Use figures for numbers greater than 999,999, followed by the word *million, billion*, and so on, even if the number could be written in two words.

EXAMPLES **1 million** **280 billion** **3.2 trillion**

RULE 5 Numbers of the same kind should be written in the same way. If one number must be written as a numeral, write all the numbers as numerals.

EXAMPLE On September 8, **383** students voted for the new rule, and **50** students voted against it.

RULE 6 Spell out ordinal numbers (*first, second, third,* and so on) under one hundred.

EXAMPLE The **ninth** of June will be the couple's **twenty-fourth** wedding anniversary.

RULE 7 Use words to write the time of day unless you are using *A.M.* or *P.M.*

EXAMPLE I usually go for a walk at **four o'clock** in the afternoon. I return home at **a quarter to five.**

EXAMPLE The first bell rang at **8:42 A.M.**, and the last one rang at **3:12 P.M.**

RULE 8 Use numerals to write dates, house numbers, street numbers above ninety-nine, apartment and room numbers, telephone numbers, page numbers, amounts of money of more than two words, and percentages. Write out the word *percent.*

EXAMPLE On June **10, 1999,** I met Jan at **41** East **329th** Street in Apartment **3**G. Her telephone number is **555-2121.**

EXAMPLE Our class meets in Room **12; 55 percent** of the students are girls.

EXAMPLE I found **two dollars** between page **250** and page **251** in this book. The book's original price was **$12.95.**

GRAMMAR/USAGE/MECHANICS

PRACTICE Writing Numbers

Write each sentence. Use the correct form for each number. If the sentence is already correct, write correct.

1. I have read 75 books this year.
2. From 1920 to 1930, the population of the United States grew from one hundred six million to one hundred twenty-three million, an increase of sixteen percent.
3. In this ballpark, the distance from home plate to the fence in center field is 410 feet.
4. I'll need $20 for fees and supplies by Monday, September thirtieth.
5. We picked ten bushels of apples and 12 bushels of peaches.
6. Only thirty-three % of the voters turned out for the election on November second, 1999.
7. I called nine one one when I saw the accident at the corner of West 150th Street and Madison Avenue.
8. Josh has collected twenty-seven hundred baseball cards.
9. 423 students were in my sister's graduating class; my sister ranked 10th in the class.
10. Please arrive between half past 7 and 8 o'clock.

PRACTICE Proofreading

Rewrite the following passage, adding missing punctuation. Write legibly to be sure one letter is not mistaken for another. There are ten errors.

Robert Frost

[1]Robert Frost was a well loved poet. [2]He was born on March 26 1874. [3]He spent his first ten years in San Francisco California. [4]His father William Frost died when Frost was ten. [5]After his father's death, Frost moved east to Massachusetts with his mother. [6]At the age of twenty one, Frost attended Harvard.

[7]After several years as a teacher, Frost moved to England he wrote many poems there and lived on a farm. [8]He published his first book of poems, A Boy's Will, at the age of forty. [9]Readers loved his poems. [10]He won the Pulitzer Prize four times; furthermore twenty-eight universities gave him honorary degrees.

[11]Frost once talked to a friend about poetry. [12]He said "It begins as a lump in the throat." [13]These are some of Frost's poems "Stopping by Woods on a Snowy Evening," "The Telephone," and "To Earthward."

POSTTEST Commas, Semicolons, Colons, and End Punctuation

Write each sentence. Add commas, semicolons, colons, and end punctuation where needed.

1. Wow Can you imagine rowing a galley in the Spanish Armada
2. Rowers grow hot tired sweaty and unhappy after several hours of rowing
3. When the Spanish ships met the English ships in 1588 what happened
4. "The English ships were faster" said Joyce "and no Spaniards boarded them."

5. "Yes I too heard that" said Heather. "The captains of the Spanish Armada gave up went home and repaired their ships."
6. Dawn Moffa Ph.D. has studied the American Revolution consequently she will talk with our class about the war
7. "Does anyone know what happened on March 5 1770 in Boston?" she asked.
8. Choose one of the following events the Boston Tea Party the Battle of Bunker Hill or the Boston Massacre
9. "Dr. Moffa was it the Boston Massacre?" asked Al who moved here from Boston.
10. Yes that's right. Will you tell me how many people died what started the fight and how the Americans reacted
11. The event that interests me most is the writing of the Declaration of Independence I wish I could hear more about the person who wrote it
12. Visit Philadelphia Pennsylvania which was the home of the Continental Congress
13. Freezing at Valley Forge some soldiers died before the winter ended
14. By the end of the summer Jane had read *Treasure Island Robinson Crusoe The Wind in the Willows* and *Bridge to Terabithia* and her friend Tom had read *Tom Sawyer Huckleberry Finn* and *Kon-Tiki*
15. The night before the storm had destroyed most of Xenia a small town in central Ohio

GRAMMAR/USAGE/MECHANICS

POSTTEST Quotation Marks, Italics, and Apostrophes

Write each sentence. Add quotation marks, underlining (for italics), apostrophes, and other punctuation marks where they're needed. If the sentence is already correct, write correct.

16. For every rule said our guest speaker there is someone or something that doesnt fit it
17. Consider the idea that cats hate water he said.

18. Did you know that one cat loves water he asked.
19. Did you say Cats love water
20. The fishing cat earns its name by fishing for its food.
21. A scientists videotape shows a fishing cat swimming in the water added the speaker.
22. Youre teasing us said Jessica.
23. Why dont you ask for some zookeepers opinions he said.
24. Ill read this article Little Cats in the Wild or look at the March 1998 issue of the magazine Zoobooks.
25. Well store everyones equipment in the mens locker room.

POSTTEST Hyphens, Dashes, Parentheses, and Numbers

Write each sentence. Add hyphens, dashes, and parentheses where they're needed. Use the correct form for each number.

26. The crowd of 32,000 fans booed when the umpire threw 1/5 of the players out of the game in the 7th inning.
27. The part time secretary asked the 6 job applicants to wait in Room 32.
28. 2 days into the trip, the all terrain vehicle broke down in the middle of a stream.
29. Sherry's brother in law, who is 27, broke his ankle on July 16, 1998, at Sixty One East Two Hundred Twenty Second Street.
30. Is 120 12% of 1,000?
31. The game begins at seven thirty five P.M.; it will end about nine o'clock.
32. Turn to page 58 to read about four endangered animals; then answer the questions on page sixty.
33. Mrs. Mandrake she's our school librarian has collected thirty seven dollars and ninety five cents in fines.
34. A one gallon container holds one gallon 4 quarts.
35. More than 267,000,000 people live in the United States.

Chapter 14

Sentence Combining

PRETEST Compound Elements

Combine the sentences in each numbered item by using a coordinating conjunction. Add commas where they're needed. (Hint: Combine the elements listed in brackets at the end of each pair of sentences.)

1. a. Rosalia has a new computer game.
b. Norman has a new computer game. [subjects]

2. a. Virginia Hamilton wrote *M. C. Higgins, the Great.*
b. She also wrote *Zeely.* [direct objects]

3. a. Sandra went to the mall with Carlotta.
b. Sandra went to the mall with An-Mei. [objects of preposition]

4. a. Geraldo fixed a sandwich.
b. Geraldo poured a glass of milk. [predicates]

5. a. Zack gave the dog a bath.
b. Zack gave the cat a bath. [indirect objects]

6. a. It was a holiday weekend.
b. Traffic was heavy. [sentences]

7. a. Lana will grill hamburgers.
b. Seth will order a pizza. [sentences]

8. a. Melissa sings in the chorus.
b. Nikki plays in the band. [sentences]

9. a. Shawna wanted to call her friend.
b. She had too much homework. [sentences]

10. a. I could write a letter to Grandma.
b. I could watch a movie. [sentences]

GRAMMAR/USAGE/MECHANICS

PRETEST Prepositional Phrases and Appositive Phrases

Combine the sentences in each numbered item by adding the new information in the second sentence to the first sentence in the form of a prepositional phrase or an appositive phrase.

11. a. I found my boots.
b. They were in the closet.

12. a. Shannon Miller won seven Olympic medals.
b. She is a gymnast.

13. a. Edmund Hillary reached the top of Mount Everest in May 1953.
b. Hillary was an adventurer from New Zealand.

14. a. I read a good book last week.
b. It was about volcanoes.

15. a. Mount Etna is located in southern Italy.
b. Etna is the most active volcano in Europe.

16. a. The committee will meet tomorrow.
b. It will meet at three o'clock.

17. a. The principal presented an award to Mr. Scott.
b. Mr. Scott is a science teacher.

18. a. I baked a chocolate cake.
b. The cake is for Theo's birthday.

19. a. We collected several autographs.
    b. We collected them from the players.
20. a. The heads of four presidents are carved into Mount Rushmore.
    b. The presidents are Washington, Jefferson, Lincoln, and Theodore Roosevelt.

GRAMMAR/USAGE/MECHANICS

PRETEST Adjective and Adverb Clauses

Combine the sentences in items 21–25 by changing the new information in the second sentence to an adjective clause and adding it to the first sentence. Begin your clause with the word in brackets. Add commas if they're needed.

Combine the sentences in items 26–30 by changing the information in one sentence to an adverb clause and adding it to the other sentence. Begin your clause with the word in brackets. Add a comma if it's needed.

21. a. Dr. Hershfield will remove my tonsils.
    b. My parents respect her. [whom]
22. a. Kelly Starr tutors me after school.
    b. Kelly is very good in math. [who]
23. a. The snacks contained no sugar.
    b. They tasted great. [which]
24. a. Mother has a beautiful old quilt.
    b. The quilt has been in her family for generations. [that]
25. a. Shel Silverstein writes for both children and adults.
    b. His poems are humorous. [whose]
26. a. Juan spent more time on his studies. [When]
    b. His grades improved.
27. a. I finish my homework.
    b. I play computer games. [before]
28. a. I wash the dishes. [After]
    b. I play outdoors.

29. a. You were tired. [Because]
b. You fell asleep.

30. a. The general raised the flag.
b. The trumpets played a song. [as]

14.1 COMPOUND SENTENCES

When you have written a few simple sentences that are closely related in meaning, try combining them to form compound sentences. A compound sentence often states your meaning more clearly than a group of simple sentences. By using some compound sentences, you can also vary the length of your sentences.

EXAMPLE **a.** Sam had three sisters.

b. Matt had only one. **[but]**

Sam had three sisters**, but** Matt had only one.

In this example, simple sentence *a* is joined to simple sentence *b* with the coordinating conjunction *but.* Note that a comma is used before the conjunction.

A **compound sentence** is made up of two or more simple sentences. You can combine two or more simple sentences in a compound sentence by using the conjunction *and, but,* or *or.*

GRAMMAR/USAGE/MECHANICS

PRACTICE **Combining Simple Sentences**

Combine the sentences in each numbered item by using a comma and a coordinating conjunction. For the first three items, use the coordinating conjunction shown in brackets at the end of the first sentence.

1. a. John may work for his uncle this summer. [or]
b. His parents may send him to camp.

2. a. Sharon has a bad cold. [and]
b. Her sister has the flu.

3. a. Mrs. Malone had many problems. [but]
   b. She was happy in spite of them.

4. a. Mom prepares dinner.
   b. Dad cleans up afterward.

5. a. Jacob smiled at the other boy.
   b. He did not trust him.

6. a. The sun was shining brightly.
   b. The birds were singing in the trees.

7. a. For her week of community service, Tessa might volunteer at a hospital.
   b. She might help the patients at a nursing center.

8. a. Maria made the first team.
   b. Nicole made the second team.

9. a. Mr. McCall could not afford a new car.
   b. He bought one anyway.

10. a. This afternoon I could clean the garage.
   b. I could lie on the couch and read a book.

14.2 COMPOUND ELEMENTS

Sometimes several sentences share information—for example, the same subject or verb. By combining such sentences and using compound elements, you can avoid repeating words. Sentences with compound elements also add variety to your writing.

EXAMPLE **a.** Helen wore a purple dress.

b. She **carried a red handbag.** [and]

Helen wore a purple dress **and carried a red handbag.**

Sentences *a* and *b* share information about Helen. The combined version takes the new information from sentence *b*, *carried a red handbag*, and joins it to sentence *a*, using the coordinating conjunction *and.*

You can avoid repeating information by using **compound elements.** Join compound elements with the conjunctions *and, but,* or *or.*

PRACTICE Combining Sentences with Compound Elements

Combine the sentences in each numbered item by using a coordinating conjunction to form a compound element. Add the new information from the second sentence to the first sentence. For the first three items, the new information is in italics, and the conjunction you should use is shown in brackets at the end of the first sentence.

1. a. We planted flowers in the garden. [and]
b. We also planted *vegetables* in the garden.

2. a. Mr. Gonzales owns a bicycle. [but]
b. He does *not* own *a car.*

3. a. Carmelita might become a chemist. [or]
b. She might become *a writer.*

4. a. The designer decorated the hat with buttons.
b. He also decorated it with bows.

5. a. The newlyweds may buy a house.
b. They may rent an apartment.

6. a. We paid Carla in cash.
b. We also paid Carlos in cash.

7. a. Mrs. Ito speaks Japanese.
b. She does not speak English.

8. a. The day was cold.
b. It was windy.

9. a. You could wear a blue tie with that suit.
b. You could wear a red tie with that suit.

10. a. Melinda helped us with the children.
b. Stephanie also helped us with the children.

14.3 PREPOSITIONAL PHRASES

Prepositional phrases are useful in sentence combining. Like adjectives and adverbs, they present more information about nouns and verbs. Because prepositional phrases show relationships, they can often express complicated ideas effectively.

EXAMPLE **a.** The family took a trip.

b. It was a **hot summer day. [on]**

c. They went **to the beach.**

On a hot summer day, the family took a trip **to the beach.**

The new information in sentence *b* is added to sentence *a* as a prepositional phrase, and the new information in sentence *c* is moved to sentence *a.* In the new sentence, the prepositional phrase *On a hot summer day* modifies the verb, *took.* The phrase *to the beach* modifies the noun *trip.* Notice that a prepositional phrase that modifies a noun follows the noun it modifies. Prepositional phrases that modify verbs can occupy different positions in a sentence. (For a list of common prepositions, see page 174.)

A **prepositional phrase** is a group of words that begins with a preposition and ends with a noun or a pronoun. Prepositional phrases most often modify nouns and verbs.

GRAMMAR/USAGE/MECHANICS

PRACTICE Combining Sentences with Prepositional Phrases

Combine the sentences in each numbered item by adding the prepositional phrase from the second sentence to the first sentence. For the first three items, the prepositional phrase in the second sentence is shown in italics. In the last item, you will need to combine three sentences.

1. a. The store was full of customers.
b. The store was *opposite the barber shop.*

2. a. We stood in line.
b. We were *with several other people.*

3. a. Our dog, Lottie, was swimming.
b. She was *in the pool.*

4. a. Mrs. Morgenstern planted daffodils.
b. She planted them along the fence.

5. a. The team plays its next game on Saturday.
   b. The game is against the Bulldogs.
6. a. The horses trotted.
   b. They trotted around the track.
7. a. The party finally ended.
   b. It was after midnight.
8. a. The Tylers moved here last month.
   b. They came from St. Louis.
9. a. The mail carrier delivered a package.
   b. It was for Tanya.
10. a. My report is due.
    b. It's about racehorses.
    c. It's due by tomorrow.

GRAMMAR/USAGE/MECHANICS

14.4 APPOSITIVES

You can use appositives to combine sentences in a compact and informative way. Appositives and appositive phrases identify or rename nouns.

EXAMPLE **a.** Maya Lin designed the Vietnam Veterans Memorial.

b. She was **an architecture student.**

Maya Lin**, an architecture student,** designed the Vietnam Veterans Memorial.

The appositive phrase *an architecture student* identifies the noun *Maya Lin.* Note that the appositive phrase is set off with commas because it gives nonessential information about Maya Lin. If an appositive or an appositive phrase gives information that is essential for identifying a noun, it's not set off with commas. (For more information about appositives, see pages 89–90.)

An **appositive** is a noun placed next to another noun to identify it or give additional information about it. An **appositive phrase** includes an appositive and other words that modify it.

GRAMMAR/USAGE/MECHANICS

PRACTICE Combining Sentences with Appositives

Combine the sentences in each numbered item by changing the new information in the second sentence to an appositive or an appositive phrase and adding it to the first sentence. For the first three items, the appositive or appositive phrase in the second sentence is shown in italics. Add commas where they're needed.

1. a. The first man on the moon was born in Wapakoneta, Ohio.
b. He was *Neil Armstrong.*

2. a. Mr. and Mrs. Kelly have bought a new car.
b. They're *our neighbors.*

3. a. Meteors are often called shooting stars.
b. Meteors are *chunks of metal or stone.*

4. a. Graceland is in Memphis, Tennessee.
b. Graceland is the home of Elvis Presley.

5. a. Suzy loves to go for walks in the woods.
b. Suzy is my pet terrier.

6. a. The house stood on a bare hill.
b. The house was a mansion with thirty-five rooms.

7. a. The students traveled to Lexington, Kentucky.
b. They were all band members.

8. a. My mother lost her favorite earrings.
b. They were a gift from my father.

9. a. The Missouri River flows from southwestern Montana to St. Louis, Missouri.
b. It is the longest river in the United States.

10. a. Jalitza is six feet two inches tall.
b. She is our star basketball player.

14.5 ADJECTIVE AND ADVERB CLAUSES

When two sentences share information, one of the sentences can often be made into an adjective clause modifying a word in the other sentence.

EXAMPLE **a.** Carla and Darla entered the dance contest.

b. Carla and Darla **are identical twins.** **[, who . . . ,]**

Carla and Darla**, who are identical twins,** entered the dance contest.

The new information (in blue type) in sentence *b* becomes an adjective clause modifying *Carla and Darla. Who* now connects the clauses. Notice the commas in the new sentence. Adjective clauses that add nonessential information are set off with commas. Those that add essential information are not. (For more information about adjective clauses, see page 195.)

An **adjective clause** is a subordinate clause that modifies a noun or a pronoun in the main clause. A relative pronoun, such as *who, whom, whose, which,* or *that,* is used to tie the adjective clause to the main clause. The words *where* and *when* can also be used as connectors.

GRAMMAR/USAGE/MECHANICS

You can also use adverb clauses to combine sentences. Adverb clauses are especially effective in showing relationships between actions. For example, an adverb clause can show when one action takes place in relation to another.

EXAMPLE **a.** Lee read a great deal as a boy.

b. He was recovering from an accident. **[while]**

Lee read a great deal as a boy **while he was recovering from an accident.**

In the new sentence, the adverb clause *while he was recovering from an accident* modifies the verb *read.* The adverb clause tells when Lee read a great deal. Note that the subordinating conjunction *while* makes the relationship between the two actions clear. An adverb clause may occupy different positions within a sentence. If it begins the sentence, it's followed by a comma. (For more information about adverb clauses, see pages 198–199.)

An **adverb clause** is a subordinate clause that often modifies the verb in the main clause. Adverb clauses are introduced by subordinating conjunctions, such as *after, although, as, because, before, if, since, unless, until, when, whenever, where, wherever,* and *while.*

GRAMMAR/USAGE/MECHANICS

PRACTICE Combining Sentences with Adjective and Adverb Clauses

Combine the sentences in items 1–5 by changing the new information in the second sentence to an adjective clause and adding it to the first sentence. For items 1–3, the new information in the second sentence is shown in italics. Begin your clause with the word in brackets. Add commas if they're needed.

Combine the sentences in items 6–10 by changing the information in one sentence to an adverb clause and adding it to the other sentence. Begin your clause with the word in brackets. Add a comma if it's needed.

1. a. Pietro made sculptures of marble.
b. The marble *came from Italy.* [that]

2. a. My sewing scissors are missing.
b. They *were in this drawer.* [which]

3. a. The Petersons have gone on a cruise.
b. Their *child is staying with us.* [whose]

4. a. The boys earned ten dollars.
b. They fixed my bicycle. [who]

5. a. Felicia will accompany us.
b. You have already met her. [whom]

6. a. Delia made an outline.
b. She wrote her report. [before]

7. a. Dante works hard.
b. He wants to be a success. [because]

8. a. We lost the game. [Although]
b. We played our best.

9. a. The driver approached the stop sign. [As]
b. She slowed down.

10. a. There was a phone call for you.
b. You were sleeping. [while]

GRAMMAR/USAGE/MECHANICS

PRACTICE Proofreading

Rewrite each of the following passages, combining sentences that are closely related in meaning. Write legibly to be sure one letter is not mistaken for another.

Robert Browning

On his fourteenth birthday, Robert Browning received a book. It was a book of poems. It was by Percy Bysshe Shelley. Browning loved these poems. The poems inspired his own poem *Pauline.*

Browning married Elizabeth Barrett. She was also a poet. She is famous for her love poems. Browning is famous for his dramatic monologues. Browning was one of the great poets of the Victorian era. He was buried in the Poets' Corner of Westminster Abbey.

T. S. Eliot

Thomas Stearns Eliot was born in the United States. He spent most of his life in England. Eliot wrote poems in his spare time. He was working as a bank clerk.

Eliot wrote about modern problems. He was a famous poet. He wrote "The Waste Land." He also wrote "The Love Song of J. Alfred Prufrock" and "The Hollow Men." Eliot won the Nobel Prize. He won the prize in 1948.

POSTTEST Compound Elements

Combine the sentences in each numbered item by using a coordinating conjunction. Add commas where they're needed. (Hint: Combine the elements listed in brackets at the end of each pair of sentences.)

1. a. Shelly is taking trombone lessons.
b. Ricardo is taking trombone lessons. [subjects]

2. a. Mr. Estevez grows tomatoes in his garden.
b. Mr. Estevez grows carrots in his garden. [direct objects]

3. a. Meg Ryan starred in *Sleepless in Seattle.*
b. She also starred in *You've Got Mail.* [objects of preposition]

4. a. Maria plays the piano.
b. Maria sings in the choir. [predicates]

5. a. Grandma knitted Su-Lin socks and mittens.
b. Grandma knitted Maya socks and mittens. [indirect objects]

6. a. Dad likes a thick, juicy steak occasionally.
b. Mom refuses to eat meat. [sentences]

7. a. Buddy will play Romeo.
b. Cissy will play Juliet. [sentences]

8. a. Sidney may enlist in the army.
b. She may attend a community college. [sentences]

9. a. Cinderella had no gown for the ball.
b. She did have a fairy godmother. [sentences]

10. a. Samuel Taylor Coleridge was a poet.
b. Samuel Coleridge Taylor was a composer. [sentences]

POSTTEST Prepositional Phrases and Appositive Phrases

Combine the sentences in each numbered item by adding the new information in the second sentence to the first sentence in the form of a prepositional phrase or an appositive phrase.

11. a. Jim, Natalie, and Singh received awards.
b. They received the awards for perfect attendance.

12. a. Confucius lived from 551 to 479 B.C.
b. He was a famous Chinese philosopher.

13. a. Shanda hid the present.
b. She hid it under her bed.

14. a. Eddie plays the drums.
b. He plays them with enthusiasm.

15. a. The monument stood on the steps of the capitol.
b. The monument was a statue of Christopher Columbus.

16. a. This story takes place during the Civil War.
b. The story is by Irene Hunt.

17. a. A hundred students participated in the production of the play.
b. The play was a musical comedy.

18. a. My drawing won a prize in the competition.
b. The drawing was a sketch of the river.

19. a. My grandparents' portrait hangs in the living room.
b. It hangs over the fireplace.

20. a. On Sunday mornings, my parents enjoy a cup of mocha.
b. Mocha is a mixture of chocolate and coffee.

POSTTEST Adjective and Adverb Clauses

Combine the sentences in items 21–25 by changing the new information in the second sentence to an adjective clause and adding it to the first sentence. Begin your clause with the word in brackets. Add commas if they're needed.

Combine the sentences in items 26–30 by changing the information in one sentence to an adverb clause and adding it to the other sentence. Begin your clause with the word in brackets. Add a comma if it's needed.

GRAMMAR/USAGE/MECHANICS

21. a. The park ranger was kind.
b. She helped me find my family. [who]

22. a. My cast comes off soon.
b. It has been on my leg for five weeks. [which]

23. a. The city will build a new stadium.
b. The new stadium will seat twice as many people as the old one. [that]

24. a. My brother has been accepted at Northwestern University.
b. His grades are excellent. [whose]

25. a. Mayor Roberts is improving the city's parks.
b. The voters elected him two years ago. [whom]

26. a. The skunk smells terrible to people. [Although]
b. The stinkbug smells terrible to other insects.

27. a. We hiked to the lake.
b. The sun was rising. [as]

28. a. Yoko takes out the trash. [While]
b. Her brother sweeps the floor.

29. a. Harriet missed her ballet class.
b. She overslept. [because]

30. a. Mrs. Cuentres gave the baby a bath.
b. She put him to bed. [before]

Chapter 15

Spelling and Vocabulary

15.1 SPELLING RULES

English spelling often seems to make no sense. Usually there are historical reasons for the spellings we use today, but you don't need to study the history of the English language to spell correctly. The rules in this section work most of the time, but there are exceptions to every rule. When you're not sure how to spell a word, the best thing to do is check a dictionary.

Spelling *ie* and *ei*

An easy way to learn when to use *ie* and when to use *ei* is to memorize a simple rhyming rule. Then learn the common exceptions to the rule.

Reprinted by permission of Sidney Harris.

RULE	EXAMPLES
WRITE *I* BEFORE *E*	achieve, believe, brief, chief, die, field, friend, grief, lie, niece, piece, pier, quiet, retrieve, tie, yield
EXCEPT AFTER *C*	ceiling, conceit, conceive, deceit, deceive, receipt, receive
OR WHEN SOUNDED LIKE *A*, AS IN *NEIGHBOR* AND *WEIGH*.	eight, eighty, freight, neigh, reign, sleigh, veil, vein, weigh, weight

Some exceptions: caffeine, either, foreign, forfeit, height, heir, leisure, neither, protein, seize, species, their, weird; words ending in *cient (ancient)* and *cience (conscience);* plurals of nouns ending in *cy (democracies);* the third-person singular form of verbs ending in *cy (fancies);* words in which *i* and *e* follow *c* but represent separate sounds *(science, society)*

Words Ending in *cede, ceed,* and *sede*

The only English word ending in *sede* is *supersede.* Three words end in *ceed: proceed, exceed,* and *succeed.* You can remember these three words by thinking of the following sentence.

EXAMPLE If you **proceed** to **exceed** the speed limit, you will **succeed** in getting a ticket.

All other words ending with the "seed" sound are spelled with *cede: precede, recede, secede.*

Adding Prefixes

Adding prefixes is easy. Keep the spelling of the root word and add the prefix. If the last letter of the prefix is the same as the first letter of the word, keep both letters.

un- + happy = unhappy	co- + operate = cooperate
dis- + appear = disappear	il- + legal = illegal
re- + enlist = reenlist	un- + natural = unnatural
mis- + spell = misspell	im- + migrate = immigrate

GRAMMAR/USAGE/MECHANICS

Adding Suffixes

When you add a suffix beginning with a vowel, double the final consonant if the word ends in a **single consonant following a single vowel *and***

- the word has one syllable

mud + -y = muddy	sad + -er = sadder
put + -ing = putting	stop + -ed = stopped

- the word is stressed on the last syllable and the stress remains on the same syllable after the suffix is added

occur + -ence = occurrence	repel + -ent = repellent
regret + -able = regrettable	commit + -ed = committed
begin + -ing = beginning	refer + -al = referral

Don't double the final letter if the word ends in *s, w, x,* or *y: buses, rowing, waxy, employer.*

Don't double the final consonant before the suffix *-ist* if the word has more than one syllable: *druggist* but *violinist, guitarist.*

Adding suffixes to words that end in *y* can cause spelling problems. Study these rules and note the exceptions.

When a word ends in a **vowel and *y*,** keep the *y.*

play + -s = plays	joy + -ous = joyous
obey + -ed = obeyed	annoy + -ance = annoyance
buy + -ing = buying	enjoy + -ment = enjoyment
employ + -er = employer	enjoy + -able = enjoyable
joy + -ful = joyful	boy + -ish = boyish
joy + -less = joyless	coy + -ly = coyly

SOME EXCEPTIONS: gay + -ly = gaily, day + -ly = daily, pay + -d = paid, lay + -d = laid, say + -d = said

When a word ends in a **consonant and *y*,** change the *y* to *i* before any suffix that doesn't begin with *i.* Keep the *y* before suffixes that begin with *i.*

carry + -es = carries	deny + -al = denial
dry + -ed = dried	rely + -able = reliable
easy + -er = easier	mercy + -less = merciless
merry + -ly = merrily	likely + -hood = likelihood
happy + -ness = happiness	accompany + -ment = accompaniment
beauty + -ful = beautiful	
fury + -ous = furious	carry + -ing = carrying
defy + -ant = defiant	baby + -ish = babyish
vary + -ation = variation	lobby + -ist = lobbyist

SOME EXCEPTIONS: shy + -ly = shyly, dry + -ly = dryly, shy + -ness = shyness, dry + -ness = dryness, biology + -ist = biologist, economy + -ist = economist, baby + -hood = babyhood

Usually a **final silent *e*** is dropped before a suffix, but sometimes it's kept. The following chart shows the basic rules for adding suffixes to words that end in silent *e*.

ADDING SUFFIXES TO WORDS THAT END IN SILENT *E*

RULE	EXAMPLES
Drop the *e* before suffixes that begin with a vowel.	care + -ed = cared dine + -ing = dining move + -er = mover type + -ist = typist blue + -ish = bluish arrive + -al = arrival desire + -able = desirable accuse + -ation = accusation noise + -y = noisy
Some exceptions	mile + -age = mileage dye + -ing = dyeing
Drop the *e* and change *i* to *y* before the suffix *-ing* if the word ends in *ie.*	die + -ing = dying lie + -ing = lying tie + -ing = tying
Keep the *e* before suffixes that begin with *a* and *o* if the word ends in *ce* or *ge.*	dance + -able = danceable change + -able = changeable courage + -ous = courageous
Keep the *e* before suffixes that begin with a vowel if the word ends in *ee* or *oe.*	see + -ing = seeing agree + -able = agreeable canoe + -ing = canoeing hoe + -ing = hoeing
Some exceptions	free + -er = freer free + -est = freest
Keep the *e* before suffixes that begin with a consonant.	grace + -ful = graceful state + -hood = statehood like + -ness = likeness encourage + -ment = encouragement care + -less = careless sincere + -ly = sincerely

RULE	EXAMPLES
Some exceptions	awe + -ful = awful judge + -ment = judgment argue + -ment = argument true + -ly = truly due + -ly = duly whole + -ly = wholly
Drop *le* before the suffix *-ly* when the word ends with a consonant and *le.*	possible + -ly = possibly sniffle + -ly = sniffly sparkle + -ly = sparkly gentle + -ly = gently

When a word ends in *ll,* drop one *l* when you add the suffix *-ly.*

dull + -ly = dully
chill + -ly = chilly
full + -ly = fully
hill + -ly = hilly

Compound Words

Keep the original spelling of both parts of a compound word.

Remember that some compounds are one word, some are two words, and some are hyphenated. Check a dictionary when in doubt.

foot + lights = footlights
busy + body = busybody
book + case = bookcase
light + house = lighthouse
fish + hook = fishhook
with + hold = withhold
book + keeper = bookkeeper
heart + throb = heartthrob

Spelling Plurals

A singular noun names one person, place, thing, or idea. A plural noun names more than one. To form the plural of most nouns, you simply add *-s.* The following chart shows other basic rules.

GENERAL RULES FOR FORMING PLURALS

NOUNS ENDING IN	TO FORM PLURAL	EXAMPLES
ch, s, sh, x, z	Add *-es.*	lunch → lunches bus → buses dish → dishes box → boxes buzz → buzzes
a vowel and *y*	Add *-s.*	boy → boys turkey → turkeys
a consonant and *y*	Change *y* to *i* and add *-es.*	baby → babies penny → pennies
a vowel and *o*	Add *-s.*	radio → radios rodeo → rodeos
a consonant and *o*	Usually add *-es.*	potato → potatoes tomato → tomatoes hero → heroes echo → echoes
	Sometimes add *-s.*	zero → zeros photo → photos piano → pianos
f or *fe*	Usually change *f* to *v* and add *-s* or *-es.*	wife → wives knife → knives life → lives leaf → leaves half → halves shelf → shelves wolf → wolves thief → thieves
	Sometimes add *-s.*	roof → roofs chief → chiefs cliff → cliffs giraffe → giraffes

GRAMMAR/USAGE/MECHANICS

The plurals of **proper names** are formed by adding *-es* to names that end in *ch, s, sh, x,* or *z.*

EXAMPLE The **Woodriches** live on Elm Street.

EXAMPLE There are two **Jonases** in our class.

EXAMPLE Have you met your new neighbors, the **Gomezes?**

Just add *-s* to form the plural of all other proper names, including those that end in *y.*

EXAMPLE The **Kennedys** are a famous American family.

EXAMPLE I know three **Marys.**

EXAMPLE The last two **Januarys** have been especially cold.

To form the plural of a **compound noun written as one word,** follow the general rules for plurals. To form the plural of **hyphenated compound nouns** or **compound nouns of more than one word,** usually make the most important word plural.

EXAMPLE A dozen **mailboxes** stood in a row at the entrance to the housing development.

EXAMPLE The two women's **fathers-in-law** have never met.

EXAMPLE The three **post offices** are made of brick.

Some nouns have **irregular plural forms** that don't follow any rules.

man → men

woman → women

child → children

foot → feet

tooth → teeth

mouse → mice

goose → geese

ox → oxen

Some nouns have the same singular and plural forms. Most of these are the names of animals, and some of the plural forms may be spelled in more than one way.

deer → deer

sheep → sheep

head (cattle) → head

Sioux → Sioux

series → series

species → species

fish → fish *or* fishes

antelope → antelope *or* antelopes

buffalo → buffalo *or* buffaloes *or* buffalos

PRACTICE Spelling Rules

Find the misspelled word in each group and write it correctly.

1. recieve, believe, their
2. reelect, imature, unnecessary
3. reference, taxable, occasionnal
4. payed, merriment, hurrying
5. loving, probably, noticable
6. nightime, knickknack, taillight
7. potatoes, monkies, foxes
8. womens, mice, geese
9. succeed, secede, procede
10. livelihood, fryed, pitiful

15.2 IMPROVING YOUR SPELLING

You can improve your spelling by improving your study method. You can also improve your spelling by thoroughly learning certain common but frequently misspelled words.

HOW TO STUDY A WORD

By following a few simple steps, you can learn to spell new words. Pay attention to unfamiliar or hard-to-spell words in your reading. As you write, note words that you have trouble spelling. Then use the steps below to learn to spell those difficult words.

1. Say It

Look at the word and say it aloud. Say it again, pronouncing each syllable clearly.

2. See It

Close your eyes. Picture the word in your mind. Visualize the word letter by letter.

3. Write It

Look at the word again and write it two or three times. Then write the word without looking at the printed spelling.

4. Check It

Check your spelling. Did you spell the word correctly? If not, repeat each step until you can spell the word easily.

Get into the habit of using a dictionary to find the correct spelling of a word. How do you find a word if you can't spell it? Write down letters and letter combinations that could stand for the sound you hear at the beginning of the word. Try these possible spellings as you look for the word in a dictionary.

SPELLING PROBLEM WORDS

The following words are often misspelled. Look for your problem words in the list. What words would you add to the list?

GRAMMAR/USAGE/MECHANICS

Often Misspelled Words

absence
accidentally
accommodate
achievement
adviser
alcohol
all right
analyze
answer
athlete
attendant
ballet
beautiful
beginning
believe
beneficial
blaze
business
cafeteria
canceled
canoe
cemetery
changeable
choir
college
colonel
commercial
convenient
courageous
curiosity
definite
descend
develop
discipline
disease
dissatisfied
eligible
embarrass
envelope
environment
essential
familiar
February
foreign
forty
fulfill
funeral
genius
government
grammar
guarantee
height
humorous
hygiene
imaginary
immediate
incidentally
incredibly
jewelry
judgment
laboratory
leisure
library

license
maintenance
medicine
mischievous
misspell
modern
molasses
muscle
necessary
neighborhood
niece
ninety
noticeable
nuisance
occasion
original
pageant
parallel
permanent
physical
physician
picnic
pneumonia
privilege
probably
pronunciation
receipt
receive
recognize
recommend
restaurant
rhythm
ridiculous
schedule
sense
separate
similar
sincerely
souvenir
succeed
technology
theory
tomorrow
traffic
truly
unanimous
usually
vacuum
variety
various
Wednesday

PRACTICE Spelling Problem Words

Find each misspelled word and write it correctly.

1. That child is a notisable newsence.
2. What is the occassion for the pajent?
3. Would you recomend that resterant?
4. Should I close this letter with *Yours sinserely* or *Yours truely?*
5. Do you beleive the reason for his absense?
6. He said his father's busness was in a blase.
7. Do you have an anser for the problems in the cafateria?
8. I have a definate curiousity about that cemetary.
9. Don't embarras yourself at the funral.
10. Is absolute quiet neccesary in the liberry?

15.3 USING CONTEXT CLUES

The surest way to learn the meaning of a new word is to use a dictionary. However, you won't always have a dictionary handy. You can often figure out the meaning of an unfamiliar word by looking for clues in the words and sentences around it. These surrounding words and sentences are called the context.

USING SPECIFIC CONTEXT CLUES

Writers often give clues to the meaning of unfamiliar words. Sometimes they even tell you exactly what a word means. The following chart shows five types of specific context clues. It also gives examples of words that help you identify the type of context clue.

GRAMMAR/USAGE/MECHANICS

INTERPRETING CLUE WORDS IN CONTEXT

TYPE OF CONTEXT CLUE	CLUE WORDS	EXAMPLES
Definition The meaning of the unfamiliar word is given in the sentence.	in other words or that is which is which means	Jamake *inscribed* his name; **that is,** he wrote his name on the card. Jaleesa put the wet clay pot in the *kiln,* **or** oven, to harden.
Example The meaning of the unfamiliar word is explained through familiar examples.	for example for instance including like such as	Some people are afraid of *arachnids,* **such as** spiders and ticks. The new program has been *beneficial* for the school; **for example,** test scores are up, and absences are down.

chart continued on next page

TYPE OF CONTEXT CLUE	CLUE WORDS	EXAMPLES
Comparison The unfamiliar word is compared to a familiar word or phrase.	also identical like likewise resembling same similarly too	Maria thought the dress was *gaudy.* Lisa, **too,** thought it was flashy. A *rampant* growth of weeds and vines surrounded the old house. The barn was **likewise** covered with uncontrolled and wild growth.
Contrast The unfamiliar word is contrasted to a familiar word or phrase.	but however on the contrary on the other hand unlike	Robins are *migratory* birds, **unlike** sparrows, which live in the same region all year round. Martin didn't *bungle* the arrangements for the party; **on the contrary,** he handled everything smoothly and efficiently.
Cause and effect The unfamiliar word is explained as part of a cause-and-effect relationship.	as a result because consequently therefore thus	**Because** this rubber raft is so *buoyant,* it will float easily. Kevin is very *credulous;* **consequently,** he'll believe almost anything.

USING GENERAL CONTEXT

Sometimes there are no special clue words to help you understand an unfamiliar word. However, you can still use the general context. That is, you can use the details in the words or sentences around the unfamiliar word. Read the following sentences:

> Joel was chosen student **liaison** to the faculty. Everyone hoped his appointment would improve communication between the students and the teachers.

The first sentence tells you that Joel is serving as a kind of connection between the students and the faculty. The word *communication* helps you figure out that being a liaison means acting as a line of communication between two groups.

Calvin and Hobbes **by Bill Watterson**

PRACTICE Using Context Clues

Use context clues to figure out the meaning of the italicized word. Write the meaning. Then write definition, example, comparison, contrast, cause and effect, *or* general *to tell what type of context clue you used to define the word.*

1. Dr. Patel specializes in *oncology,* which is the study of tumors.
2. The *susurration* of voices from the next room was like the whisper of the breeze in the trees.
3. Cyril is the most *pusillanimous* person I've ever known; Raji, on the other hand, is as brave as a lion.
4. My *olfactory* senses became irritated as a result of the foul-smelling smoke.
5. The author takes an *omniscient* point of view; she reports what all her characters are thinking and feeling.
6. *Bovines,* including domestic cattle and the American bison, are an important source of food for many cultures.

GRAMMAR/USAGE/MECHANICS

7. How I hate these *ubiquitous* commercial advertisements! They're in your mailbox, on television, on the radio, on billboards, even on the Internet!
8. *Indolence* is not a characteristic of successful people. In other words, lazy people don't succeed.
9. His handwriting is *illegible.* It resembles chicken scratchings in a barnyard.
10. Kareem does his chores *conscientiously,* but his sister, Rani, must be reminded constantly.

15.4 ROOTS, PREFIXES, AND SUFFIXES

You can often figure out the meaning of an unfamiliar word by dividing it into parts. The main part of the word is called the root, and it carries the word's basic meaning. A root is often a word by itself. For example, *read* is a word. When a prefix or a suffix is added to it, *read* becomes a root, as in *unreadable.*

Prefixes and suffixes can be added to a root to change its meaning. A prefix is added to the beginning of a root. A suffix is added to the end of a root. A word can have both a prefix and a suffix: *un* + *read* + *able* = *unreadable.*

ROOTS

The root of a word carries the main meaning. Some roots, like *read,* can stand alone. Other roots may have parts added to make a complete word. For example, the root *port* ("carry") by itself is a place to which ships carry goods. Combined with a prefix, it can become *report, deport,* or *transport.* Add a suffix and you can get *reporter, deportment,* or *transportation.*

Learning the meanings of common roots can help you figure out the meanings of many unfamiliar words. The following chart shows some common roots.

ROOTS

ROOTS	WORDS	MEANINGS
bio means "life"	biography	a written story of a person's life
	biosphere	the part of the atmosphere where living things exist
dec or *deca* means "ten"	decade	ten years
	decathlon	an athletic contest consisting of ten events
dent means "tooth"	dentist	a doctor who treats the teeth
	trident	a spear with three prongs, or teeth
dict means "to say"	dictionary	a book of words
	dictator	one who rules absolutely
	predict	to say before (something happens)
duc or *duct* means "to lead"	conductor	one who leads or directs
	produce	to bring into existence
flect or *flex* means "to bend"	flexible	able to bend
	reflect	to bend back (light)
graph means "to write" or "writing"	autograph	one's own signature
	biography	a written story of a person's life
lect means "speech"	lecture	a speech
	dialect	the speech of a certain region
miss or *mit* means "to send"	omit	to fail to send or include
	missile	something sent through the air or by mail
phon means "sound" or "voice"	phonograph	an instrument for playing sounds
	telephone	a device for transmitting voices over a distance
port means "to carry"	transport	to carry across a distance
	porter	one who carries baggage

GRAMMAR/USAGE/MECHANICS

ROOTS	WORDS	MEANINGS
script means "writing"	prescription	a written order for medicine
	postscript	a message added at the end of a letter
spec or *spect* means "to look" or "to watch"	spectator	one who watches
	inspect	to look closely
	prospect	to look for (mineral deposits)
tele means "distant"	telephone	a device for transmitting voices over a distance
	television	a device for transmitting pictures over a distance
tri means "three"	triathlon	an athletic contest consisting of three events
	tricycle	a three-wheeled vehicle
vid or *vis* means "to see"	vision	the ability to see
	videotape	a recording of visual images
voc or *vok* means "to call"	vocation	an inclination, or call, to a certain pursuit
	revoke	to recall or take back

PREFIXES

The following chart shows some prefixes and their meanings. Notice that some prefixes, such as *dis-*, *in-*, *non-*, and *un-*, have the same or nearly the same meaning. A single prefix may have more than one meaning. The prefix *in-*, for example, can mean "into," as in *inject,* as well as "not," as in *indirect.* The prefix *re-* can mean "again" or "back."

Note that *il-*, *im-*, *in-*, and *ir-* are variations of the same prefix. *Il-* is used before roots that begin with *l (illegal); im-* is used before roots that begin with *m (immature);* and *ir-* is used before roots that begin with *r (irregular). In-* is used before all other letters.

PREFIXES

CATEGORIES	PREFIXES	WORDS	MEANINGS
Prefixes that reverse meanings	*de-* means "remove from" or "reduce"	defrost devalue	to remove frost to reduce the value of
	dis- means "not" or "do the opposite of"	disagreeable disappear	not agreeable to do the opposite of appear
	in-, il-, im-, and *ir-* mean "not"	incomplete illegal immature irregular	not complete not legal not mature not regular
	mis- means "bad," "badly," "wrong," or "wrongly"	misfortune misbehave misdeed misjudge	bad fortune to behave badly a wrong deed to judge wrongly
	non- means "not" or "without"	nonathletic nonfat	not athletic without fat
	un- means "not" or "do the opposite of"	unhappy untie	not happy to do the opposite of tie
Prefixes that show relationship	*co-* means "with," "together," or "partner"	coworker coexist coauthor	one who works with another to exist together an author who writes as a partner with another
	inter- means "between"	interscholastic	between schools
	post- means "after"	postseason	after the regular season
	pre- means "before"	preseason	before the regular season

GRAMMAR/USAGE/MECHANICS

CATEGORIES	PREFIXES	WORDS	MEANINGS
	re- means "back" or "again"	repay recheck	to pay back to check again
	sub- means "under" or "below"	submarine substandard	under the sea below standard
	super- means "more than"	superabundant	more than abundant
	trans- means "across"	transport	to carry across a distance
Prefixes that show judgment	*anti-* means "against"	antiwar	against war
	pro- means "in favor of"	progovernment	in favor of the government
Prefixes that show number	*bi-* means "two"	bicycle	a two-wheeled vehicle
	semi- means "half" or "partly"	semicircle semisweet	half a circle partly sweet
	uni- means "one"	unicycle	a one-wheeled vehicle

SUFFIXES

A suffix added to a word can change the word's part of speech as well as its meaning. For example, adding the suffix *-er* to *read* (a verb) makes *reader* (a noun). Adding *-less* to *faith* (a noun) makes *faithless* (an adjective).

The following chart shows some common suffixes and their meanings. Notice that some suffixes, such as *-er, -or,* and *-ist,* have the same or nearly the same meaning. A single suffix may have more than one meaning. The suffix *-er,* for example, can also mean "more," as in *bigger.*

SUFFIXES

CATEGORIES	SUFFIXES	WORDS	MEANINGS
Suffixes that mean "one who" or "that which"	*-ee, -eer*	employee charioteer	one who is employed one who drives a chariot
	-er, -or	worker sailor	one who works one who sails
	-ian	physician musician	one who practices medicine (once called physic) one who plays or studies music
	-ist	pianist chemist	one who plays the piano one who works in chemistry
Suffixes that mean "full of" or "having"	*-ful*	joyful suspenseful beautiful	full of joy full of suspense having beauty
	-ous	furious famous courageous	full of fury having fame having courage
Suffixes that show a state, a condition, or a quality	*-hood*	falsehood	quality of being false
	-ness	happiness	state of being happy
	-ship	friendship	condition of being friends
Suffixes that show an action or process or its result	*-ance, -ence*	performance conference	action of performing process of conferring
	-ation, -ion	flirtation invention	action of flirting result of inventing
	-ment	argument arrangement enjoyment	result of arguing result of arranging process of enjoying

GRAMMAR/USAGE/MECHANICS

Suffixes, *continued*

CATEGORIES	SUFFIXES	WORDS	MEANINGS
Suffixes that mean "relating to," "characterized by," or "like"	*-al*	musical comical	relating to music relating to comedy
	-ish	childish foolish	like a child like a fool
	-y	witty hairy	characterized by wit characterized by hair
Other common suffixes	*-able* and *-ible* mean "capable of," "fit for," or "likely to"	breakable collectible agreeable	capable of being broken fit for collecting likely to agree
	-ize means "to cause to be" or "to become"	visualize familiarize	to cause to be made visual to become familiar
	-less means "without"	hopeless careless	without hope done without care
	-ly means "in a (certain) manner"	easily sadly	in an easy manner in a sad manner

Notice that sometimes the spelling of a word changes when a suffix is added. For example, when *-ous* is added to *fury*, the *y* in *fury* changes to *i*. See pages 301–304 to learn more about spelling words with suffixes.

More than one suffix can be added to a single word. The following examples show how suffixes can change a single root word.

peace **[noun]**

peace + ful = peaceful **[adjective]**

peace + ful + ly = peacefully **[adverb]**

peace + ful + ness = peacefulness **[noun]**

PRACTICE Roots, Prefixes, and Suffixes

Divide the following words. Write their parts in three columns headed prefix, root, *and* suffix. *In a fourth column, write another word that has the same prefix or the same suffix or both. Then write a definition for each word.*

1. semitropical
2. prediction
3. disadvantageous
4. deductible
5. mismanagement
6. reflector
7. invisible
8. transmitter
9. unmercifully
10. immeasureableness

GRAMMAR/USAGE/MECHANICS

Part Three

Composition

Chapter 16

The Writing Process

Writing is a process done in different stages. These stages are listed below.

- prewriting
- drafting
- revising and editing
- proofreading
- publishing and presenting

These stages may be repeated several times during the Writing Process, and they need not necessarily follow one another in order. You can go back and forth between steps as often as you wish. You can repeat whichever steps you need to repeat until you get the result you want. The diagram on the next page shows you how the Writing Process works for most people.

THE WRITING PROCESS

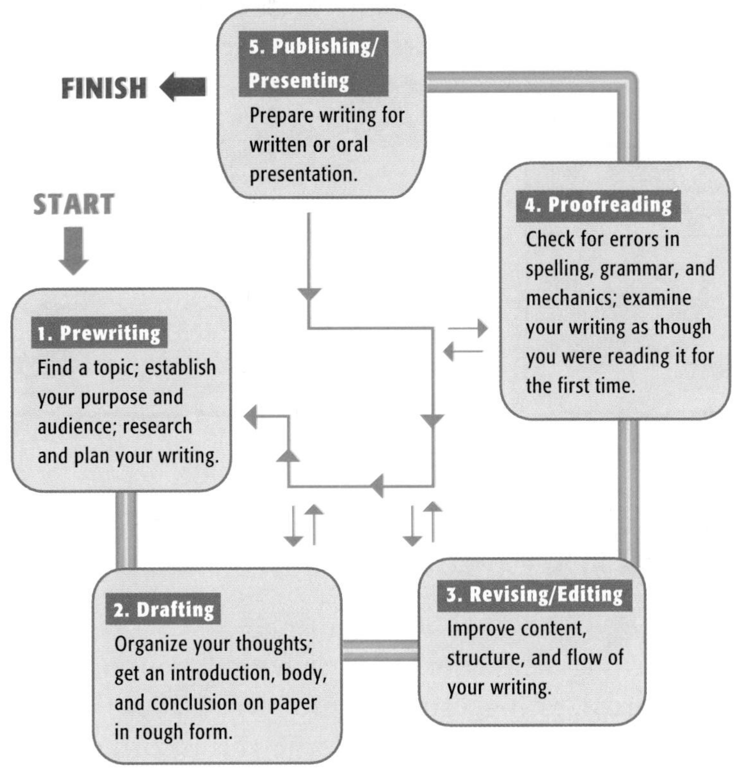

STAGE 1: PREWRITING

During Prewriting, you decide what you want to write about by exploring ideas, feelings, and memories. Prewriting is the stage in which you not only decide what your topic is, but

- you refine, focus, and explore your topic
- you gather information about your topic
- you make notes about what you want to say about it
- you think about your audience and your purpose

Your audience is whoever will read your work. Your purpose is what you hope to accomplish through your writing.

After you've decided on a topic and explored it, making notes about what you will include, you will need to arrange and organize your ideas. This is also done during the Prewriting stage, before you actually draft your paper.

There are many techniques you can use to generate ideas and define and explore your topic.

By permission of Doug Marlette and Creators Syndicate.

CHOOSING AND EXPLORING YOUR TOPIC

Keeping a Journal

Many writing ideas come to us as we go about our daily lives. A journal, or log, can help you record your thoughts from day to day. You can then refer to this record when you're searching for a writing topic. Every day you can write in your journal your experiences, observations, thoughts, feelings, and opinions. Keep newspaper and magazine clippings, photos, songs, poems, and anything else that catches your interest. They might later suggest questions that lead to writing topics. Try to add to your journal every day. Use your imagination. Be inventive and don't worry about grammar, spelling, or punctuation. This is your own personal record. It's for your benefit only, and no one else will read it.

COMPOSITION

Freewriting

Freewriting means just what it says: writing freely without worrying about grammar, punctuation, spelling, logic, or anything. You just write what comes to your mind. Choose a topic and a time limit and then just start writing ideas as they come to you. If you run out of ideas, repeat the same word over and over until a new idea occurs to you. When the time is up, review what you've written. The ideas that most interest you are likely to be the ones that will be most worth writing about. You can use your journal as a place for freewriting, or you can just take a piece of paper and start the process. The important thing is to allow your mind to follow its own path as you explore a topic. You'll be surprised where it might lead you.

1. Let your thoughts flow; write ideas, memories, anything that comes to mind.
2. Don't edit or judge your thoughts; just write them down. You can evaluate them later. In fact, evaluating your ideas at this point would probably dry up the flow. Accepting any idea that comes is the way to encourage more ideas.
3. Don't worry about spelling, punctuation, grammar, or even sense; just keep writing.
4. If you get stuck, just keep writing the same word, phrase, or sentence over and over until another idea occurs to you.

COMPOSITION

Brainstorming

Brainstorming is another technique you can use to generate ideas. It's often effective to do your brainstorming with other people because one idea can spark other ideas. Start with a key word or idea. Then list other ideas as they occur to you. Don't worry about the order. Just let your ideas flow freely from one to the next.

1. Choose someone to list ideas as they are called out. Use a chalkboard or a large pad of paper on an easel so that everyone can see the list.
2. Start with a topic or a question.
3. Encourage everyone to join in freely.
4. Accept all ideas; don't evaluate them now.
5. Follow each idea as far as it goes.

Clustering

Write your topic in the middle of a piece of paper. As you think about the topic, briefly write down everything that comes to mind. Each time you write something, draw a circle around it and draw lines to connect those circles to the main idea in the center. Continue to think about the secondary ideas and add offshoots to them. Draw circles around those related ideas and connect them to the secondary ideas. (See the model on the facing page.)

Clustering TIP

1. Start with a key word or phrase circled in the center of your paper.
2. Brainstorm to discover related ideas; circle each one and connect it to the central idea.
3. Branch out with new ideas that add details to existing ideas. Use as many circles as you need.
4. Review your chart, looking for ideas that interest you.

Clustering

Collecting Information

Whether you're deciding on your topic or exploring a topic you've already chosen, you need to get information about it. You can begin the process of collecting information with one or more of the following activities: asking questions, doing library research, observing, and interviewing. You may find that you'll want to use all four of these methods to gather information.

Asking Questions To discover the facts you need, begin by writing a list of questions about your topic. Different questions serve different purposes, and knowing what kind of question to ask can be as important as knowing how to ask it clearly. The chart on the following page will help you categorize your list of questions.

PERSONAL QUESTIONS	ask about your responses to a topic. They help you explore your experiences and tastes.
CREATIVE QUESTIONS	ask you to compare your subject to something else or to imagine observing your subject as someone else might. Such questions can expand your perspective on a subject.
ANALYTICAL QUESTIONS	ask about structure and function: How is this topic constructed? What is its purpose? Analytical questions help you evaluate and draw conclusions.
INFORMATIONAL QUESTIONS	ask for facts, statistics, or details.

Library Research If your topic requires information you don't already have, your school or public library is the best place to find what you need. The following tips can aid you in your search.

COMPOSITION

Library TIP

1. Search for books by title, author, and subject, using either the card catalog or the online computer system.
2. Use the subject headings for each listing as cross-references to related material.
3. Browse among other books in the section in which you locate a useful book.
4. Jot down the author, title, and call number of each book you think you will use.
5. Record the titles of books that don't provide help (so you won't search for them again).
6. Examine each book's bibliography for related titles.
7. Try to be an independent researcher but ask a librarian for help if you can't locate much information on your topic.

If you do your research on the Internet, evaluate your sources carefully and always find at least one more source to verify each point. The reliability of Internet information varies a great deal. It's a good idea to use print sources to verify information you find on the Internet, if possible.

Observing One good starting point for exploring a topic is simply to observe closely and list the details you see. After you've listed the details, arrange them in categories. The categories you choose depend on the details you observe and your writing goal. For example, you might want to organize your details by space order, by time order, or by order of importance.

Interviewing Get your information directly from the source: Interview someone. By asking questions, you can get the specific information you need or want. Follow these steps:

BEFORE THE INTERVIEW	Make the appointment.
	Investigate your topic and learn about your source.
	Prepare four or five basic questions.
DURING THE INTERVIEW	Ask informational questions (who, what, where, when, why, and how).
	Listen carefully.
	Ask follow-up questions.
	Take accurate notes (or tape-record with permission).
AFTER THE INTERVIEW	Write a more detailed account of the interview.
	Contact your source to clarify points or to double-check facts.

IDENTIFYING PURPOSE AND AUDIENCE

Purpose

Before you start to write, you must determine the primary purpose for your writing: to inform or explain, to persuade, to amuse or entertain, to narrate, or to describe. Sometimes you might want to accomplish more than one purpose, so you will have a primary purpose and a secondary purpose. To determine the primary purpose, answer these questions:

1. Do I want to tell a story?
2. Do I want to describe someone or something?
3. Do I want to inform my readers about the topic or to explain something about it?
4. Do I want to persuade my readers to change their minds about something or take some action?
5. Do I want to amuse or entertain?

Audience

Your audience is anyone who will be reading your writing. Sometimes you write just for yourself. Most often, however, you write to share information with others. Your audience might include a few friends or family members, your classmates, the population at large, or just your teacher. As you write, consider these questions:

1. Who will my audience be? What do I want to say to them?
2. What do my readers already know about my topic?
3. What types of information will interest my audience?

COMPOSITION

ARRANGING AND ORGANIZING IDEAS

Once you've gathered your information and ideas, you can choose from many kinds of details—examples, facts, statistics, reasons, and concrete and sensory details—to support your main idea. As a writer, you need to organize these details and put them in order. Your purpose and main idea will determine which kinds of supporting details you include as well as the order in which you arrange them. Some possible patterns of organization are

- chronological order (by time)
- spatial order (relationships based on space, place, or setting)
- order of importance
- cause and effect (events described as reason and result, motive and reaction, stimulus and response)
- comparison and contrast (measuring items against one another to show similarities and differences)

The technique you choose to organize details might be as simple as making a list or an outline that shows how the details will be grouped under larger subtopics or headings. You can also organize details visually by making a chart. You might better be able to see a plan for organizing your paper when you see the relationships among the parts of your topic.

STAGE 2: DRAFTING

When you write your draft, your goal is to organize the facts and details you have accumulated into unified paragraphs. Make sure each paragraph has a main idea and does not bring in unrelated information. The main idea should be stated in a topic sentence, and it must be supported by details that explain and clarify it. Details can be facts and statistics, examples or incidents, or sensory details.

Writing a draft, or turning your ideas into paragraphs, is a stage in the Writing Process and a tool in itself. During Prewriting, you started to organize your details. You will continue to do this as you write your draft because you might find links between ideas that give new meanings to your words and phrases. Continue to organize your details using one of the methods discussed in Prewriting.

To make your sentences interesting, vary their length. Don't use too many short sentences. Doing so will make your writing sound choppy. Use some short sentences and some long ones, but don't connect all your ideas with the word *and*.

You can use the ideas on sentence combining in Chapter 14 to combine and vary your sentences. You can use prepositional phrases, appositive phrases, and adjective and adverb clauses to make your sentences more interesting.

Your writing will also be easier for your audience to understand if you follow the Writing Tip below.

Writing Tip

Your composition should consist of three parts: the introduction, the body, and the conclusion (see the outline on page 370). Begin your paper with an **introduction** that grabs the reader's interest and sets the tone. The introduction usually gives the reader a brief explanation of what your paper is about and often includes the **thesis.** The thesis states your paper's main idea. The main idea is what you're trying to prove or what you're supporting.

Each paragraph in the **body,** or main part, of your paper should have a topic sentence that states what the paragraph is about. The rest of the paragraph should include details that support the topic sentence. Similarly, each topic sentence should support the thesis, or main idea of the paper.

End your paper with a good **conclusion** that gives a feeling of completeness. You might conclude your paper in any of the following ways:

- Summarize what you've said in the body of your paper.
- Restate the main idea (using different words).
- Give a final example or fact.
- Make a comment on the topic or give a personal reaction to it.
- End with a quotation that sums up the topic or comments on it.
- Call for some action (especially in persuasive papers).

STAGE 3: REVISING/EDITING

The purposes of Revising are to make sure that your writing is clear and well organized, that it accomplishes your goals, and that it reaches your audience. The word *revision* means "seeing again." You need to look at your writing again, seeing it as another person might. To accomplish this, you might just read your paper very carefully, or you might tape-record yourself reading your paper aloud and then listen to the tape to evaluate what you've written. The revision phase, however, often includes other people. You might share your writing with another student, a small group of students, or your teacher, who can suggest improvements. The ideas and opinions of others will tell you whether you're achieving your goals. After you evaluate your work, you might want to move some sentences around or change them completely. You might want to add or cut information. Mark these changes right on your draft and then include them in your final copy.

The revision stage is the point at which you can

- improve paragraphs
- use self-evaluation and peer evaluation
- check content and structure
- make sure the language is specific and descriptive
- check unity and coherence
- check style and tone

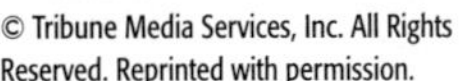

COMPOSITION

Writing Tip

It was once acceptable to use the masculine pronouns *he*, *him*, and *his* to refer to nouns that might be either male or female. This practice is now considered unfair and outdated. Instead of writing *A reporter must check his facts*, you can write *Reporters must check their facts* or *Reporters must check the facts* or *A reporter must check his or her facts.* Of course, if you're writing about a specific person, you should use a suitable pronoun: *This reporter loves her work.*

Parallelism

The phrases and clauses of a sentence must be **parallel**. This means that elements that have the same function in a sentence must be written in the same form.

Jo likes swimming and to go to the library.

In this sentence, *swimming and to go to the library* is a compound direct object. It tells what Jo likes. However, the first element, *swimming,* is a gerund. The second, *to go to the library,* is an infinitive phrase. To make the elements parallel, make both gerunds or make both infinitive phrases:

Jo likes swimming and going to the library.

Jo likes to swim and to go to the library.

Identify the elements that should be parallel in each sentence below. Then revise the faulty parallelism in each sentence.

1. The tennis player's assets were a fast serve, a strong backhand, and playing a good baseline game.
2. Symptoms of chicken pox include a rash and having a fever.
3. To visit Africa and climbing Mt. Kilimanjaro are Ted's dreams.
4. The actor is a funny comedian and talented in dramatic roles.
5. The city streets were neither clean nor safety.

COMPOSITION

STAGE 4: PROOFREADING

The purposes of Proofreading are to make sure that you've spelled all words correctly and that your sentences are grammatically correct. Proofread your writing and correct mistakes in capitalization, punctuation, and spelling. Refer to the following chart for Proofreading symbols to help you during this stage of the Writing Process.

Proofreading Marks		
Marks	**Meaning**	**Example**
∧	Insert	My granmother is eighty-six years old.
℘	Delete	She grew up on a dairry farm.
# ∧	Insert space	She milkedcows every morning.
⁀	Close up space	She fed the chickens in the barn yard.
≡	Capitalize	times have changed.
/	Make lowercase	Machines now do the Milking.
◯ sp	Check spelling	Chickens are fed autommatically. sp
∽	Switch order	Modern farms are like more factories.
¶	New paragraph	¶ Last year I returned to the farm.

STAGE 5: PUBLISHING/PRESENTING

This is the stage at which you share your work with others. You might read your work aloud in class, submit it to the school newspaper, or give it to a friend to read. There are many avenues for Presenting your work.

For Better or For Worse **by Lynn Johnston**

Chapter 17

Modes of Writing

17.1 DESCRIPTIVE WRITING

An effective written description is one that presents a clear picture to the reader. You can use descriptive writing to help your reader see what you see, hear what you hear, and feel what you feel. Good descriptive writing involves these skills:

- using your senses to observe
- selecting precise details
- organizing your ideas

OBSERVING AND TAKING NOTES

Writing a good description begins with careful observation. You use your sight, touch, smell, hearing, and taste to experience the world. These sensory details can add richness to your descriptions of people, places, things, and experiences. Before you take notes, close your eyes and picture what you want to describe. Then list words and phrases that tell how it looks, feels, smells, sounds, or tastes.

If you can't find just the right word, turn to a **thesaurus.** A thesaurus is a reference book that groups together words with similar meanings.

Using Your Experience and Imagination

You are able to describe people, places, things, and situations because you first perceive the details through your senses. You see that your friend has curly red hair. You smell the hot, buttered popcorn at the movies. You can take those details from your own experience and use them in descriptive writing.

Focusing on the Details

Descriptive writing often starts with a memory or an observation—something that catches your attention. The details that make someone or something stay in your mind become the raw material for composing a description.

Start with your first impressions—the things you first notice about a person, a place, a thing, or an experience. Then start gathering details. One way is to identify the small things that help produce each impression.

Asking yourself questions can also help you choose details. For example, you might ask how something appears at different times of the day, what senses you use to observe it, or to what you might compare it.

WRITING THE DESCRIPTION

Using Specific Words

A good description includes specific nouns, vivid verbs, and exact adjectives.

- A specific noun, *beagle* or *Rover,* is more informative than the general noun *dog*.
- A vivid verb such as *stroll, amble, saunter, march, tramp,* or *hike* tells the reader more than a pale verb like *walk.*

- Exact adjectives—*seventy-six* rather than *many; lanky, gaunt, bony,* or *gangly* instead of *thin*—give a clearer picture than vague, indefinite ones.

Technology Tip

Your word-processing program may have a built-in thesaurus to help you find the precise word you need.

Ordering Descriptive Details

When details are presented in a sensible order, readers get a picture in their minds. To order your own descriptive details, you might think of your eye as a camera lens. First, choose a starting point. Then decide on the best way to move your eye's camera across your subject. One way is to start at the front and move toward the back. Another way is to start at one side and move toward the other side. Still another way is to start from a far point and move to a near one. The order you use should be one that will make sense to your readers. When you're writing a description, make a sketch of the scene. The sketch can help you decide how to order your details.

A painter arranges details so the viewer sees an ordered picture. A writer describes details so the reader imagines a scene clearly. Writers, like painters, arrange the details of a scene in a certain order and for a particular reason. How you order your details depends on your purpose. Describing a skyscraper from bottom to top emphasizes the building's height. A description of the Grand Canyon might show details in the order a descending hiker sees them. Writers can order details in several ways, depending on the point in space that seems a logical starting place. Details can be ordered from top to bottom, from near to far, or from left to right. Ordering your details according to their place in the picture is called **spatial order.**

COMPOSITION

Using Transitions

When you use spatial order, you must give your audience a way to picture the scene as you move from one detail to the next. Transition words, such as *under, to the right,* and *behind,* help link details so readers can follow the path you've made.

Transition words show how the details in a description are related, and they make the description easier to follow. Transitions are powerful tools. Without them, you just have a list of details—not a description. Transition words and phrases can turn the details into vivid images. The chart on the next page shows some additional transition words and phrases you can use.

TRANSITION WORDS AND PHRASES		
above	between	nearby
among	beyond	over
around	in back of	overhead
before	in front of	past
behind	in the distance	to the left of
below	inside	to the right of
beside	near	under

SUMMARY

As you write your description, use sensory details to bring your subject to life. Remember these tips:

- Use precise language.
- Follow spatial order.
- Include transitions.

COMPOSITION

17.2 NARRATIVE WRITING

A narrative is a story or an account of an event. There are historical narratives, fictional narratives, and real-life narratives. When you write a story, or narrative, you answer the question *What happened?* Your story will need a beginning, a middle, and an end. It will also need a setting, a conflict and solution, characters, and, perhaps, dialogue.

Plot Suppose you've seen a movie, and a friend asks you what the movie was about. You would probably tell what happened through a series of events. What happens in a narrative is called the **plot.**

Characters As you talk about the events of the plot, you will find yourself talking about the **characters.** Characters are the people or animals that take part in the events.

Setting A story also has a **setting.** The setting puts the characters in a certain place at a certain time. Stories can be set in the present, the past, or the future. What happens in the story and how characters look and act often depend on the time when the events take place.

EXPLORING NARRATIVE IDEAS

The plot of most good stories centers on a problem faced by a character. Focusing on a problem that needs solving is one good way to come up with story ideas.

Once you have an idea you like, you can start developing it into a full-length story. Asking yourself questions like those listed in the chart below will help you plan a series of events. Some events will help solve the problem in your story. Others may make the solution more difficult.

QUESTIONS ABOUT STORY IDEAS
1. What is the problem?
2. What characters are involved?
3. What happened before?
4. What will happen next?
5. What is the solution to the problem?

COMPOSITION

Planning Your Story

Plan some elements of your story before you begin writing. Think about the characters and events and how the setting affects them. Writing down some details about the important story elements—plot, characters, and setting—can ease you into writing.

Establishing Your Point of View

In narrative writing, the point of view is important. Some stories are told by a main character in the first person—using *I* or *we*. First-person narratives tell only what the narrator witnesses and thinks. The reader sees all the events through the narrator's eyes and views them as the narrator views them. Other stories are told by an observer in the third person—using *he, she,* or *they.* The narrator of a third-person story may describe events from a single character's view, or the narrator may reveal the thoughts and feelings of all the characters.

WRITING YOUR STORY

Your narrative will eventually bring together plot, setting, and characters. As you write, focus on one of these three elements. Choose the element that seems most striking. Then start writing about this element and notice how the other elements find their way into the story.

Writing Tip

1. Start writing and keep writing.
2. Let your story tell itself.
3. Try to see and hear your story as you write. Think of your story as a movie unfolding before your eyes.
4. Take a break if you get stuck.

Beginning Your Story

A good story begins by grabbing the reader's attention. Think about what makes you keep reading a story. Is it an exciting plot? Intriguing characters? An unusual writing style? Some writers work and rework the beginning of a story until they get it just the way they want it. Other writers draft the entire story first. Then they look for the catchiest line or the first dramatic moment and move that to the beginning.

Sometimes revising a story opening means looking at the rest of what you've written to find the best place to start. You might look for the most engaging sentences and start your story at that point.

Other times you may keep the beginning you have but make a few changes. Cutting unimportant words or adding descriptive details can give more impact to your story beginning. Remember that a good story beginning is what gets your readers interested and keeps them reading.

Keeping a Story on Track

When you begin to write your narrative, you may find that you have too many details to tell. Choose only the details that are essential to your story. If you do this, your readers won't get confused by ideas that don't really matter. Sometimes you may have to cut out some details in order to keep the most important details clear. You may be able to use the details you cut out at another time in another story.

Putting Events in Order

To tell a story that is clear, the events and details must be arranged in a logical order. After you've chosen the important events for your narrative, you need to place them in some particular order. **Chronological order** is an effective way to organize your story. A story is in chronological order when the events are presented in the time order in which they occurred. When you use time order, you tell what happened first, second, and so on. You may use words like *then, next,* and *later* or phrases like *in the meantime, early in the morning,* and *about nine o'clock that night.* These words will help your readers follow your story.

THE FAR SIDE By GARY LARSON

COMPOSITION

Using Transitions

Certain words and phrases, called **transitions,** can help readers keep track of the order of events in your writing. Some examples of transitions are *before, after, until then, next, first, later, afterward,* and *finally.*

Writing Tip

In writing a narrative, vary your transitions. If you always use *first, next,* and *finally,* your writing may sound dull.

Writing Dialogue

Dialogue is the words spoken by the characters in a narrative. Well-written dialogue can help bring characters and events to life. What characters say, and how they say it, will often reveal what they're like. Dialogue can help show the moods, interests, and personalities of different characters.

Your dialogue will sound natural if your characters talk the way real people talk. You can use slang, sentence fragments, contractions, and descriptions of facial expressions and body language.

When you write dialogue, you need to help your readers keep track of who is speaking.

- Enclose the exact words of a speaker in quotation marks.
- Use phrases such as *Molly said* or *Jake replied.*
- Begin a new paragraph for each speaker.

Finishing the Job

Every well-written narrative has a conclusion. One type of conclusion sums up the story and reflects on what happened. The conclusion should give your audience the feeling that the story is complete.

SUMMARY

A narrative has plot, characters, and setting. These three elements contribute to a conflict and a solution. In writing a narrative, remember these tips:

- Establish a point of view.
- Reveal your characters' personalities through appropriate dialogue.
- Make the order of the events clear with transitions.

COMPOSITION

17.3 EXPOSITORY WRITING

The goal of expository writing is to explain or inform. The following chart shows four approaches to expository writing.

These approaches can be used alone, or they can be combined in any expository piece of writing.

APPROACHES TO EXPOSITORY WRITING	
APPROACH	**Example**
DEFINITION	*Sivuquad,* a name for St. Lawrence Island, means "squeezed dry." The islanders believed that a giant had made the island from dried mud.
COMPARE-CONTRAST	Coastal fishing fleets often stay at sea for days or weeks. Long-range fishing vessels may remain at sea for months.
PROCESS	To breathe, a whale surfaces in a forward rolling motion. For two seconds, it blows out and breathes in as much as twenty-one hundred quarts of air.
CAUSE-EFFECT	The discovery of oil and gas in Alaska in 1968 led to widespread development in that region of the world.

DEFINING

Defining a term or an idea is one approach to expository writing. You can give a formal definition or a personal definition. In a formal definition, you should provide specific qualities of the term you're explaining to help your audience understand it. For a personal definition, you might use real-life examples and vivid details. These examples and details will express your personal feelings about the idea or term.

COMPOSITION

Organize Your Definition Begin your research with a dictionary or other reliable source. After you've written the basic definition or idea, you can add details. When you write your draft, try different orders of organization. You might want to start with the basic definition and move to a broader sense of the term, or you could begin with details and examples and conclude with the basic definition.

COMPARING AND CONTRASTING

Comparison-contrast is another kind of expository writing. When you compare two things, you explain how they're similar. When you contrast two things, you explain how they're different. Comparing and contrasting two items can be a useful way of explaining them.

Examine Your Subjects A good way to begin your comparison-contrast piece is with a careful examination. First, think about one subject and list descriptive details that go with that subject. Then make a list of the same kinds of details for your other subject. For example, if you were going to compare Superman and Batman, you might note that Batman travels by car and wears a mask and a cape. Then you would make a list of the same kinds of details for Superman.

Sort What You See Once you've listed some details, you can sort them for comparison and contrast. At this point, some writers use a Venn diagram like the one below. A Venn diagram is made of two ovals or circles. Each circle contains the details of one of the subjects. Details that the two subjects have in common go where the circles overlap.

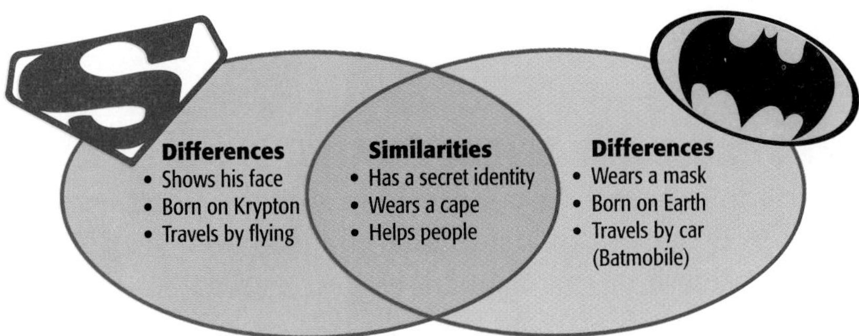

After you've made a Venn diagram, you're ready to write. Details you pull from the middle of the Venn diagram are similarities. Details pulled from the outsides are differences.

Organize the Details There are two ways to organize a comparison-contrast piece.

- One way is by subject. In this method, you discuss all the details about one subject first and then all the details about the other subject.
- The second way to organize your details is by feature. In this method, you choose one feature and discuss the similarities and differences for both subjects. Then you do the same thing for another feature and so on until you've covered all the features.

EXPLAINING A PROCESS

To explain a process, choose a topic you know well. Then identify your audience and what they may already know. Locate terms they'll understand and those you'll have to explain. Be clear about your purpose.

Make the Order Clear Before you write about a process, gather information through research, observation, or interviews. List the steps of the process in chronological order. Then write. Use transition words to help make the order of the steps clear for the reader. *First, then, after, next, later, while,* and *finally* are some useful transition words in explaining a process.

USING CAUSE-AND-EFFECT RELATIONSHIPS

Sometimes events are connected in a cause-and-effect relationship. A cause is an identifiable condition or event. An effect is something that happens as a direct result of that condition or event.

A cause-and-effect explanation may show one cause and one effect. It may explain a series of effects resulting from a single cause. It can also present multiple causes and multiple effects.

Sometimes a cause and its effect form part of a chain of events. One cause may lead to an effect, and that effect may in turn change circumstances and lead to another effect. The example below shows how this cause-and-effect chain works.

> Below-freezing weather occurs. ➡ Frost damages the orange crop. ➡ Fewer oranges are available than in other years, but demand doesn't fall. ➡ Oranges and orange juice become more expensive.

Organize Your Explanation You can organize your cause-and-effect explanation in one of two ways. One method involves identifying a cause and then explaining its effects. The other method involves stating an effect and then discussing its cause or causes. After you've completed your draft, review it to be sure the cause-and-effect relationships are clear. Use transition words such as *so, if, then, since, because, therefore,* and *as a result* to clarify the relationships.

Using Details Supporting details are the heart of expository writing. The details you select will depend on the approach you've chosen. The chart below shows different kinds of details that might be included in a report about the planet Mercury.

KINDS OF DETAILS	
FACTS	Mercury is nearer the sun than any other planet in our solar system.
STATISTICS	Mercury rotates once in about fifty-nine Earth days. Its orbit around the sun takes about eighty-eight Earth days.
EXAMPLES/ INCIDENTS	The temperature on Mercury could melt lead.
REASONS	Because Mercury is so close to the sun, the daylight side of the planet is extremely hot.

Arranging Details Once you've selected supporting details for your explanation, you're ready to organize them. Ask yourself what you're trying to do in your essay. For example, are you going to show the cause and effect of tornadoes? Are you going to use a comparison-contrast essay to point out the similarities and differences between two planets? Questions such as these can help you organize your ideas—the supporting details—logically.

You might choose a number of ways to arrange information and supporting details. If you're defining something, you might arrange features from most to least significant. If you're writing about a process, then **chronological order,** or time order, might be more logical.

SUMMARY

Expository writing explains and informs. You can include one or more of these elements:

- definitions
- step-by-step processes
- comparison and contrast
- cause-and-effect relationships

You can support your explanation with facts, statistics, examples, incidents, and reasons. Use appropriate transition words and phrases to make relationships clear.

COMPOSITION

17.4 PERSUASIVE WRITING

Look around you. Magazines, newspapers, books, posters, letters, radio and television programs—almost anything you read, see, or hear can include persuasion. One purpose of persuasive writing is to make readers, listeners, or viewers think or feel a certain way about an idea or a product. Another purpose is to make people take action. Sometimes it does both. When you write to persuade, you try to convince your audience to think or act in a particular way. In order to persuade, you must catch and hold the attention of your audience.

Often persuasive writing begins by stating the writer's goal. Then evidence—information to support that goal—follows. Some supporting statements will make you think ("The rain forest is disappearing at the rate of. . . ."). Some supporting statements will make you feel a certain way ("You won't fit in unless you wear. . . ."). Finally, there is usually a reminder of what the writer wants you to do or think.

FORMING AN OPINION

In most persuasive writing, the writer states an opinion or urges an action and then offers reasons to convince readers to accept the opinion or support the action. Reasons are often supported by facts, statistics, and examples.

Once you take a stand on an issue, you must provide support for it. At the same time, you should also consider arguments your opponents might make against your position.

When you're searching for a topic, explore experiences from your daily life that inspire strong opinions. Make a list. Write names of people, places, or things and jot down your thoughts about each. Freewrite for about ten minutes to see where your writing leads you. Journal entries can also help you find a topic. Sometimes just reading your entries will remind you of something you feel strongly about.

When you have a topic or a goal you really care about, the challenge is to win over your audience. As you choose a goal for your persuasive piece, answer the questions in the chart below. If you can answer yes to each question, you've found a good topic.

FINDING A PERSUASIVE WRITING TOPIC
1. Do I feel strongly about this topic?
2. Do people disagree about this topic?
3. Do I have enough to say about this topic to persuade others to accept my position?

Once you have a topic, think about your position on it. Sometimes when you learn more about a topic, your position changes. Other times you may discover that your opinion is the same as everyone else's. Exploring a topic helps you discover whether it's a suitable one for a writing project.

In persuasive writing, a key ingredient is the statement of what you want your audience to do or think. You can express that in a topic sentence, which may appear either at the beginning or at the end of your opening paragraph.

One way to explore a topic is to list the reasons people might agree or disagree with you. You can put these reasons in a chart headed "Pro" and "Con." A pro-and-con chart can help you organize your thoughts, make your opinion clearer, and help you determine why or how others might argue against your opinion.

CONSIDERING YOUR AUDIENCE

Why should people adopt your ideas? You need to provide convincing reasons. Whenever you try to convince someone of something, you need to keep your audience in mind. Consider the following questions.

THINKING ABOUT YOUR AUDIENCE
1. Who is my audience?
2. How much does my audience know about my topic?
3. Does my audience care about this topic?
4. What evidence will be most interesting to my readers?
5. What evidence will be most convincing to my readers?

Different people have different interests and different levels of knowledge. Choose reasons that will appeal to your audience. When your goal is to influence opinions, you need to know who your readers are and how they think.

SUPPORTING YOUR OPINION

Research is an important step in persuasive writing. Your opinions will carry weight only if you can back them up. To gather support, investigate your topic by reading, observing, and discussing, and sometimes by interviewing experts—people with special knowledge about the issue.

One way to build an argument is to list reasons that support your opinion. Your list of pros and cons is a good source of reasons. The next step is to gather evidence to support your reasons. What kinds of evidence will you use to support your position and your reasons? Persuading people to change their attitudes or to take action requires evidence. Evidence comes in two forms: facts and opinions.

Facts Facts are statements that can be proved. For example, the statement "Snakes are not slimy" is a fact. You could prove it by touching a snake or by reading about snakes. Statistics, or facts expressed in numbers, are one form of factual support. Examples are another.

Opinions An opinion is a personal belief or feeling. It can't be proved. The opinions of experts, however, can be powerful evidence. Personal experience can also be good evidence.

Test your argument to discover possible arguments against it. Use your list of pros and cons to discover any weak links or places where your evidence is unconvincing. Decide how to strengthen any weaknesses you discover.

COMPOSITION

EVIDENCE IN PERSUASIVE WRITING	
KINDS	**Examples**
FACT	Americans spent 33 billion dollars on the diet industry in 1990.
STATISTIC	In 1990, 34 percent of men and 38 percent of women spent 33 billion dollars on diets.
EXAMPLE	A preteen boy guzzles protein drinks, hoping to increase his size and strength.
OPINION	Well-known diet specialist Dr. Luz Waite recommends regular exercise along with any weight-loss plan.

Not all pieces of evidence are equally strong. Some "facts" are really opinions in disguise. When you write persuasively, check your facts to make sure they back up your point.

ORGANIZING YOUR ARGUMENT

After you gather your evidence, review it piece by piece. Which evidence is the strongest or most convincing? Sometimes you might want to put the strongest piece of evidence first in your paper. Other times you might want to save it until the end. Decide which order of evidence best supports your goal.

Make a list of your evidence in the order that seems most persuasive. Use this list to draft your persuasive argument. Of course, you may change the order of the evidence during revision.

The structure of a persuasive piece can resemble the three-part structure of a report. The introduction states the topic and your opinion on it. The body provides evidence to support your opinion. The conclusion summarizes your argument and suggests action.

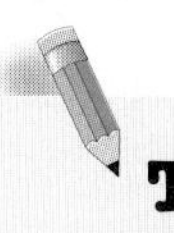

Tips for Structuring a Persuasive Piece

1. Decide how to arrange your evidence.
2. Write a strong opening that states your position clearly.
3. Present suitable supporting evidence in the best order.
4. Anticipate and answer opposing arguments.
5. Begin or end with your strongest point.
6. Sum up your argument and give your conclusions.

SUMMARY

The goal of persuasive writing is to make people think or act in a certain way. Remember these tips:

- State your position clearly and forcefully.
- Consider your audience.
- Include suitable supporting details in the form of facts and opinions.
- Arrange your evidence in the most effective way.

COMPOSITION

Chapter 18

Research Report Writing

When you write a research report, you investigate a topic and present information about the topic to your readers. You've probably seen such reports in newspapers and magazines. Journalists write these reports to investigate such topics as politics, environmental issues, and business concerns. They use a variety of sources to find information, and then they present this information to their readers.

To write a report, you should

- choose a topic that interests you
- decide on a purpose for your report
- gather information from sources
- take notes, organize your notes, and write an outline
- write about your purpose and main idea in a thesis statement
- present the information about your topic to your readers in your own words
- prepare a list of your sources

18.1 PREWRITING

CHOOSE A GOOD TOPIC

Keep two important things in mind when you're planning a research report.

1. Select a topic that interests you. Ask yourself, What are my favorite subjects? What would I like to know more about?
2. Narrow the topic so that you can cover it thoroughly.

When you prepare to write a research report, write down a list of things that interest you. You may find it helpful to freewrite in your journal to see where your thoughts lead you.

Miss Rogers, Sally Green. Is it true my son's research project is "the effect of too much television on atypical ten-year-old?"

Narrow Your Topic

Every subject contains both broad general topics and narrower topics. Before you can begin writing your research report, you need to choose an appropriate topic.

- If you choose a topic that is **too broad**—such as sports—you won't be able to cover the topic thoroughly.
- If you choose a topic that is **too narrow**—such as a particular type of mountain bike—you may not find enough facts and statistics for your report.

Are you writing a two-page report or a five-page report? Use a chart like the one that follows to narrow your topic so that you can present it to your readers' satisfaction.

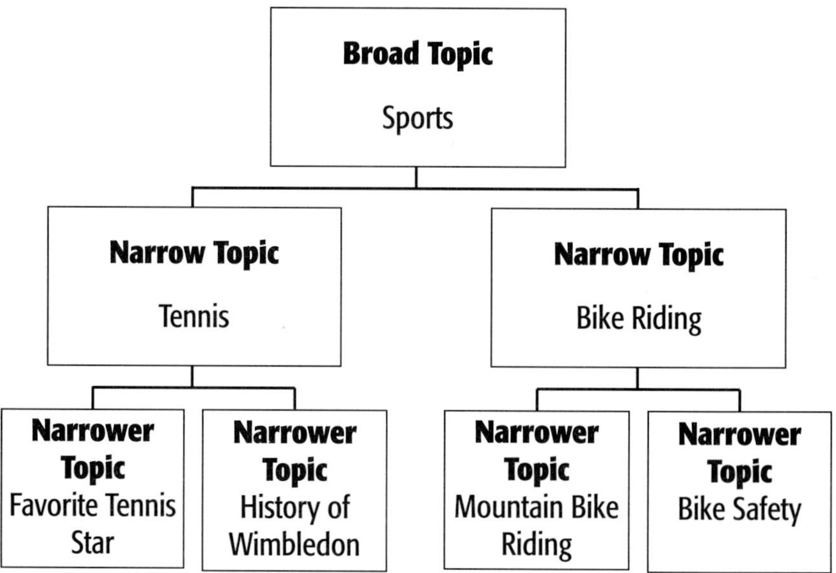

Answer the following questions to make sure you have chosen the right topic.

1. How long is your report supposed to be?
2. How much information about your topic can you find?
3. What element of the general subject interests you most?

FIND THE INFORMATION

Now it's time to gather the information you'll need to begin drafting your report. Reports are built on facts, statistics, examples, and expert opinions, so you'll need to do some research.

Encyclopedias and other reference books are a good place to begin looking. The information in these books can help you pinpoint your search. They can also help you to ask questions about your topic and lead you to other resources. Here is a list of the sources you can use to investigate your topic.

- reference books, such as encyclopedias, almanacs, atlases, and dictionaries
- books
- magazines
- newspapers
- pamphlets
- nonprint resources, such as videotapes and audiotapes
- Internet sources
- computer software programs
- experts—anyone who has valuable information about the topic you're investigating

Evaluate the Information

As you look for information from these sources, you must decide how reliable the information is. One way to do this is by identifying facts and opinions.

Facts Facts can be proved. Statistics and other information that can be proved true are facts.

Opinions Opinions cannot be proved; they are what people think about facts. You should include only the opinions of experts in your report. The opinions of experts are more reliable than the opinions of nonexperts.

Another way to decide if a source is reliable is to consider bias. Authors who are biased support a particular point of view. They'll probably include only information that supports their point of view. Because of this, you may not get a complete picture from a biased source.

Technology Tip

Evaluate Internet Sources Not all Internet sites contain accurate information. To make sure the information from a site is accurate, find another source with the same information.

Use Primary and Secondary Sources

Primary Sources Primary sources give you information that has not been gathered and shaped in a certain way by someone else. Examples of primary sources include these:

- A person close to the event or topic you're investigating. For example, someone who lives on a farm would be a primary source for a report on farm life.
- A real journal, a letter, or a document from the period you're investigating

Research TIP

A teacher may be a valuable primary source for you. For a report about tennis, for example, you might interview a school tennis coach.

Secondary Sources Books and magazines are generally considered secondary sources, which means that another writer has gathered the information and shaped it in a certain way. For example, a newspaper article about life on a farm would be a secondary source.

Conduct an Interview

When possible, your research should include primary sources. Interviews with people who know about your topic can give you firsthand information you probably couldn't find anywhere else.

Once you've identified an expert on your subject, contact him or her to see if and when an interview is possible. Prepare interview questions ahead of time. The most effective interview questions are open-ended; that is, they ask for more than a yes or no answer.

QUESTIONS THAT INVITE A YES OR NO ANSWER	OPEN-ENDED QUESTIONS
1. Is it dangerous to ride a bike without a helmet?	**1.** Why is it dangerous to ride a bike without a helmet?
2. Do young cyclists wear bike helmets?	**2.** What might happen to young cyclists who don't wear helmets?

When you conduct an interview, use a notebook, a tape recorder, or both to help you remember important points.

COMPOSITION

Form a Purpose

You should have a purpose, or reason, for writing your research report. After surveying your topic, choose a purpose by

- writing down three questions you hope to answer in your report
- considering which question will guide your research

An example of a question that might guide your research is, What can cyclists do to make bike riding safer? The purpose of your report will be to show your readers how to ride a bike safely.

Research TIP

As you learn more about your topic, you may discover an element that looks more interesting than the one you originally chose. It's not too late to change direction.

Make Note Cards

After you've found some sources, you can start to gather information. As you read, think about what is important and worth remembering. Take notes on three-by-five index cards, being sure to jot down the title and the author of each source.

- Take notes as you read—not later!
- At the top of each note card, write the subject of the note. Later this heading will help you organize your note cards and find the information you need.
- At the bottom of each note card, write the author's name, the title of your source, and the page number where you found the information.
- Don't copy information word for word. This is called plagiarism. Instead, think about what you're reading, and then write your notes in your own words.
- If you do copy some words from a source, use quotation marks on your note card (and later in your report) to show that you're using someone else's words and ideas.
- Begin a new card each time you start a new topic or go to a new source.

Look at the following source, which was taken from a book on cycling.

Helmets come in more styles, shapes, and prices than most shops can handle. As I write this, there are at least a hundred models on the market competing for your attention. Average weight is about 9 ounces though some are as light as 6 or 7 ounces.

James C. McCullagh. Cycling for Health, Fitness, and Well-being, 182–183. New York: Dell Publishing, 1995.

Now look at the handwritten notes that one student made after reading the selection. Notice the differences.

Helmets
- different styles (This might encourage young people to wear them.)
- many weigh less than ten ounces

James C. McCullagh. Cycling for Health, Fitness, and Well-being, 182-183.

COMPOSITION

Editing TIP

Don't throw away your notes before your report is finished. If you need to check a fact as you edit your report, you can look back at your notes.

Writing Tip

When you're planning your report, remember that visual aids, such as photos, maps, and charts, can help your readers understand your points.

Make Source Cards

Keep a record of your sources (the books, magazines, encyclopedias, Internet sites, and people you interview) by using source cards. (A source card is simply a three-by-five index card.) On these source cards, you will list the information about the source. You should make a source card for each of your sources. Be sure to copy this information exactly. You will use it later to prepare a list of your sources. The information included on the example source cards that follow is recommended by the Modern Language Association.

Source Cards for Books List the author, the title of the book, the city where the book was published, the publisher, and the date of publication.

> McCullagh, James C. <u>Cycling for Health, Fitness, and Well-being</u>. New York: Dell Publishing, 1995.

Source Cards for Magazines Magazines can be useful for gathering up-to-date information. On your source card, list the author of the article, the title of the article, the title of the magazine, the date of the issue, and the first and last page numbers of the article. (If there's a break between the first and last pages, list only the first page number and a plus sign.)

Rathbun, Mickey. "Play It Safe! What Is the Best Armor Against Kids' Sports Injuries? An Informed Parent." Sports Illustrated for Kids May 1, 1998: 10+.

Source Cards for Encyclopedias List the author (if he or she is named), the title of the article, the name of the encyclopedia, and the year of publication followed by the abbreviation *ed.*, which stands for *edition.* If the encyclopedia articles are arranged in alphabetical order, you don't need to write the volume and page numbers.

Shepherd, Ron. "Cycling." Encyclopedia of World Sport: From Ancient Times to the Present. 1996 ed.

Source Cards for Online Sources Electronic resources are cited much as print resources are, but additional information is needed. You must indicate whether your source is online, CD-ROM, diskette, magnetic tape, or DVD.

Cite the information in the order that it is given in the following list. You might not be able to find everything in the list. If you can't find all the information listed here, provide as much information as you can find.

1. Author, editor, or compiler of the source
2. Title of an article, poem, or short work (in quotation marks) or title of a book (underlined); or title of a posting to a discussion line or forum followed by the phrase *Online posting*
3. Title of the scholarly project, database, or professional or personal site (underlined). If the professional or personal site has no title, use a description such as *Home page.*
4. Editor or director of the scholarly project or database

COMPOSITION

5. Date of electronic publication, of the last update, or of the posting
6. Name of the institution or organization sponsoring the Internet site or associated with it
7. Date you used the source
8. Electronic address of the source (in angle brackets)

"A Consumer's Guide to Bicycle Helmets." Mar. 8, 1998. Bicycle Helmet Safety Institute. July 15, 1998 <http://www.bhsi.org/webdocs/guide.htm>.

Interviews List the name of the person you interviewed, the type of interview (personal, telephone, or e-mail), and the date of the interview.

Smith, John. Personal Interview. July 17, 1998.

COMPOSITION

CHOOSE AN APPROACH

When you prepare your research report, decide what approach you want to take toward your topic. Here are some common approaches. You may want to look at the chart on page 348 for more information about these approaches.

- Explain how something works, using a step-by-step process.
- Compare and contrast.
- Define something.
- Point out a cause-and-effect relationship.

Different approaches work with different topics. For example, if you want to tell your readers how to use the Internet, you may find that a step-by-step approach works best.

Write a Thesis Statement

As you were doing your research, you chose a purpose for your report. Now you should write about your purpose in the form of a thesis statement. A thesis statement is a sentence that tells briefly and clearly the main idea you want your readers to understand. It tells what you want to show, prove, or explain, and it gives your report a focus.

Answer the following questions to help you compose a thesis statement for your research report:

- What is your report's purpose or main idea?
- What are some of the most important ideas you learned in your research?
- What exactly do you want your readers to know?

After you've written a thesis statement that explains exactly what you want your readers to know, you're ready to write an outline.

Write an Outline

Make a list of ideas that support your thesis statement; then organize the ideas to form an outline.

1. Review your note cards and sort them into groups with similar headings.
2. Ask yourself, What main idea does each group represent?
3. Think of the most logical way to arrange your main ideas.
4. Read every note card in each group. Which ideas support other ideas? Identify the **main headings,** or main ideas, and then identify the **subheadings,** or supporting details.
5. When you write your outline, use roman numerals to indicate main headings and capital letters to indicate subheadings.

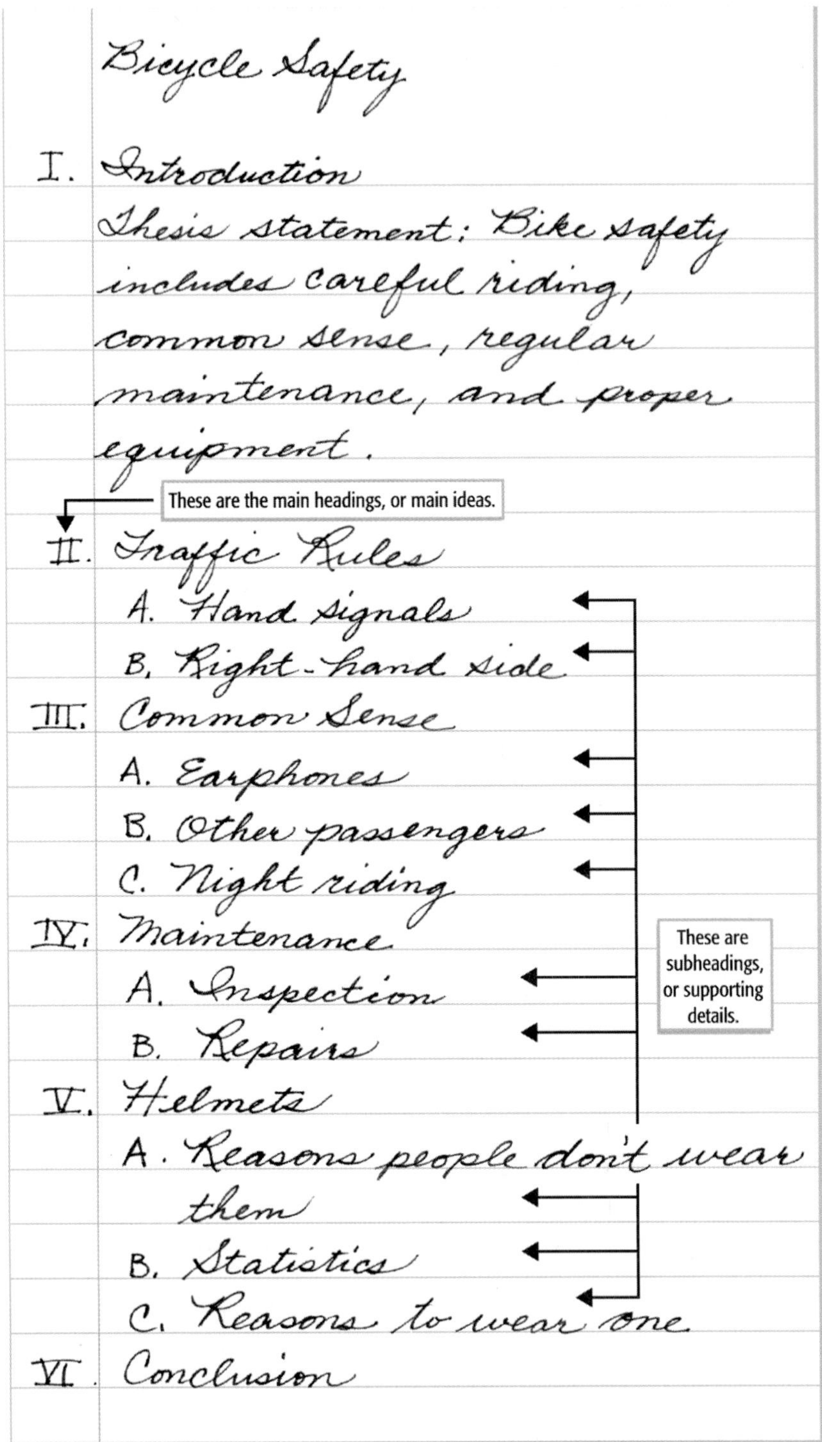

COMPOSITION

Study Your Draft Outline Ask yourself the following questions as you study your draft outline:

1. Is every subheading, or supporting detail, under the correct main heading, or main idea?
2. Does every main heading have at least two subheadings? If not, either do more research or delete the main heading.
3. Is your outline as complete as it can be? You should be able to write your report directly from your outline by adding details about your main headings and your subheadings.

18.2 DRAFTING

KNOW YOUR AUDIENCE

Who will read your report? You should have a certain audience in mind as you write your report. Consider this audience's interests as well as their knowledge of the subject. Remember that your readers don't have the benefit of all the background research you've done. Be sure to explain any term or process your audience might not know.

ORGANIZE YOUR REPORT

A report has three parts: an introduction, a body, and a conclusion.

1. In the **introduction,** you will catch your readers' interest and show your position on your topic. You can begin your report in several ways.
   - with a question
   - with a surprising fact or statistic
   - with a fascinating story related to the topic
   - with a striking quotation
2. In the **body** of the report, you will develop your topic. As you write the body, answer the question, What did I discover? You should include at least one paragraph for each main heading in your outline.

3. In the **conclusion,** you will summarize your topic or state your final thoughts about it.

WRITE YOUR DRAFT

Use your outline and your note cards to write a draft of your research report. To begin, arrange your note cards in the same order as the ideas in your outline. Read each roman numeral heading on your outline and skim your notes for information about that heading. As you write, you may find that you need to put your information in a different order. Your outline is only a guide. You can always change it as you write.

Don't worry about details of punctuation, spelling, or grammar as you write your draft. You can fix those later. The important thing is to express your ideas in a clear, organized way.

LIST YOUR SOURCES

When you were doing research for your report, you made source cards. These cards contain the sources of your information. Now it's time to make a list of these sources. This list will appear on a separate page at the end of your report. First, arrange the entries in alphabetical order according to the author's last name (or the work's title if there is no author indicated). Then copy the information for each source in the order in which it appears on your source card. Include the page numbers for magazine and newspaper articles. You may want to look at the sample source cards on pages 366–368 and the model list of sources on pages 378 and 379 for help.

18.3 REVISING/EDITING

EVALUATE YOUR DRAFT

When your draft is finished, set it aside for a while before you read it again. When you return to your draft, evaluate it to decide what you need to improve. Answer the questions on the following checklist to decide how to revise your draft to make it clearer and more accurate.

- Do I grab my readers' attention in the introduction?
- Do I stick to my topic?
- Do I accomplish my purpose?
- Do I keep my audience in mind?
- Does my main idea come across clearly?
- Does the information in the body fit the main idea of each paragraph?
- Have I followed my outline? Is there a paragraph in my report for each main heading in my outline?
- Do I give enough details? Too many?
- Are all dates, names, and numbers correct?
- Are all quotations accurate?
- Have I written a good conclusion that summarizes or restates my main idea?

GET A SECOND OPINION

One of the best ways to evaluate a draft is to have a classmate examine it. Share your draft with a partner and ask him or her the following questions.

- Is anything unclear?
- Where could I add more information?
- What do you find most interesting about my topic?
- What would you like to know more about?

You may want to ask your partner to write down his or her responses to these questions. Then you can refer to these responses as you revise.

18.4 PROOFREADING

After revising your draft, type or print a new copy of it with your corrections included. Then proofread your report one final time. You should check for one type of error at a time. For example, the first time you proofread, check for spelling errors. The second time you proofread, check for punctuation.

Proofreading Checklist

1. Have I explained or defined any words that may be unfamiliar to the reader?
2. Have I corrected all grammar errors?
3. Have I corrected all spelling errors?
4. Have I used correct punctuation?
5. Have I capitalized everything correctly?
6. Have I documented my sources properly?
7. Is my final copy neat and easy to read?
8. Have I indented each paragraph?
9. Have I left a one-inch margin on all four sides of each page?
10. Have I numbered the pages and included my name on each one?

18.5 PUBLISHING/PRESENTING

After completing your report, you're ready to share what you've learned. You can share your work in a variety of ways.

- Bind your report in book form.
- Present it on a computer disk.
- Put it into a notebook binder.
- Post it on a bulletin board.
- Print it as part of a class newsletter or magazine.

Think of things to include—covers, drawings, diagrams, clippings, or photographs—that will make your report attractive. Then share it with others!

SAMPLE RESEARCH REPORT

Kent 1

Clark Kent

Ms. Lane

Period 3

March 15, 2000

Bicycle Safety

Every year, millions of Americans take to the streets to ride their bikes. They ride them to and from work or school or on the weekend as a hobby. Although bike riding can be an enjoyable way to exercise, it's important to remember that bike riding can also be dangerous. More than a million Americans injure themselves seriously each year while riding a bicycle. The good news is that many bicycle injuries can be avoided through bike safety. Bike safety includes careful riding, common sense, regular maintenance, and proper equipment.

The thesis statement expresses the main idea of the report.

One of the most important ways that cyclists can avoid accidents is by knowing and obeying all traffic rules. Not knowing

Kent 2

these rules can be dangerous. Cyclists are at fault in nearly 90 percent of all biking accidents. When turning a corner, cyclists should use hand signals to let others know which way they are going. If there is no bicycle lane, cyclists should ride on the far right-hand side of the road.

Cyclists should also use common sense when riding. They should never wear earphones when they ride because earphones may prevent them from hearing warning signals from other traffic. They should never allow others to ride on the handlebars. A passenger can block the cyclist's vision and distract the cyclist. When riding at night, cyclists should have lights and special reflectors on their bikes so that drivers can see them.

One safeguard that people often ignore is proper bike maintenance. Cyclists should inspect their bikes regularly to make sure the tires, brakes, handlebars, seats, and spokes are in good condition. Some repairs

Kent 3

can be done easily by the cyclist, but regular inspections at a bike shop are also recommended.

The topic sentence of each paragraph supports the thesis statement. The rest of the paragraph supports the topic sentence.

The most important part of bicycle safety is wearing a helmet. Many young people don't wear helmets because they believe helmets are unattractive and not "cool." Statistics indicate that up to 85 percent of all bicycle injuries could be prevented if people would simply wear helmets. Many manufacturers produce helmets in attractive designs and styles, and helmets are now much lighter than they used to be. The Bicycle Helmet Safety Institute recommends that parents buy "snazzy" helmets to encourage their children to wear them. There is no longer any excuse for people not to wear helmets.

Bike riding can be fun, but it also carries important responsibilities. By following the proper precautions and making safety a habit, cyclists can be sure that biking remains fun for everyone.

The conclusion summarizes or restates the thesis statement.

COMPOSITION

Kent 4

SOURCES

"A Consumer's Guide to Bicycle Helmets." Mar. 8, 1998. Bicycle Helmet Safety Institute. July 15, 1998 <http://www.bhsi.org/webdocs/guide.htm>.

Fine, Kenneth C. "Bicycle Safety." The Columbia University College of Physicians and Surgeons Complete Home Medical Guide. New York: Crown Publishers, 1995.

McCullagh, James C. Cycling for Health, Fitness, and Well-being. New York: Dell Publishing, 1995.

Pessah, Jon. "Bicycle Helmets Are As Important As Seat Belts in Preventing Injuries. But How Do You Convince Your Kids to Wear Them?" Newsday Nov. 20, 1993: 21.

Rathbun, Mickey. "Play It Safe! What Is the Best Armor Against Kids' Sports Injuries? An Informed Parent." Sports Illustrated for Kids May 1, 1998: 10+.

COMPOSITION

Kent 5

Shepherd, Ron. "Cycling." Encyclopedia of World Sport: From Ancient Times to the Present. 1996 ed.

COMPOSITION

Chapter 19

Business Writing

19.1 WRITING A REQUEST LETTER

Have you ever written to someone you didn't know to ask for something? Maybe you wrote to an author to ask why she wrote a book you liked. Perhaps you wrote to the staff of a summer camp for information about a special program that interested you. Maybe you need information for a school report. You might decide to write a request letter to get the facts you need.

TIPS FOR WRITING A REQUEST LETTER

Here are some tips that will help Susan—and you—write a request letter that will get the results you want:

Be Brief Don't wander off the subject or include details that the reader doesn't need (or want) to know. Remember that business people are busy. They expect you to explain the reason for your letter in the first sentence or two. If you don't, they might not continue reading, or they might misunderstand why you're writing.

Explain Your Request Clearly Provide all the necessary information. If you have several questions or are asking for several things, number them. That way, the reader will be more likely to answer all your questions and not overlook one.

Respect the Reader's Time and Effort You shouldn't ask someone to provide basic information you could easily find in an encyclopedia or a library reference book. You shouldn't ask your favorite author, who lives several states away, to visit your school to talk to your class—for free. Be reasonable in your requests and make it easy for the reader to respond.

Ask Politely Request, don't demand. Show that you appreciate anything the reader can do to meet your request or answer your questions.

Use Business Style Include all the parts of a business letter: the heading, inside address, salutation, body, closing, and signature. Using the correct form will make a good impression on your reader. If you take your letter seriously, the reader is more likely to take it seriously too.

Proofread You should read your letter several times before you mail it. If you don't take the time to find and correct any errors in your letter, why should the reader take the time to answer it?

EXAMPLE Request Letter

Include a heading: your own address and the date.

16A Portage Road
Portland, Maine 34567
May 10, 2002

Education Department
Columbus Zoo
9990 Riverside Drive
Columbus, Ohio 44344

Address the letter to a specific person or department, if possible.

Include an inside address: the reader's name and address.

Explain your request clearly in the first sentence or two.

Dear Education Department Staff:

Please send me information about your breeding program for gorillas. I'm writing a science report about how zoos are helping to preserve endangered species, and I understand that your zoo has been very successful with gorillas.

Give the reason for your request.

I have learned quite a bit about gorillas in my research, but I would like to know more about your program. Could you please answer the questions below?

Show that you've made an effort to learn about the topic.

Write your questions in a list if there are several.

1. What species of gorillas are in your program?
2. Where do you get the gorillas for your program?
3. How many babies have been born and in what years?
4. Do you keep all the babies that are born at your zoo?

I'd also be interested in any other information that you have available about the gorillas and your program. I know you are very busy, but I'd appreciate getting the information as soon as possible. I've enclosed a large stamped, self-addressed envelope.

Make it easy for the reader to fulfill your request.

Thank you very much for your time and the information.

Show your appreciation.

Sincerely,

Susan Workman

Write your signature above your typed name.

Susan Workman

COMPOSITION

USING THE CORRECT FORM

Business letters, including request letters, can be written in two forms: block or modified block. Susan used the modified block form. Notice how she placed her heading, closing, and signature toward the right side of the page. She also indented each paragraph.

In the block form, all the parts of a letter begin at the left margin. Nothing is indented. Both the modified block and block form should be single-spaced and should include a blank line between the paragraphs (not shown in Susan's letter).

BEING BUSINESSLIKE

To write a business letter, you don't have to use long sentences. You also don't have to use old-fashioned words, such as *herein* and *the undersigned,* meaning "the writer." Business writing is supposed to communicate, to share information. Simple language does that best. A business letter should sound more like a conversation than a textbook.

Your business letters, including your request letters, will be much better if you make these kinds of substitutions:

INSTEAD OF THIS	WRITE THIS
this letter is written for the purpose of requesting	please send me
enclosed please find	I am enclosing
at this point in time	now/today
in the near future	soon
if you are in a position to	if you can
will you be kind enough	please
I would like to express my appreciation	thank you
thanking you in advance for your help	thank you

At the same time, a business letter should not sound exactly like a conversation. "Thanks a lot!" is fine for e-mail or letters to friends, but it's a little too informal for a business letter. A simple "Thank you" is more appropriate. In other words, your language should be polite but not stiff, friendly but not overly casual. You should write as you would to an adult whom you respect.

Everyone needs information and help from time to time. Now you know how to write a letter that will explain what you need, show that you respect the reader, and get you what you want!

19.2 WRITING DIRECTIONS FOR A PROCESS

Do you always read the instructions before you use a new compact-disc player or a headset or new computer software? No? You're not alone. Many people avoid reading instructions. They expect the instructions to be too confusing or too long, or maybe the instructions will be too short, leaving out important steps. Many people don't expect instructions to be helpful, so they don't bother to read them. Of course, this can lead to mistakes, wasted time, frustration, and even damaged equipment. Still, trying to figure out poorly written instructions can have the same result.

If you learn to write clear instructions, you'll gain a valuable skill. The ability to write clear instructions will help you in school and at work for the rest of your life. This section will help you develop that skill.

GETTING STARTED

Before you write anything, including instructions, the first step is always the same: Think about your readers. Ask yourself these questions:

- Who is my audience?
- What does my audience know about the topic?
- What terms will they understand? What terms will I need to explain?

If you assume that your audience understands certain things, you may fail to explain them in your instructions. If you don't explain these things, some of your readers might get stuck at a certain step and not know how to continue. On the other hand, if you explain too much, experienced readers may get impatient. "Why should I read more of this?" they may ask themselves. "I already know how to do these steps!" However, if they stop reading at Step 3, they might do Step 4 incorrectly.

How do you avoid explaining too little or too much? Find out what most of your intended readers already know about the topic. Let's say you're explaining how to get from one place to another. First, you need to find out how well your readers know your town or city. Maybe you're lending your cousin your compact-disc player, and she has asked you to write down instructions for using it. Before you start writing, ask your cousin if she has ever used a compact-disc player. Then you will know what to put in your instructions and what to leave out.

Find out what terms your readers know and use. If you're explaining how to program a videocassette recorder, will they understand such terms as *INPUT/SELECT, SP, EP, timer set mode,* and *program memory*? If you're writing the steps for adding a phone number to a speed-dial program, which of these terms are your readers likely to understand: *type, input, program*? If you're not sure whether your readers will be familiar with a certain term, it's probably best to explain it.

CHOOSING A TITLE

Start your instructions with a clear title that specifically describes what the reader will learn.

INSTEAD OF THIS	WRITE THIS
How to Use Your Videocassette Recorder	How to Set Your Videocassette Recorder to Record Automatically

WRITING AN INTRODUCTION

An introduction tells the purpose of the instructions. It explains who should follow them and perhaps when and why. For example, suppose a set of instructions in a business office tells how to reorder parts. The introduction should explain who is responsible for reordering the parts and when they should be reordered. Otherwise, everyone in the office might assume that someone else is responsible for following the steps.

In your introduction, list any needed materials or equipment so that readers can gather what they need before they begin the steps. Include any general warnings or cautions, such as "Unplug the videocassette recorder before changing the connections." Then repeat the warnings at the appropriate steps in the instructions. This is also a good time to explain any terms that may be new to readers, such as *initialize* or *airway.*

COMPOSITION

ORGANIZING THE STEPS

Now it's time to ask yourself these questions:

- What steps should readers complete?
- What other information does my audience need?

List all the steps in the process. Leave out obvious ones, such as "Locate your videocassette recorder." Then put the steps in chronological order—that is, in the order readers should complete them—and number them. List the steps in the order readers should complete them. For example:

INSTEAD OF THIS	WRITE THIS
1. Insert the disk in the slot after turning on the computer.	1. Turn on the computer. 2. Insert the disk in the slot.

List each step separately. If you try to combine two or more instructions in a single step, your readers may become confused.

INSTEAD OF THIS	WRITE THIS
1. Turn on the computer before inserting the disk in the slot.	1. Turn on the computer. 2. Insert the disk in the slot.

Start each step with a verb. A verb will tell your readers what to do.

INSTEAD OF THIS	WRITE THIS
1. The CONTROL key and the F1 key are pressed at the same time.	1. Press the CONTROL key and the F1 key at the same time.

Number only the steps that readers should complete. Below each step, add any other information they might need. For example, you may want to explain what should happen at that point in the process, or you might want to stress why that step is important. If you want to include this kind of information, indent these explanations under the steps or underline them or put them in italics or parentheses. Make it easy for readers to find and follow each step without getting confused by explanations. Below is an example of how to include an explanation.

INSTEAD OF THIS	WRITE THIS
1. After you press 3, the screen will show a menu.	1. Press 3. (The screen will show a menu.)

Sometimes a step should be carried out only under certain conditions. In that case, describe the conditions first. Otherwise, readers might carry out a step before they realize they should do it only at certain times. (This time, you will not start a step with a verb.)

INSTEAD OF THIS	WRITE THIS
1. Press ENTER if the light is flashing.	1. If the light is flashing, press ENTER.

If a diagram will help explain what to do, include it. For example, you might want to draw a diagram of the control panel of the videocassette recorder. Then you could label each knob and button.

CONSIDERING A CONCLUSION

If you wish, end your instructions with a brief conclusion. You might write one of the following:

- Tell what readers should have accomplished by following the instructions.
- Name some sources of help if readers have problems following the instructions.

Compare the following sets of instructions. It's difficult to find the steps in the first set. Notice how much easier it is to follow the numbered steps in the second set.

EXAMPLES

Confusing

Taking a Test

Be sure to take along a pencil to mark the answer form. Fill in the whole circle and stay within the lines, or the computer might make a mistake in scoring your test. Read all the answers before making your choice. One choice may seem correct, but another one may be more correct. You also need to learn all you can about the test. For example, is it going to be timed? Are you expected to

COMPOSITION

complete the test? Should you guess if you're not sure, or do incorrect answers count against you? The directions should always be read before you begin each section of the test. Directions may change from section to section. Skip a space on the answer form if you skip a question. The best approach is usually to answer all the questions you're sure of first. If there's time, go back and answer the rest.

Clear

How to Take a Standardized Test

Begin with a clear, descriptive title.

The tips below will help middle school students improve their scores on standardized tests, such as state achievement tests.

Explain the purpose of the instructions and who should follow them.

1. First, find the answers to these questions:

   Put the steps in chronological (time) order and number them.

   - Is the test going to be timed? Are you expected to complete the whole test?
   - Should you guess if you're not sure, or do incorrect answers count against you?

2. Take along a pencil to mark the answer form. Start all steps with a verb.

3. Read the directions before you begin each section of the test. (Directions may change from section to section.)

   Use parentheses (or underlining, italics, or indention) for explanations.

4. Read all the possible answers before choosing one. (One may seem correct at first, but another answer may be more accurate.)

5. Fill in the whole circle for the answer you choose and stay inside the lines. (Computers have trouble scoring messy answer forms.)

6. Answer all the questions you're sure of first. (If there's time, go back and answer the rest.)

7. If you skip a question, skip that space on the answer form.

   Describe any special conditions before explaining a step.

19.3 MAKING A PRESENTATION

Making an oral presentation can be a rewarding experience, but it can also make your stomach flutter. You're up there all alone, and everyone's looking at you. You're sure you're going to embarrass yourself somehow. Probably you'll forget what you were going to say. Maybe you'll remember, but everyone will get bored and start yawning. What if your hands shake and people notice?

But what if you walk to the front of the room, full of confidence, and give a presentation that really fascinates your audience? It could happen! This section will help it happen to you. You'll learn how to prepare for an oral presentation so that you can do it well and feel comfortable. You'll even look forward to it!

You've given oral presentations before, of course. You probably started with book reports in elementary school. In middle school, you might be asked to give oral reports in language arts or science class. You'll also have to give them in high school and in college or other training programs after high school. When you begin working, sooner or later you'll probably have to give more oral presentations. Now is the time to develop the skills and the confidence to give these presentations. You'll use these skills for many years to come and in many different settings.

Here are the steps you will learn in this section:

1. Think About Your Topic and Your Purpose
2. Analyze Your Audience
3. Decide What to Say
4. Organize Your Presentation
5. Add Visuals
6. Practice
7. Present Yourself Well

THINK ABOUT YOUR TOPIC AND YOUR PURPOSE

You might be assigned a topic, or you may get to choose your own. First, make sure you know what is expected from your presentation. Are you simply supposed to inform the audience about a topic, or are you expected to persuade the audience to do something?

Suppose your purpose is to inform. If you chose your own topic, make sure it's not too broad for a short presentation. You might want to present just one or two aspects of it. For example, if your topic is television, you might decide to talk about how commercials influence our buying decisions, or you might explain why and how the networks are trying to reduce the amount of violence on television.

Think of an approach that will interest your audience. If your topic was assigned, find out what the assigner (probably your teacher) wants the audience (probably your class) to learn about the topic.

Maybe your purpose is to persuade the audience to do something. Perhaps you're supposed to convince them to volunteer for a community clean-up campaign or enter a short-story contest. In either case, you will need to think of ways to persuade your audience. How would they benefit from helping in the campaign or participating in the contest?

Technology Tip

If you don't know your topic well, your next step will be to learn more about it. Besides the library, a good source for current information is the Internet. Before using information from the Internet, however, be sure your source is accurate. Sites sponsored by well-known organizations, such as news networks, are your best bet. Avoid home pages posted on the Internet by individuals.

COMPOSITION

ANALYZE YOUR AUDIENCE

To analyze your audience, answer these questions:

- How will your listeners respond to this topic? Will they be eager to learn about it? Will they be bored unless you can think of a new approach?

- What does this audience already know about the topic? Have they studied it in school? What terms will they understand? Which ones will you have to explain? If your topic is television commercials, for example, which ones will be familiar to your audience? If you will be talking about television violence, which shows does your audience watch that tend to contain violence?
- How can you show your audience that the topic is important in their lives? For example, have students in your school bought products advertised by commercials and been disappointed? Has something happened in your community that might have been inspired by violence on television?

Analyzing your audience will help you decide what your presentation should include. You can first gain your audience's interest and then inform or persuade them, depending on your purpose in speaking.

DECIDE WHAT TO SAY

Knowing a great deal about your topic and your audience will help you decide what to include in your presentation. The amount of time you have to speak will also help you decide how much information you can include.

Instead of saying a little about many elements of your topic, choose two or three main points that will be meaningful to your audience. They will not remember a large number of details. However, they are likely to remember two or three points if you offer interesting examples.

While you're planning what to say, ask yourself one or both of these questions:

- What do I want the audience to learn?
- What do I want the audience to do after my presentation?

ORGANIZE YOUR PRESENTATION

A presentation has a beginning, a middle, and an end. An effective presentation begins with a strong opening to interest the audience in the topic. Then the speaker tells the audience the points he or she will cover so that they know what to expect. Next, the speaker presents those points in an organized way. The speaker ends with a strong closing to remind the audience of what they've learned or to motivate them to act.

The Beginning

Plan an opening that will grab your audience's attention. It should also introduce your topic. Here are some ways to do this:

Tell a Story It can be a true story about yourself or others, but make sure it won't embarrass anyone else. (You can embarrass yourself if you want to!) For example, you might mention a recent news story that relates to your topic, or you could tell about a time when you believed a commercial's claims and spent your whole allowance on a useless product.

Ask a Question Questions can get the audience thinking about the topic. For example, you might ask, "When was the last time you bought a product because it was advertised on television?" or "Did you watch television last night? How many times did you see a character hit, punch, shove, kick, shoot, or stab someone?"

Offer a Surprising Fact Get the audience's attention with a fact that startles them. For example: "By the time you are legally old enough to drink alcoholic beverages, you will have seen more than 100,000 beer commercials on television."

Tell a Joke Do this only if you're good at it. Choose your joke carefully. Select one that relates to your topic, and *make sure it doesn't insult any person or group of people.* Most libraries have books of jokes written especially for speakers to use. After you choose a joke, try it out on friends to see if they think it's funny, doesn't insult anyone, and isn't too silly. Telling a joke can relax both the audience and you, but be careful. You may embarrass yourself if the joke flops.

The Middle

After you've decided how to begin your presentation, organize your main points into a logical order. Writing them in an outline helps. Then you will locate examples, quotations, or statistics to back up each point and add them to your outline. Here are some ways to organize your points:

Chronological Explain a series of events in the order they occurred or give steps in the order they should be completed. For example, you might tell what was done over the past few years during the school clean-up campaign, or you could explain the steps in writing a short story.

Priority Arrange the reasons to do something from least to most important. For example, here are three reasons we should ignore television commercials:

Least important:	They waste our money on products that don't work as promised. ("Buy this face cream, and your pimples will disappear!")
Next important:	They encourage our fears. ("Use this mouthwash, or no one will want to be near you!")
Most important:	Some advertised products can harm our health. For example, drinking beer leads to thousands of automobile accidents.

Problem/Cause/Solution Describe a problem, explain why it is happening (or will happen), and offer a solution. For instance, you might point out specific areas at school where trash has accumulated, such as the outdoor areas near the cafeteria. Next, you will explain the cause of this problem: students dropping trash from their lunches. Then you will describe the solution: the clean-up campaign, more trash containers, signs to remind students not to litter.

Compare and Contrast Show how two events, people, or objects are similar and different. Using this approach, you might compare the amount of violence in two popular television shows. If one show can be popular without violence, is violence necessary in the other one?

Categories Divide your topic into categories and explain each one. You might use this approach to explain several of the persuasive techniques used in television commercials.

The Ending

The ending of your presentation is as important as the beginning. Here are two effective endings:

Summarize Restate your main points and then go back to your opening. Finish the story you started, repeat the question you asked, or show the audience how the fact or joke you shared relates to your main points.

Repeat Your Strongest Point Rephrase your strongest point and then ask the audience to do something specific. For example, you might urge them to sign up for the clean-up campaign or write a short story for the contest.

After organizing your opening, your main points, and your closing, write them on note cards. Put each main point on its own card and include any important details you want to mention, along with any quotations or statistics you have gathered.

Writing Tip

Write on your note cards in words and phrases, not sentences. You're not going to *read* these cards. The cards will just remind you of what you planned to say. Number the cards so you can keep them in order during your presentation.

Three persuasive techniques:

1. bandwagon – everyone's buying it

2. testimonial – a famous person says it's good

3. snob appeal – rich people buy this brand.

ADD VISUALS

Different people prefer to learn in different ways. Some people like to listen to someone tell them new information. Other people would rather see new information printed out, perhaps in a book or on a chart. Most people, especially the second group, will be more interested in your presentation—and understand it better—if you use some visuals.

A visual can be as simple as a list printed on poster board. It can be as complicated as animated computer graphics. Visuals can include charts, tables, graphs, maps, models, samples, videotapes, drawings, photographs, and diagrams. They can be presented on individual sheets of paper to be distributed to the audience, on poster board, or on slides. Visuals can be made by hand or by computer.

If your presentation is about television commercials, you might videotape two or three of them. Then you could show them to your audience and discuss the persuasive techniques used in each one, or you could make a line graph to show the decrease in television violence and display the graph using an overhead projector or an opaque projector.

Visuals should not only give the audience something to look at. They should also help explain your points. If you use a number of visuals, they can serve as an outline for your presentation. Then you can use the visuals as reminders of what you were going to say instead of looking at note cards. Using visuals makes you look well organized. Visuals also give you something to do with your hands!

Designing Visuals

- Explain only one point on each visual. Keep the visual simple so that your audience will immediately understand its point. Don't make your audience struggle to figure out what your visual means.
- Give every visual a title that helps explain it.
- Use big letters so your audience can read the words on your visual. But don't use all capital letters. WRITING THAT'S IN ALL CAPITAL LETTERS IS MUCH HARDER TO READ!

Writing Tip

Keep it simple!

- Use only one idea for each visual.
- Use no more than thirty-five words on one visual.
- Give each visual a title.

- Don't try to include every detail from your note cards on visuals. Focus on your main points.
- Don't make your visuals too cluttered. That is, don't use too many colors, sizes of letters, or pictures. Three colors are plenty, and two sizes of letters are enough. Choose pictures to help explain your points, not to decorate your visual.
- Don't forget to proofread. If you skip this step, an overhead might display a misspelled word in three-inch letters!

Using a Computer Presentation Program

If you have a computer and software available, they can help with your presentations. PowerPoint software, for example, can produce slides and send them directly from your computer to an overhead screen for your audience to see. PowerPoint allows you to make words, paragraphs, or pictures appear and disappear from the slide. You can also add sound effects. In addition, PowerPoint can make overhead transparencies and print handouts for the audience.

ARE YOUR VISUALS

- easy to understand?
- interesting?
- related to your topic?
- neat?

Using Visuals

Visuals can add a great deal to your presentation. However, they do require some planning so that your presentation will flow smoothly. Follow these tips:

- Check any equipment you plan to use. Just before the presentation, check it one more time to make sure it still works. A computer program that worked at home may not work in another setting. The bulb on the overhead projector may have burned out. Be ready with another way to share the information in case of problems.
- Don't show a visual until you're ready to talk about it. Then leave it displayed until you're ready for the next one. Turning equipment on and off can annoy an audience. Empty white screens can also be distracting.

- Face your audience and stand to one side of your visual so that everyone can see it. *Do* explain your visuals, but *don't* read them to the audience.

PRACTICE

Rehearse your speech two or three times. Use your visuals so you can figure out when to show each one to the audience. After the opening of your speech, tell the audience the points you will cover so they know what to expect. Then practice moving smoothly from one point to the next. Finally, close with the strong ending you have planned.

Ask a few friends or family members to listen to you and give you their opinions. Ask them to pay attention to the way you organized your presentation and the way you gave it. You might videotape yourself and watch the tape. Listen for times when you were difficult to understand or you didn't clearly explain what you meant. Were any of your points a little boring? If so, find more interesting examples to liven them up.

Check your timing to make sure your presentation is not too long or too short. Remember that you might speak more quickly in front of a larger audience. Don't practice so many times that you memorize your presentation. You want it to be fresh and interesting for you and for the audience.

Calvin and Hobbes **by Bill Watterson**

PRESENT YOURSELF WELL

If you feel nervous before speaking to a group, congratulations! You're just like most speakers! You can still make an excellent presentation. Just admit to yourself that you're feeling a little nervous. Then use that energy to do your best. Many professional athletes also feel nervous just before a competition begins. They welcome their nervousness because it gives them extra energy.

Getting Ready

Get a good night's sleep. To prevent burps, avoid drinking any kind of carbonated beverage for several hours before your presentation.

Just before you speak, help yourself relax by taking several deep breaths. Next, tighten and relax your muscles, one set at a time. Start at your toes and work to the top of your head. Then take a few more deep breaths for good measure. Finally, gather your note cards and your visuals and take your place in front of the group. Pause and smile at the audience. DON'T apologize for being nervous—and begin.

Looking Good

- Stand up straight, but don't be stiff.
- Look at the audience. Pick out one person and pretend you are talking just to him or her. Then pretend you are talking to a different person. Keep changing so you look at people in every part of the audience. Audiences like speakers who look at them. They believe that speakers who look at them are better informed, more experienced, friendlier, and more sincere than speakers who do not make eye contact.
- Use gestures, just as you would during a conversation. They help show your enthusiasm for your topic.
- Move around. Unless you're standing on a stage or must stay close to a microphone, try walking among the audience members. It will help make you and them feel more relaxed.

Sounding Good

- Speak clearly and slowly. Let your voice rise and fall naturally, as if you were having a conversation. Try not to rush.
- Speak loudly enough to reach people in the back of the room. If you're using a microphone, let it do the work. Don't shout.
- Get excited about your topic! Your audience will catch your excitement. Enthusiasm is contagious.

PUTTING IT ALL TOGETHER

Now you know how to do well on your next presentation. If you still feel nervous about it, imagine the worst thing that could happen. Here are some disasters that might come to your mind:

- You'll forget what you were going to say, or you'll lose your place. (No, you won't. Your note cards and your visuals will keep you on track.)
- Your presentation will be boring. (Not after all the planning you've done! You know your audience and your topic well. You've thought of an interesting opening, and you've found good examples to support your main points. You have also designed excellent visuals.)

So when *is* your next presentation? Think about how you can use the steps in this section to get ready for it. Then you will feel confident and comfortable as you make your presentation. You might even look forward to it!

Part Four

Resources

So much has already been written about everything that you can't find out anything about it.

–James Thurber

HD

Chapter 20

The Library or Media Center

Although you've probably been in a library, you might not realize all the resources the library has to offer or how to find them. This chapter will guide you through the library and help you understand how and where to find what you need.

CIRCULATION DESK

At the circulation desk, you'll find a library worker to answer your questions and check out your books.

CATALOG

A computer or card catalog will tell you what books are available in the library and where to find them. You'll learn more about using both kinds of catalogs in Chapter 21.

THE STACKS

The stacks are rows of bookshelves. They're called the "adult section" in some libraries, but you usually need not be an adult to use these books. In most libraries, the stacks are divided into these sections:

- fiction (novels and short stories)
- biography (books about the lives of real people)
- nonfiction (everything that is not included in fiction or biography)

RESOURCES

YOUNG ADULT AND CHILDREN'S SECTION

The young adult and children's section includes picture books for very young readers, but you can also find excellent resources here for your school reports and for fun. Fiction, biographies, and nonfiction are usually grouped separately, as in the adult section. All these books are listed in the library's computer or card catalog.

REFERENCE AREA

The reference area might include encyclopedias, dictionaries, almanacs, and other reference materials. Books in the reference area can be used only in the library. The library doesn't allow anyone to check them out. Thus, these materials are always available when someone needs them.

NEWSPAPERS AND PERIODICALS

In the newspapers and periodicals section, you can read newspapers from your town or city, from other major cities, and perhaps from other countries. You can also look through periodicals, which include magazines and journals. You probably can't check out the most recent issues. However, you can usually check out older issues to read at home. You'll learn more about finding articles in newspapers and periodicals in Chapter 21.

AUDIO-VISUAL MATERIALS

From the audio-visual section of the library, you can borrow books on tape, videotapes, and audiocassettes and compact discs (CDs) of your favorite music.

COMPUTER AREA

Many libraries offer personal computers you can use for research. Some computers might also be available for writing reports and papers and for using the Internet.

STUDY AREAS

Your library might have quiet areas set aside for people who want to read or study.

SPECIAL COLLECTIONS

Some libraries set up special displays and change them every few weeks. A display might consist of rare books, student art, or a collection of antique dolls, carved figures, or items from another country.

School librarian Nelda Limpkin was pretty pleased with her new book classifying system.

Chapter 21

Using Print Resources

In the course of doing research for a report, you will no doubt look at books and periodicals. One reason that print resources, especially books, are tremendous sources of information is that they survive for years, enabling you to gain access to information from the past.

Periodicals, because they're printed more quickly and more often than books, are sources of current information and opinion. You can use periodicals to find varying viewpoints on the same subjects. In this chapter, you'll learn about some of the different kinds of print resources available to you.

RESOURCES

21.1 UNDERSTANDING CATALOGING SYSTEMS

Maybe you're looking for information on a particular subject. Maybe you want to see books by a certain author, or you want to check out a specific book. The library's catalog will help you find what you're looking for. Most libraries now use computerized catalogs, but some still have card catalogs.

COMPUTER CATALOGS

Each computer catalog is different. Before you use one for the first time, read the instructions. They might be posted beside the computer or printed on the screen. If you need help, ask a librarian.

Most catalog programs begin by asking whether you want to search by author, title, or subject. If you want to search for an author's name, type the last name first, followed by a comma and the first name. Here is an example:

Thurber, James

If you want to search by title, start with the first important word in the title. Ignore *A, An,* and *The* at the beginning of a title. For the book *A Thurber Carnival,* you would type the following:

Thurber Carnival

When you're entering names and titles, be sure the words you enter are spelled correctly. A computer catalog can't recognize misspelled words. It will search for exactly what you type.

For a subject search, you will use a key word. A key word is a word that names or describes your topic. Whenever you search a computer database, such as a library catalog or the Internet, the key word you use will greatly affect the results you get. On the next two pages are several tips to help you get the best results from a subject search.

RESOURCES

1. **Be specific.** A general key word, such as *experiments,* will get you many screens of sources, sometimes called matches or hits. Although these sources will relate in some way to your key word, few of them will be mainly about your topic. To save time, choose a key word that better names or describes your topic, such as *cloning.* You will get a much shorter list of hits, but more of them will be useful to you.

2. **Use Boolean search techniques.** Boolean search techniques can help you look for books in a computer catalog, find articles in magazine databases, or locate information on the Internet. (You'll learn to search magazine databases and the Internet later in this chapter.) Boolean techniques use the words *and, or, not,* and sometimes *near* or *adj (adjacent).*

   And: You can combine two key words with *and,* such as *cloning and animals.* Then the computer will list only sources that contain both words. This kind of search results in far fewer hits, but more of them will relate to your topic. (Some programs use + instead of *and,* as in *cloning* + *animals*.)

   Or: If you want information on two different topics, link them with *or,* as in *cloning or twins.* The word *or* tells the computer to conduct two searches at once.

   Not: To stop the computer from searching for information you don't want, use *not.* For example, if you wanted information about cloning but not about cloning sheep, you could enter *cloning not sheep.*

   Near or *adj:* Some computer programs allow you to use *near* or *adj (adjacent).* These words tell the computer to locate sources with two key words near each other. For example, you might use *cloning near dog.* (You could also enter *cloning and dog.* However, the computer might then list articles that contain the word *cloning* and the word *dog*–but nothing about cloning dogs.)

Not all computer programs recognize Boolean search instructions. For some programs, you must begin a Boolean search with *b/* (for Boolean search), as in *b/cloning near dog.*

3. **Use quotation marks.** Enclosing a phrase in quotation marks tells the computer to find every book or article with *exactly* those words. For instance, you might enter *"cloning dogs."*

4. **Try truncating.** You can truncate, or shorten, your key word by using an asterisk (*). Then the computer will search for all words that begin with the letters before the asterisk. For example, you might use *clon** as a key word. The computer will list books or articles containing the words *clone, clones, cloning,* and *cloned.* By truncating your key word, you make sure the computer doesn't overlook various forms of the word.

You can also use this technique when you aren't sure how to spell a word. For example, you could use *Doll** as a key word if you weren't sure whether the first cloned sheep was named *Dollie* or *Dolly.*

If you need help with the computer catalog of your library, you can always ask a librarian for help. Many libraries also offer classes on how to use the computer catalog.

Understanding Search Results

To use a library computer catalog, type in the author's name, the book title, or a key word for a subject search. The screen will list related sources that are available at that library. Let's say you start a subject search by typing in *cloning.* The screen shows you a list similar to the one on the next page.

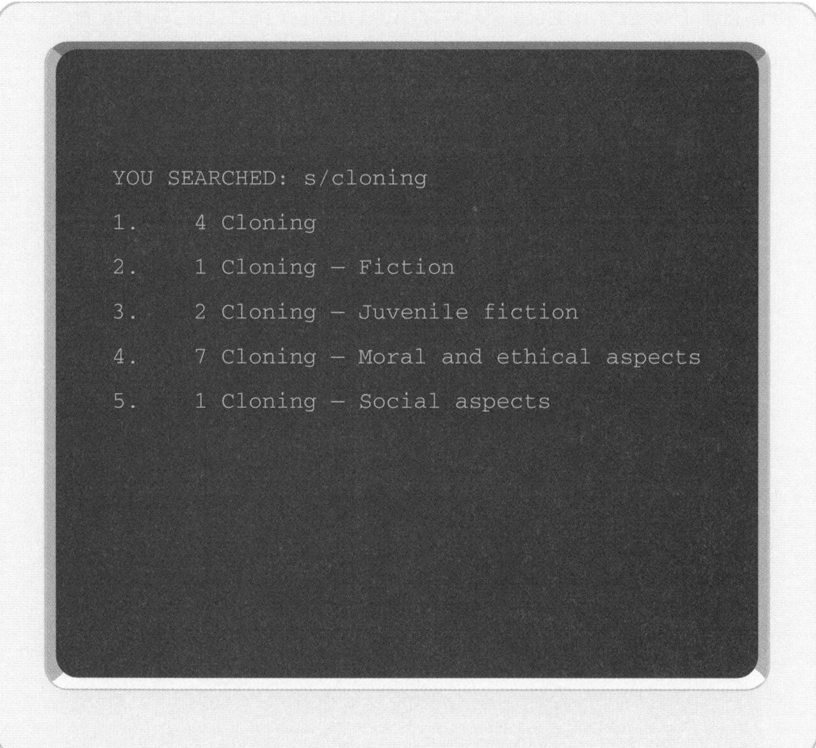

RESOURCES

The first listing (1) tells you the library has four books about cloning in general. Because they aren't marked "fiction," they're nonfiction. Because they aren't marked "juvenile," they're meant for adults. The second (2) and third (3) listings are fictional books, one for adults and two for young readers. The fourth (4) and fifth (5) listings are adult nonfiction books.

You don't know much about cloning yet, so you were hoping the library would have some books on this topic in the "juvenile nonfiction" category. Those books would give you the basic information you need. You don't want to read a fictional story about cloning, even one meant for young readers. You need facts for your report, not a story. You decide to try a different but closely related key word.

Follow the computer's instructions to return to the first page and type in your new key word: *genetics.*

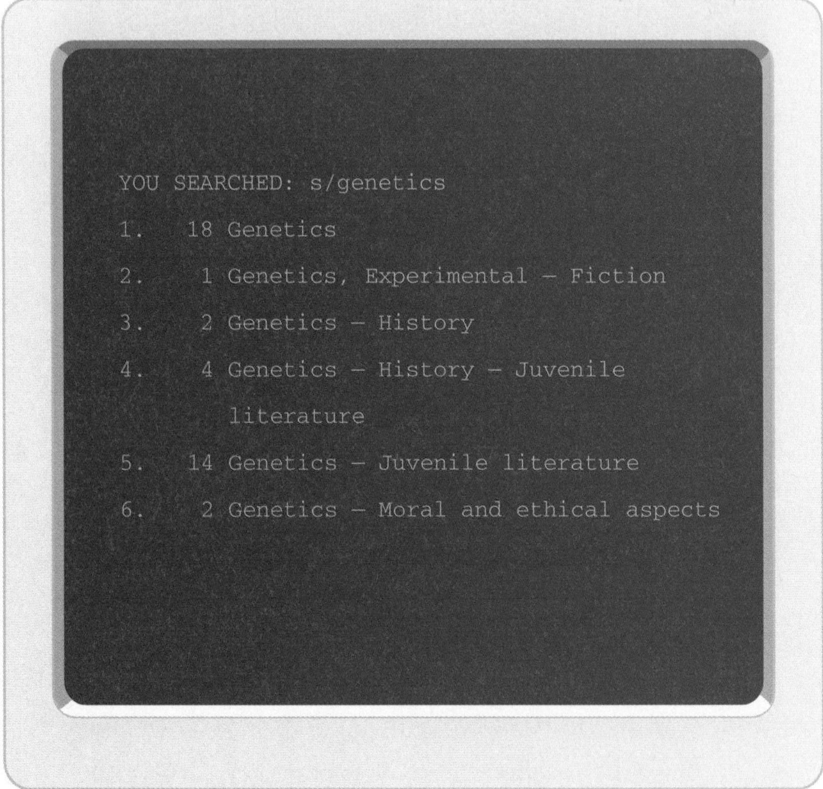

You're glad to see listings 4 and 5; they offer a total of eighteen nonfiction books about genetics for young readers. You follow the directions on the screen to see what books are listed under 4 and 5. The computer instructions tell you how to move forward and backward through a library listing. For example, you might enter *ns* (next screen) or *f* (forward) to see the next page of a listing. To go backward, you might enter *ps* (previous screen) or *b* (backward). Each catalog program is different, so carefully read the onscreen instructions.

You decide to find out more about a book that was listed under 5. The screen on the next page offers this information about that book:

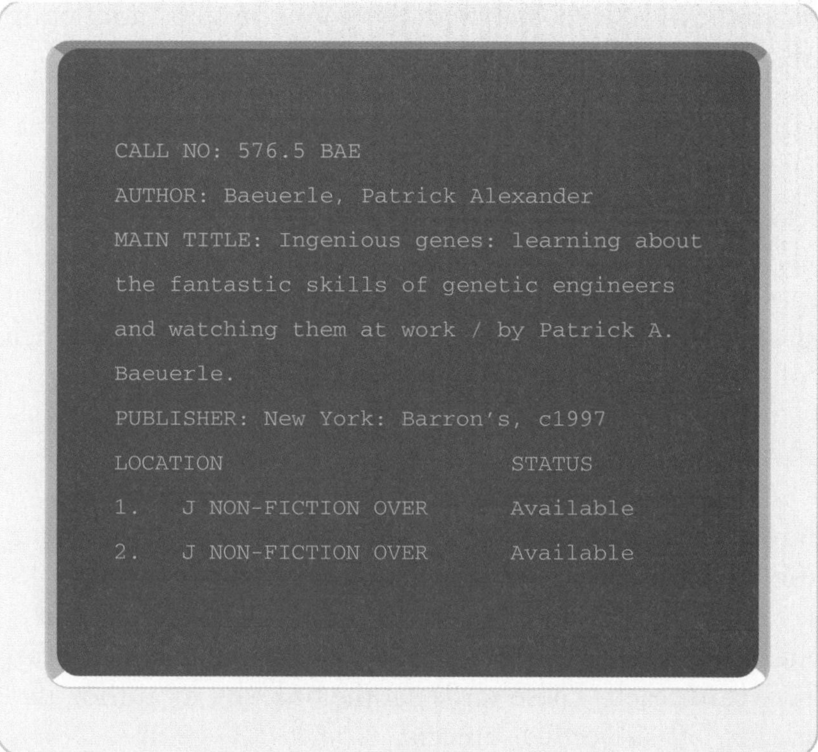
CALL NO: 576.5 BAE
AUTHOR: Baeuerle, Patrick Alexander
MAIN TITLE: Ingenious genes: learning about the fantastic skills of genetic engineers and watching them at work / by Patrick A. Baeuerle.
PUBLISHER: New York: Barron's, c1997

LOCATION	STATUS
1. J NON-FICTION OVER	Available
2. J NON-FICTION OVER	Available

This book may provide the basic information you need. The library has two copies. The status column on the screen indicates that no one has checked out either copy, so both should be in the library. If someone had checked one out, the status column would list the date it was due back at the library.

Some catalog entries also include the number of pages in the book. Some tell whether the book is illustrated or has a bibliography. Some state whether the work is a book or a videotape. Many entries list additional headings you could use as key words to find more information about the same topic.

Write down the call number shown at the top of the listing. (Call numbers are numbers and letters used to classify books. They're explained on pages 414–417.) Then go to the location listed: the oversized shelves in the young readers' nonfiction area. (The word *OVER* in the listing means "oversized.") Oversized books are located in their own section because they need taller shelves than most books.

Find the shelf in the oversized section with call numbers between 570 and 580. Then look along the rows for the book marked 576.5 BAE. The books are in numerical order, so it's easy to find the one you're looking for. As you glance through the table of contents, you're sure this book will help you learn more about cloning.

CARD CATALOGS

Card catalogs are stored in long, narrow drawers. The drawers hold two or more small cards for every book in the library. The cards are arranged alphabetically. Fiction books have two cards each. One lists the book by its author, and one lists the book by its title. Nonfiction books have at least three cards each. These cards list the book by its author, its title, and its subject or subjects.

The cards list the same information as the computer catalog. However, they don't tell you whether someone has checked out the book. A library may separate its card catalog into two categories: subject cards in one category and author and title cards in another.

21.2 LOCATING BOOKS: DEWEY DECIMAL SYSTEM OF CLASSIFICATION

The purpose of call numbers is to help you locate books. Most school and community libraries use call numbers based on the Dewey Decimal System of Classification. The Dewey Decimal System divides nonfiction books into ten categories.

RESOURCES

DEWEY CATEGORIES		
NUMBERS	**CATEGORY**	**EXAMPLES OF SUBCATEGORIES**
000–099	General Works	encyclopedias, bibliographies, periodicals, journalism
100–199	Philosophy	philosophy, psychology, personality
200–299	Religion	mythology, bibles
300–399	Social Sciences	sociology, education, government, law, economics, vocations, customs
400–499	Language	dictionaries, languages, grammar
500–599	Pure Sciences	chemistry, astronomy, biology, mathematics
600–699	Technology and Applied Sciences	medicine, engineering, agriculture, home economics, business, radio, television, aviation
700–799	Arts	architecture, painting, music, photography, recreation
800–899	Literature	poetry, plays, essays, criticism
900–999	Geography and History	geography, history, travel

Let's say you want to know more about James Thurber. You'd begin by entering his last name as a key word in a computer catalog or by looking under *T* in a card catalog.

The library might have many books by Thurber and about Thurber. One book might be *My Life and Hard Times,* a book by James Thurber. This book is placed in the 800 category, literature. Literature is broken into subcategories; for example, 810 is American literature, and 820 is English literature.

James Thurber was an American author, so *My Life and Hard Times* has a call number in the 810s: 817 THU. Some subcategories of the Dewey system contain hundreds of books. To make sure each book has its own call number, a decimal point and more numbers (and sometimes letters) are added to the number of the subcategory. For example, the book about genetics by Patrick Baeuerle has a call number of 576.5 BAE. Many libraries also add the first three letters of the author's last name to the call number, such as THU for Thurber or BAE for Baeuerle.

Library TIP

Two librarians may assign the same book to different Dewey categories. That's why books may have different call numbers in your library than those noted here.

Our imaginary library has another book, called *Remember Laughter: A Life of James Thurber,* by Neil A. Grauer. Its call number is *B Thurber James. B* stands for biography. Many libraries group their biographies together in a separate section of the library. Often there is one biography section in the adult stacks and another in the young adult and children's section. Biographies are shelved alphabetically according to the subject of the book. *Remember Laughter: A Life of James Thurber* is located in the *T* section of the biographies.

The library also has a book called *Thurber: A Biography,* by Burton Bernstein. It, too, has a call number of *B Thurber James.* Two biographies with the same call number but different authors are shelved alphabetically by the last name of the author. That puts Bernstein's book before Grauer's book in the *T* section of the biographies.

One book of short stories by James Thurber, *92 Stories,* is located in the fiction section. Most libraries using the Dewey system identify fiction with the call number *F, Fic,* or *Fiction.*

The call number also includes the first three letters of the author's last name or the author's entire last name. The call number of *92 Stories* is *Fic Thurber.*

Fiction is shelved alphabetically by the authors' last names. Books by the same author are shelved by the first important word in each title, ignoring *A, An,* and *The.* (The book *92 Stories* is shelved as if the number were spelled out: *Ninety-two.*)

Reference books, such as encyclopedias, have an *R* or *Ref* before their call numbers. This means you cannot check out these sources and must use them in the library.

21.3 LOCATING ARTICLES IN NEWSPAPERS AND OTHER PERIODICALS

You can find the latest information on a topic in newspapers, magazines, and journals. The two tools described below will make your search easier.

COMPUTER DATABASES

You may be able to use the library's computers to locate magazine and newspaper articles on your topic. These articles are organized and stored in a database. The library may store databases on CD-ROMs, or it may subscribe to an online service that provides databases. Some libraries do both. Most databases allow you to search by topic, by type of publication (magazine or newspaper), or by specific publication, such as the *New York Times.*

To search for information in a database, begin by entering a key word. The database will then list articles about that topic. The listing usually includes the title, the author, the publication, the date, and a sentence or two about the article. You can select any articles that seem useful. Then the database will allow you to read a brief summary or the whole article on the computer screen. For a small fee, you can print a copy of the article.

RESOURCES

READERS' GUIDE TO PERIODICAL LITERATURE

Not every library can subscribe to computer databases. However, nearly every library has the print edition of the *Readers' Guide to Periodical Literature.* This guide includes titles of articles from about two hundred magazines and journals. Both subjects and authors are listed alphabetically and cross-referenced.

An update of the print edition of *Readers' Guide* is published every two weeks. Information about all the articles published that year is reprinted in a hardbound book at the end of the year. The guide is also available on a CD-ROM that you can search using a computer.

Libraries often keep issues for the current year in their newspapers and periodicals section. Issues from the previous one to five years may be stored in a different area. Older issues may be on **microfilm** (a roll or reel of film) or **microfiche** (a sheet of film). Both types of film must be inserted into special projectors that enlarge the pages so that you can read them easily. You can usually make copies of these articles to take home.

Not every book in the library or article in library databases offers current, reliable information. The tips below will help you avoid sources that have outdated information or biased opinions.

1. **Evaluate the author of each source of information.** Look for information about the author's background. Consider whether this person is an expert or just someone with many opinions.
2. **Make sure the information is directly related to your topic.** If you try to include facts that are slightly off your topic, your report will seem unorganized.

3. **Check the publication date.** You may use older sources for information that's not likely to change, such as facts about the battles of World War II. However, your sources must be as recent as possible for topics that are in today's headlines, such as cloning.
4. **Evaluate the author's thinking.** Are the "facts" in a source really facts, or are they just opinions? Can they be proved or disproved? Does the author offer evidence to support his or her ideas?
5. **Gather information on the same topic from several sources.** By doing this, you'll discover different opinions on the issue or topic, but the facts should remain the same.

21.4 USING OTHER REFERENCE SOURCES

General reference sources are easy to use and provide information on thousands of topics. Below are some excellent examples of these sources.

TYPE OF REFERENCE	EXAMPLES
General Encyclopedias General encyclopedias fill many volumes. Subjects are arranged alphabetically. An index at the end helps you find topics.	*World Book Encyclopedia* *Encyclopaedia Britannica* *Collier's Encyclopedia* *Grolier Encyclopedia* *Encarta Encyclopedia*
Specialized Encyclopedias Specialized encyclopedias focus on specific topics. You might be surprised at the number of specialized encyclopedias available.	*Encyclopedia of World Art* *Van Nostrand's Scientific Encyclopedia* *Encyclopedia of World Crime* *Encyclopedia of the Opera* *Encyclopedia of the Third Reich* *Encyclopedia of Vitamins, Minerals, and Supplements* *Encyclopedia of Western Movies* *Encyclopedia of the Geological Sciences*

RESOURCES

TYPE OF REFERENCE	EXAMPLES
Almanacs and Yearbooks Almanacs and yearbooks are usually published annually. They provide current facts and statistics. Check the most recent issues for the latest information.	*Information Please Almanac* *World Almanac and Book of Facts* *Guinness Book of Records* *Statistical Abstract of the United States*
Atlases Atlases may contain current or historical information. They include maps and statistics about countries, climates, and other topics.	*Hammond World Atlas* *Cambridge Atlas of Astronomy* *Historical Atlas of the United States* *Goode's World Atlas* *National Geographic Atlas of the World* *Atlas of World Cultures*
Biographical References Biographical reference works include brief histories of notable people, living or dead.	*Contemporary Authors* *American Authors 1600–1900* *Cyclopedia of Literary Characters* *Webster's New Biographical Dictionary* *Biographical Dictionary of World War I* *Biographical Dictionary of World War II* *Biographical Dictionary of Scientists (by field)* *Biographical Dictionary of Artists*
Government Publications Some large libraries have government publications on agriculture, population, economics, and other topics.	*Monthly Catalog of United States Government Publications* *United States Government Publications Catalog* (Both are also available on CD-ROMs and as online publications.)
Books of Quotations In a book of quotations, you can find quotations by famous people or about certain subjects. The quotation from James Thurber at the beginning of Part Four can be found in *The International Thesaurus of Quotations.*	*Bartlett's Familiar Quotations* *The Harper Book of Quotations* *The Oxford Dictionary of Quotations* *The International Thesaurus of Quotations*

RESOURCES

21.5 MAKING THE MOST OF WORD RESOURCES

A dictionary and a thesaurus can help you put more words on the tip of your tongue and at the tip of your pencil. Both references are essential tools for writers.

DICTIONARIES

A dictionary contains entries in alphabetical order. An entry is a single word or term along with its pronunciation, definition, and other information.

"DICTIONARY."

RESOURCES

Finding Words in a Dictionary

The guide words at the top of each dictionary page can help you find words quickly. Guide words are the first word and the last word on the page. If the word you're looking for falls between these words alphabetically, it will be on that page.

For example, let's say the guide words on a page are *lintel* and *lisp.* You'll find the words *lioness, lip-synch,* and *liquid* on this page. However, *linguistic* comes before *lintel,* so it will be on an earlier page. *Lithium* comes after *lisp,* so it will be on a later page.

If you're looking for a phrase beginning with *St.,* the abbreviation will be spelled out: *Saint.* Look for *Saint Bernard,* not *St. Bernard.*

Understanding Dictionary Entries

Let's analyze a dictionary entry to see what kinds of information it offers.

1 2 3 4 5

in•fer (in fur´) *v.* **in•ferred, in•fer•ring 1.** to conclude by reasoning from facts known or assumed: *I infer from your frown that you're angry.* **2.** to guess: *We inferred that the stranger was our new teacher.* 5

6 **—in•fer•able** (in fur´ ə bəl) *adj.* **—in•fer•rer** (in fur´ər) *n.* [from Middle French *inferer,* from Latin *inferre,* literally, "to carry or bring into," from *in-* + *ferre* "to carry"] 7

8 **Synonyms:** *Infer, deduce,* and *conclude* all mean "to arrive at a conclusion." *Infer* implies arriving at a conclusion based on specific facts. *Deduce* includes the special meaning of drawing a conclusion from a general idea. *Conclude* suggests arriving at an inference based on a chain of reasoning.

1. *The Entry Word:* The entry word itself shows the correct spelling of the word. A raised dot or a blank space within the entry word shows where the word may be divided at the end of a line of writing. The entry word will also show you when a compound word should be written as one solid word (as in **landfill**), when it should be hyphenated (as in **land-poor**), and when it should be written as two words (as in **land mine**).

2. *The Respelling:* The respelling, or pronunciation, is shown immediately after the entry word. An accent mark follows the second syllable in *infer* to show that the second syllable should be stressed in pronouncing the word. So that you can check the pronunciation of the letters and symbols in the respelling, a pronunciation key is shown on every page or every other page in most dictionaries.
3. *Part of Speech Label:* An abbreviation in italic type gives the part of speech of the entry word. The abbreviation *v.* stands for *verb; adj.* stands for *adjective;* and *n.* stands for *noun.*
4. *Inflected Forms:* Inflected forms include plurals of nouns, principal parts of verbs (past, past participle, and present participle), and comparative and superlative forms of adjectives and adverbs. These forms are included in a dictionary entry only when they have irregular spellings. When the past and the past participle of a verb are the same, only one form is shown for both. The sample entry shows that *inferred* is the past form and the past participle of *infer,* and *inferring* is the present participle. These forms are considered irregular because the final consonant is doubled when the ending is added.

   This part of a dictionary entry can help you spell irregular plural forms, such as *quizzes* for *quiz* and *rodeos* for *rodeo.* This section will also show you when to double a final consonant *(stop, stopping; sad, sadder),* when to drop a final *e (dine, dining),* and when to change a final *y* to *i (easy, easiest)* before adding an ending.
5. *Definitions:* Definitions are the heart—and the longest part—of a dictionary entry. If an entry word has more

than one meaning, each definition is numbered. Example sentences are often included to make meanings clearer.

6. *Run-on Entries:* Definitions in a dictionary entry may be followed by one or more run-on entries. A run-on entry is a form of the entry word to which a suffix has been added. In the sample dictionary entry, **in•fer•able** and **in•fer•er** are run-on entries. Each run-on entry is preceded by a dash and followed by its pronunciation and its part of speech. The meanings of these words can be inferred by combining the meaning of the entry word and the meaning of the suffix. (See the list of suffixes and their meanings on pages 319–320.)
7. *Etymology:* Many dictionary entries include an etymology, which gives the origin or history of the word. The entry for *infer* explains that this word is based on a Middle French word. The Middle French word was based on a Latin word with a literal meaning of "to carry or bring into." When you infer, you carry or bring your knowledge into a new situation. You use what you know to reach a conclusion. You can see that the Middle French and Latin versions of the word are both similar to the English spelling.
8. *Synonyms:* Some dictionary entries list synonyms, or words with the same or nearly the same meanings. Understanding small differences in meaning will help you use the right word in the right place. Some dictionaries also include antonyms, words with opposite meanings.

Some words have more than one meaning or word history; some may be used as more than one part of speech. In such cases, a dictionary may have multiple entries for a word. Let's look at three entries for the word *rest:*

> ^{1}**rest** (rest´) *n.* **1.** REPOSE, SLEEP **2.** freedom from activity or disturbance **3.** something that acts as a stand or a support **4.** a place for resting or lodging **5.** *Music.* a

silence between musical notes **6.** a brief pause in reading [Middle English, from Old English; akin to Old High German *rasta* "rest"]

[2]**rest** *v.* **1.** to get rest by lying down or stopping activity **2.** to lie dead **3.** *Farming.* to remain idle or without a crop **4.** *Law.* to finish presenting evidence in a legal case: *The defense rests, Your Honor.*

[3]**rest** *n.* something that remains over; REMAINDER: *Jada ate the rest of the fruit salad.* [Middle English, from Middle French *reste,* from *rester* "to remain," from Latin *restare,* from *re-* + *stare* "to stand"]

RESOURCES

Numbered Entries Notice the small raised numeral to the left of each entry word in the preceding dictionary sample. This number indicates there is more than one entry for the word. Some dictionaries show separate entries for each part of speech. Some show separate entries for each meaning that has a different word history, or etymology.

In the first and second entries, the meanings have to do with pausing, sleeping, or remaining idle, but the entry words are different parts of speech. The third entry word is the same part of speech as the first, but the word's meaning and its etymology are different.

Cross-References Synonyms within an entry are sometimes printed in small capital letters. In the entries for *rest,* the words *repose, sleep,* and *remainder* are synonyms for specific meanings of *rest.* You can learn more about these meanings of *rest* by looking up the words in small capital letters.

Subject Labels Some dictionary entries include subject labels. A subject label preceding a definition indicates that the definition applies to the subject named. In the sample entries for *rest,* there are three subject labels. In [1]*rest* definition 5 applies to music. In [2]*rest* definition 3 applies to farming, and definition 4 applies to law.

The following chart gives examples of other kinds of information you may find in a dictionary entry.

TYPE OF INFORMATION	DESCRIPTION	EXAMPLE FROM AN ENTRY
Capitalization	Indicates that certain uses of a word should be capitalized	**earth** . . . *Often capitalized.* the planet that is third in order from the sun
Out-of-date label	Identifies meanings that are no longer used or used only in special contexts	**anon** . . . *Archaic.* at once; immediately
Style label	Indicates a meaning that is appropriate only in a very informal context	**cool** . . . *Slang.* very good; EXCELLENT
Regional label	Indicates a meaning used in a certain geographical area	**bon•net** . . . *British.* an automobile hood
Usage note	Offers guidelines for using–or not using–a word	**ain't** . . . Although inappropriate in formal speech or writing, *ain't* is sometimes used to attract attention or add humorous emphasis.

OTHER KINDS OF INFORMATION IN GENERAL DICTIONARIES

You can find other kinds of information in the back of some dictionaries. Here is a list of some of the kinds of information you may find in a dictionary.

Biographical Names

Do you remember James Thurber? Who was he? When was he born? When did he die? A section of biographical names gives the spelling and pronunciation of thousands of people's names, from Berenice Abbott (an American photographer who lived from 1898 to 1991) to Stefan Zweig (an Austrian writer who was born in 1881 and died in 1942).

RESOURCES

Geographical Names

How do you pronounce *Kilimanjaro*? What is it, and where is it? In a section of geographical names, you can find the correct spelling, pronunciation, and location of countries, cities, mountains, lakes, rivers, and other geographical features. Entries range from Lake Abitibi, in Ontario, Canada, to Zimbabwe, a country in southern Africa.

Abbreviations, Signs, and Symbols

Is the postal abbreviation for Maine MA, MN, or ME? A dictionary may include lists of abbreviations, signs, and symbols. Check this section if you can't remember, for example, what *NOAA* stands for (National Oceanic and Atmospheric Administration) or what the symbol *&* means *(and).*

Style Handbook

Some dictionaries include a style guide. This section may include rules for spelling, punctuation, and capitalization. It may also include other matters of writing style. Investigate your dictionary to find out what it has to offer.

THESAURI

A thesaurus lists synonyms, words with the same or nearly the same meaning. A thesaurus may be organized in traditional style or in dictionary style.

Traditional Style

Let's say you've used the word *continue* several times in a report, and you want to find a synonym. To use a traditional thesaurus, begin by looking in the index. There you might find these choices:

RESOURCES

continue endure 110.6
protract 110.9
go on 143.3
extend 201.9
persevere 623.2

Let's say that *extend* seems like a good word to replace *continue* in your report. You could use *extend,* or you could look in the front of the book under 201.9 for more choices. Guide numbers at the top of each page help you find the number you want quickly. They're similar to a dictionary's guide words.

On the page with the guide numbers 201.3–203.7, you find paragraph 201.9, a group of synonyms for *extend.* The most commonly used words are printed in bold type.

VERBS **9. lengthen, prolong,** prolongate, **elongate, extend,** produce [geom.], **protract,** continue, lengthen out, let out, **draw out,** drag out, string out [coll., U.S.], spin out; **stretch,** draw; tense, strain.

A page in the back of the thesaurus explains that *geom.* stands for *geometry* and *coll.* stands for *colloquial,* or *informal.*

Dictionary Style

A dictionary-style thesaurus is organized much like a dictionary. Using the guide words at the top of the page, locate the word *continue.* Checking the front of the book, you learn that an asterisk (*) indicates that a term is colloquial or slang.

CONTINUE

Verb. **1.** [To persist] persevere, carry forward, maintain, carry *or* roll *or* keep *or* go *or* run *or* live on, never stop, sustain, remain, press onward, make headway, move ahead, *leave no stone unturned; see also ADVANCE.

Antonyms: cease, end, give up

2. [To resume] begin again, renew, begin *or* carry over, return to, take up again, begin where one left off, be reinstated *or* restored; see also RESUME.

Antonyms: discontinue, halt, postpone

FRANK AND ERNEST reprinted by permission of Newspaper Enterprise Association, Inc.

RESOURCES

Chapter 22

Accessing Electronic Resources

When you're looking for up-to-date information, electronic resources can provide an excellent starting point. The Internet is an increasingly important source of information for people of all ages around the world. CD-ROMs and other electronic resources that are not connected to the Internet also offer vast amounts of information.

22.1 USING THE INTERNET

The Internet is a computer-based, worldwide information network. The World Wide Web, or WWW, is software that determines what is displayed on the Internet. Working together, the Internet and the World Wide Web allow you to gather information without leaving your home, school, or library.

GAINING ACCESS

Computers in your library can probably link you to the Internet for free. If you're using a computer at home, you'll need a modem. A modem connects your computer to a telephone line. You must also subscribe to an Internet service, such as America Online or CompuServe. That service will connect you to the Internet for a monthly fee.

UNDERSTANDING ADDRESSES

The information on the Internet is organized by locations, or sites. Each site has its own address. An address is also called a Uniform Resource Locator, or URL.

ACCESSING WEB SITES

Let's say you're connected to the Internet, and you want to view the information at a certain site or address. You can enter the address on the computer screen and be connected to the site.

You can also access specific reference sources, such as the *New York Times* or *Encyclopædia Britannica,* in this way. Some of these sources are free. For others you must subscribe and perhaps pay a fee. A screen will explain any extra charges that are required. Then you can choose whether to continue.

USING SEARCH ENGINES AND SUBJECT DIRECTORIES

If you don't have a specific address in mind, you can search by key word. A search engine or a subject directory can help.

Search Engines A search engine uses your key word to produce a list of related Web sites. Each Internet service provider uses a certain search engine, but you can switch to a different one by entering its address.

A key word that is too general may generate hundreds of thousands of possible Web sites. It will take you a very long time to search through them to find a few helpful sources!

Subject Directories If you haven't selected a specific topic yet, start with a subject directory. It will begin by listing general topics, such as arts and humanities, science, education, entertainment, recreation and sports, health, and other general subjects. After you choose one, the directory will offer a list of possible subtopics from which to choose. The directory then offers several more lists of subtopics for you to consider. In this way, you can narrow your topic. Finally, the directory will show a page of Web sites that are related to the specific topic you have chosen.

MOVING AROUND WEB SITES

Often words or phrases at one Web site provide links to related Web sites. These special words or phrases are called hyperlinks. They may be underlined or printed in a different color to make them easy to spot. When you click on a hyperlink, you will be transferred to another Web site. To get back, you can click on the back arrow at the top of the computer screen.

HOMESPIN

RESOURCES

No one oversees Web sites to make sure they offer accurate information. You must evaluate each site yourself. First, review the "Evaluating Tip" on pages 418–419. The tips listed there also apply to Internet sources. The following tips will also help you evaluate Internet sources.

1. Determine whether a Web site actually relates to your topic. A search engine will use every possible meaning of your key word to produce its list of sites.
2. Check the source of the information at a Web site. (You may have to press the "move back" key several times to identify a source.) Many Web sites are personal pages. Just because you find information on the Web doesn't mean it's true or accurate.

22.2 USING CD-ROMS AND DVDS

CD-ROMs (Compact Disc Read-Only Memory) and DVDs (Digital Video Discs) can be used with a personal computer at home, at school, or at a library. They don't require a connection to the Internet.

CD-ROM databases store both sights and sounds. Some CD-ROMS offer short versions of historical events. Some have moving pictures that show, for example, how bees "dance" to communicate with one another.

One CD-ROM can store the same amount of information as seven hundred computer diskettes. Many dictionaries, encyclopedias, and other reference sources are now available as CD-ROMs. A DVD can store even more information, as much as a full-length movie.

Library computer catalogs are another example of electronic resources that are not part of the Internet. Some of the databases available at a library are also on CD-ROMs. Other databases on library computers are part of the Internet.

James Thurber died in 1961, long before the Internet existed and long before there was as much information available as there is today. He would be amazed to discover how much has been "written about everything" at this point, and more is being written every minute!

Now you know how to find the information you need. Use your new skills to gather information for school reports and to find out more about this challenging and exciting world!

INDEX

Entries with bold page numbers represent terms and definitions in the Glossary of Terms, pages 4–28.

B

C

I

O

T